Writing Below the Belt

A RICHARD KASAK BOOK

Writing Below the Belt

Conversations
with
Erotic
Authors

Michael Rowe

First Richard Kasak Book Edition 1995

First Printing September 1995

ISBN 1-56333-363-5

Manufactured in the United States of America
Published by Masquerade Books, Inc.
801 Second Avenue
New York, N.Y. 10017

A portion of the author's royalties from the sale of *Writing Below the Belt* will be given to Vancouver's Little Sister's Bookstore legal defense fund, in recognition and support of their lawsuit against Canada Customs, and their fight for freedom of expression against the censorship and book-banning practices of the Canadian government.

Donations may be sent to:

Little Sister's Book and Art Emporium
1221 Thurlow Street, Vancouver, B.C.
V6E 1X4, Canada

Writing Below the Belt

Introduction   1

Dorothy Allison   9

Laura Antoniou   35

Michael Bronski   55

Pat Califia   73

Lars Eighner   101

Nancy Kilpatrick, writing as "Amarantha Knight"   123

Will Leber   139

Michael Lowenthal   153

Scott O'Hara   177

V. K. McCarty   201

John Preston   223

Leigh W. Rutledge   251

Steven Saylor, writing as "Aaron Travis"   273

Caro Soles, writing as "Kyle Stone"   299

Larry Townsend   323

For John Preston

1945–1994

*We are all in the same boat, in a stormy sea,
and we owe each other a terrible loyalty.*
—G. K. Chesterton

Acknowledgments

I am deeply grateful to my friend Lyn Underwood, who acted as my assistant on this project. Her clerical and typing skills were invaluable, and her friendship is one of the treasures I most miss from my former hometown of Milton, Ontario.

On a personal level, the support of certain friends has been a constant source of encouragement and joy to me. They are Brian Ashworth, Claire Birks, Wayne Brown, Ron Bigelow, Nancy and Jay Bowers, Scott Clevely, Lesley Durnin, Dan Duic and Tracy Jobe, Barney Ellis-Perry and Douglas Brockway, Glenn Hall, Tasia Hazisavvas and Rod MacNeil, Owen Keehnen, Kathy Lefroy, Gabriella Martinelli, Rob McNutt, Mark Monaghan, Wolfgang Mueller, Dylan Neal and Becky Southwell, Sean Reycraft, Mark Saskoley, Jan-Louise Sasseville and Alexandra Hazisavvas, Pat Smelser, Uncas the Wonder Mutt, Barry Wallace, Werner Warga, Christopher Wirth and Claire Price, and Pat Woods.

And Randy Murphy, above all, for reasons he knows well.

To the gifted writers profiled in this book: Thank you for your honesty, your openness, your willingness to share your lives with us, and for your writing, which arouses and inspires us.

With your indulgence, I would like to acknowledge my three most important personal debts. First, to my parents, Penny and Alan Rowe, who have always prized education, self-reliance, and independent thought. They raised us to be strong individuals, in a home where no topic of discussion—least of all sexuality—was ever off-limits.

Second, to my big brother Ron Oliver, a gifted screenwriter with a keener eye for hypocrisy than anyone I have ever met. He has taught me much. The luckiest among you may find a friendship like ours. This is Ron's book as much as it is mine.

Third, and most important, from beginning to end, to my life partner Brian, the author of all good things.

I'm one of those people who believe that you have a right to cry "Fire!" in a crowded theater. I don't believe in any kind of censorship—before or afterward—at all. I think if you go into a crowded theater, you'd best be prepared to evaluate all cries of "Fire!" on the objective evidence.   —Lars Eighner
from the interview with Michael Rowe

I would have you know that this kingdom of mine is not so scant of men but there be a rogue or two among them.   —Elizabeth I

Introduction

I discovered pornography at Knox College, a Presbyterian seminary attached to the University of Toronto, where I lived when I was in college.

I was visiting my friend Rob one afternoon. Rob was a law student who lived in West House, across the quad from East House, where I had rooms. It seems somehow appropriate that I discovered porn in Robbie's room—he was an Adonis: pale, pale skin, black hair, with the most beautifully muscled body I had ever seen. Years later, when I read Steven Saylor's electrifying story, "Blue Light," the character of Michael had Rob's face and sculpted-marble body.

Robbie also had the distinction of being the first gay man I had known who was kind, *and* masculine, *and* intelligent, all at the same time. I had come out eighteen months earlier, and I had known men with all three of those individual attributes, but they never seemed to have them at the same time. I had a crush on Rob for about a week. Nothing came of it. I decided very soon in the game that he would be a much better friend than a boyfriend. In retrospect, it seems to have been an excellent choice on my part. If he had been my boyfriend, the pornography I discovered in his room would have been a distraction, and I would have had to pay attention to *Rob* instead of paying attention to the magazines his friend David, who was in the process of moving, had asked him to take care of until the move was complete.

Poor David. I wonder if he missed the ones I stole. Rob never even noticed. He never once looked up from his torts and briefs.

Like many gay kids in the seventies, I was far too repressed to ever do more than steal surreptitious peeks at *Playgirl* in the drugstore, back before they had closed-circuit security television cameras in drugstores. I read Gordon Merrick novels in the psychology sections of bookstores, fantasizing desperately about Peter and Charlie.

At boarding school, my friend Barney (who already knew his way around in the dark at fifteen) told me about how he'd found stacks of gay porn magazines outside a neighbor's apartment in Vancouver during Easter vacation. I remember the gleam in his eye the night he described them to me just before study hall ("They were *hard-core!*" Barney rhapsodized). That night, as I tried to concentrate on my tedious Canadian-history assignment, my mind wandered to the exotic foreign territory Barney had described in such exquisite detail.

Ah, me. If I'd been able to tear myself away from the teenage navel-gazing angst I felt in those days over my emerging homosexuality, I might have had the wherewithal to explore that hot territory for myself, before I turned twenty. With or without Barney.

The magazines I discovered in Rob's room at Knox College were ragged copies of a magazine I had never heard of, called *Drummer.* I made a discovery between those pages that was to alter the course of my life. I happened upon a story called "Mr.

Benson," written by a man named Jack Prescott, which I assumed was a pseudonym.

(Please—I was an *English major.* There was no way anyone would use their own name writing *pornography.)*

But God, it was hot. It was rough.

About six weeks later, I discovered a novel of the same name at the old Glad Day Bookstore on Yonge Street, as well as a collection of short fiction called *I Once Had a Master,* both by a man named John Preston. I didn't linger on my smugness over having been right about the pseudonym. I bought both books and took them back to my dorm. What began for me that afternoon was effectively both a love affair with the work of John Preston, and an intoxication with a kind of champagne prose with which I was completely unfamiliar—writing that spoke to my groin and my mind at the same time.

The political flavor-of-the-month on campus that year was an earnest, if melodramatic, polemic against pornography called *Not a Love Story*, produced by the National Film Board of Canada, and required viewing for my sociology course. We all watched it, and we all walked away from the film convinced that pornography was the scourge of enlightened society. It would destroy women. Like Circe, it would turn men into swine, and into rapists as well. It would threaten the well-being of children. Given half a chance, it would probably raise storms and sour milk. I had no trouble identifying *pornography.* Pornography was smut, the cheap stuff, the badly written books, the badly photographed slick magazines that Barney found in the trash. Not my well-thumbed and stained copy of *I Once Had a Master*. No, that was erotica. That was *erotic literature.*

What spectacular crap.

I find it painful to remember that particular adolescent pomposity, more painful still to write it down. When I met John Preston years later, I told him that story. He fixed me with his most sardonic smirk, and gave one of the short laughs he reserved for the most preposterous pretensions: a cross between a sharp bark and a snort. It was most effective, and I've never looked back.

In actual point of fact, however, I wasn't completely wrong

in my assessment of the difference between the two types of material. One type *was* what I called (and would still call) smut. It was cheap; it was written by cheesy formula-hacks with no respect for the intelligence of their readers. Furthermore, it was too clumsy and stupid to be arousing. It was *bad writing*.

The other type was sterling prose from a gifted American author at the height of his literary powers. The fact that he was using those powers to strip-mine my erotic fantasies and drive me to sleepless nights of grinding my pelvis against the mattress was, if not incidental, at least secondary to the fact that it was excellent fiction.

Gourmet magazine makes me hungry. Travel magazines make me want to roam. Stephen King's earlier fiction still chills me. And I still cry at the end of *Out of Africa*, when the lions lie down on Robert Redford's grave, and Meryl Streep's voiceover implies that she never returned to Africa. That movie won several Academy Awards.

Pat Califia, Steven Saylor, John Preston, and Leigh Rutledge all arouse me with their stories. Why is it that when one is made hungry, or claustrophobic, or maudlin and sentimental, awards are given, but when one is sexually aroused by writing—which has one's arousal as its primary goal—one has been "debased"?

As for the two categories of erotic fiction, was one "pornography" and the other "erotica"? Not at all. Either appellation was appropriate for either type. The words are meaningless in and of themselves.

The questions are all rhetorical, of course. We have long since had our fill of the endless, tedious discussions about the difference between "pornography" and "erotica." In light of the tremendous volume of good erotic fiction published in the last twenty-five years, we ought to have bigger fish to fry than to deal in that tiresome debate.

The fifteen writers you will meet in this book are some of the best practitioners of what I have referred to as "sterling writing." Thirteen of them are American. Two are Canadian. Fourteen of them are fiction writers, and one of them is an esteemed historian and culture critic.

Many of them are successful crossover writers who have

achieved success in other literary genres. Between them, they have won and/or been nominated for the National Book Award, the Lambda Literary Award, the Pushcart Prize, the Nebula Award, and the Bram Stoker Award.

They range in age, and in personal history, from before the beginnings of gay liberation to Generation X. All but one of them accepts the mantle of "pornographer," whatever that might mean. None of them apologizes for writing about sex.

I am reluctant to call these profiles "interviews." As a journalist, I have come to think of interviews as a search for specific answers to specific questions. Rather, I approached them as "conversations." I have attempted to keep my intervention at a minimum while I encouraged these writers to tell their stories, and talk about what was important to them. What you will find, I hope, is a far truer portrait than if I had gone in with a more structured agenda.

Writers are invariably the product of the environments in which they grew up, and these writers are no exception. I made a point of exploring the childhoods of these fifteen, and I found that all of them had at least some aspects of what are considered classic fodder for a writer's childhood: an almost painful shyness, a heightened sense of being *outside* and *away* from the world around them, and an insatiable curiosity as to why people treat each other the way they do. All of them were acutely aware of sexuality without being obsessed by it, and all of them turned to writing about sex as naturally as any other genre they might have reached for. Pat Califia discusses growing up as a Mormon daughter. Steven Saylor explores his Texas boyhood. Leigh Rutledge describes a childhood of physical abuse, where one of his earliest-rooted fantasies was finding the perfect father.

Many of the writers profiled have explored regionalism. Toward the end of his life, John Preston was almost as well known for the New England inflections in his writing as for his pornography. Steven Saylor and Lars Eighner pepper some of their work with their Texas roots. Caro Soles, who is Canadian, sets much of her work in outer space.

I was also deeply curious about the concept of generations. The gay-rights movement is just old enough now to begin to feel the effects of different generations: pre-Stonewall, post-Stonewall, pre-AIDS, post-AIDS. Is erotic fiction more taken for granted today? Has quality become more of a concern now that we have more time to savor pornography in the light of day, rather than flog away in the dark? Or *do* we have more time?

For the writers whose field of expertise is SM and acrobatic gender-switching, I was particularly intrigued by whether or not they felt that the days of SM's being "outlaw" sexuality are gone. Had the twin forces of Madonna's *Sex* book and the appropriation of SM iconography by popular culture brought "outlaw sexuality" irretrievably into the light, making the entire concept a quaint, silly anachronism? Or is it only a wake-up call for eroticists to work harder and dig deeper?

The issue of censorship is one that all the writers agree on; and not surprisingly, since much of their own work is under attack. Censorship is a dangerous and pernicious force, and it is based on the infantilizing premise that we are incapable of deciding what we may or may not read, and that someone else always knows the answer to that question better than we do. Several of the authors' books were unavailable to me here in Canada while I was working on *Writing Below the Belt*. In the United States, the antiporn feminists and the fundamentalists have finally found something they agree upon. But how does it apply to gay pornography? As Richard Schneider, Jr., wrote in a recent editorial in *The Harvard Gay & Lesbian Review*:

> Censorship in Canada is operating under a new theory that has ostensibly "liberal" origins, one that's been promoted by the American feminists Catharine MacKinnon and Andrea Dworkin, who argue that porn—presumably straight porn—"objectifies" women's bodies and literally *causes* men to rape women. The whole model upon which their thesis is based would seem not to apply. Who is objectifying whom?

I am reluctant to challenge the stereotype of "the pornographer" as dirty, amoral, talentless, exploitative, and money-obsessed (whoever is getting rich in pornography, it's not the writer), because challenging the stereotype gives it credence as more than a silly caricature. Doubtless there *are* pornographers who match that description. But off the top of my head, I could name one or two journalists and a talk-show host who would fit the bill far more effectively. It certainly doesn't fit any of the fifteen writers I have interviewed in this collection, but they don't need to be defended. Their work speaks for itself.

We live in a society with such harsh parameters of acceptable gender roles and behavior that anyone daring to step out of those roles, particularly gays and lesbians, is viewed as a traitor to God, their country, The Family, and his or her sex, and therefore subject to violence or death.

We live in a puritanical, church-driven culture that views the body and its appetites as sinful, dangerous, unclean, and needing strict control. Many of us either deny these appetites completely or indulge them clandestinely, and masturbate ourselves with the guilt. Much of our literature reflects that. To some, writing that isn't a painful moral duty to read must, by definition, be worthless.

However uncomfortable it might make the literary establishment, the fact remains that pornography is an excellent barometer by which to measure society's attitudes toward sex and morality. Pornography can be considered "low" and "base" for only as long as sexuality itself is considered "low" and "base." The prejudice against erotica turns on as uncomplicated an axis as that. Until this perception changes, society will continue to dismiss erotic fiction as unworthy of serious critical attention.

While waiting for hell to freeze over, we have the work of these fifteen writers to help us explore the sexual landscape and its many shadows. Their work will continue to challenge the establishment and—ultimately—society itself.

Michael Rowe
Toronto, Ontario
October 31, 1994

Dorothy
ALLISON

Sexually, I have a fetish about truth telling. It does help in my work. I find it profoundly exciting to watch somebody articulate their desires.

Dorothy Allison has been hailed as one of the most important new writers working in American letters. Her first book, *The Women Who Hate Me*, was an acclaimed volume of poetry. Her second book, *Trash*, a collection of short fiction, was awarded two Lambda Literary Awards: one for Lesbian Fiction, and another for Small Press Book. Allison's crossover triumph, however, was her acclaimed 1992 novel, *Bastard out of Carolina*, which was a National Book Award Finalist in Fiction. In 1994 Firebrand Books released a collection of essays, *Skin: Talking About Sex, Class, and Literature*, further illustrating the breadth and power of Allison's life and vision.

I had been perplexed, over the years, by the discrepancy between what I perceived to be her persona in interviews—brash, bold, occasionally harsh—and her writing, which is unparalleled in its earthy beauty. As a gay man I was stunned by the erotic power of her short story, "Her Thighs," which appeared in Joan Nestle's 1992 anthology *The Persistent Desire*, proving to me that the best erotic fiction transcends gender, and even sexual orientation.

Dorothy Allison's prose may be lush and accessible, but the world she describes is frequently less so. At one time excoriated by the women's movement, derided as "a pimp for the pornographic-incest society" because she dared to express what she felt were the complexities and truths of sexual desire—whether SM, incest, or the bittersweet pain of being a "romantic masochist"—Allison has triumphed by any objective standard, in her work and in her private life. In this interview, she speaks without rancor about her life, enfolding past hurts and mistakes in the same warm maternal embrace as her successes. Whatever personal questions I was able to resolve over the course of our conversation regarding the dichotomy of Dorothy Allison's many facets, I walked away with one dominant impression: she perfectly embodies the notion that the most beautiful, mercurial women are the ones in their middle years and later—the ones who have occupied their hearts, minds, and strengths with the daily work of being fully alive.

Today Dorothy Allison lives in California with her lover and her young son. She continues to write joyously and courageously about being queer, female, and an outlaw, in a world that often distrusts all three.

Michael Rowe: Tell me about the early and primary erotic influences in your life, growing up as you did in the rural South.

Dorothy Allison: Well, if we're going to talk about it like the great rivers, there would be two main tributaries, and one of them was porn. Raw porn, the kind my stepfather collected and kept under his bed—everything from [Henry Miller's] *Sexus, Nexus,* and *Plexus,* which I remember mostly because there was one section in one of those books where a woman smoked a cigarette with her pussy, and I just wanted to meet her. I couldn't believe anyone could actually do that. And the other was science fiction, which I kind of rewrote to my own taste, with female heroines, and lots and lots of Sturm und Drang and kidnapping, and sacrificing yourself for the object of your lust.

MR: What was it about those themes that caught your attention?

Allison: Mostly the self-sacrifice. For instance, a story in which young girls would have to be tortured, but never give the name of the beloved, the one they loved. That kind of thing.

MR: Was that a very romantic image to you, or a sexual one?

Allison: Romantic. But I didn't see a lot of difference when I was a child, and I'm not sure I do still.

MR: Was there a dearth of romance in your life when you were growing up?

Allison: (*laughs*) There was perverse romance in my life when I was growing up. I grew up in the South. It's an inherently romantic atmosphere, except that I grew up in this working-class family in which the assumption was that everybody's nerves are kind of blunted. I knew women who talked literally about dying for love, in a way that you believed them. One of my cousins fell in love, married a man, and he died. And she never married again. And the whole story was that this had been the great love of her life. So I had that kind of idea of romance, but I didn't particularly trust it because all the people I saw seemed to be victims of romance. No one had profited by it.

MR: Was your lesbianism something that was interfering with what you saw of romance around you? Gay people often have to do a double take. They have to do a double-filter to bring the stories around them into their own lives, making them applicable to them.

Allison: The funny thing is, I don't think it was a real problem. I think that it was so natural and early for me that I automatically transposed all of culture into an all-female context. It was real simple—I sometimes astonish myself by how simple it was.

MR: Did you ever share that with the people around you? Or did you just carry it around with you inside your head?

Allison: Mostly it was not safe to share it. I did, a couple of times, and the results were horrible.

MR: Would you elaborate on that?

Allison: (*laughs*) I discovered the hard way that nobody else shared my ability to transpose to an all-female environment, and that, in fact, it was considered crazy and dangerous. I got laughed at. In my earliest experiences, making up a romantic story for another girl I was madly in love with, she gave it away. She read it to all the other kids at school, and I remember it with great pain. I spent three days in bed recovering. I was terrified to go back to school, and it turned me into this object of ridicule. I just somehow knew that it was dangerous. I hadn't known how personally dangerous it was. So, very quickly, I became careful. I had this secret life that all us young queer people have. But I just could not—it's like my girlfriend, who's ten years younger, and went into the army, and got kicked out for being queer. She said the reason was she just couldn't believe they were serious. I couldn't believe everybody was so serious about this thing—proving to me that they were.

MR: Did that make you feel like a freak? Or did you ever suspect that maybe they were the ones with the problem?

Allison: Not until I grew up. I grew up from that realization.

MR: What happened with the little girl you were in love with? Did you and she ever become friends?

Allison: I had one of those childhoods in which we moved every six months, so I didn't hang on to people very easily. I lost a lot of people, and in a way that became an assumption of my life. I began to think of it as being part of being queer. It was the way I felt safe, because nobody got to know me too well.

MR: Did you keep journals as a child?

Allison: No. I wrote stories; but after that one incident, I made a fetish out of burning them, or destroying them, or tearing them up and getting rid of them.

MR: So you never had anything that you kept around you?

Allison: I kept books that began to reflect something back to me that I loved or understood. I hung on to them.

MR: Your desire to become a writer—your decision to be a writer—was that something that you were able to identify as a young girl?

Allison: I just wanted out. I wanted to be a writer, but I had no idea how to do it, and I didn't think it was possible. And, pretty quickly, people communicated to me that it wasn't possible.

MR: Was there *anyone* around you that gave you any kind of support, or reflected the good back to you?

Allison: Yes. My mother and my aunt. My mother, most power-fully. My mother believed that I was a genius. She believed I was this incredibly special, rare, exotic creature, and the most impor-tant person in her life. That kind of existed at the same time as the fact that she had very little time for me, and was constantly having to fight off my stepfather's resentment of that. That's the way it was; but at the same time, she used to be the backbone. Then there were all these incredibly strong women all around me, really, really strong, dangerous women whom I loved madly—mostly my aunts and my great-aunts.

MR: That's a very Southern archetype.

Allison: Yes, except of course, you know what you get with that—you get to watch these strong women destroy themselves.

MR: Because the culture was not amenable to strong women?

Allison: No, because they are taught how to destroy themselves, and taught that it's a thing they are supposed to do. That's what comes of that romanticism. It's one reason that it makes such stubborn, brittle little lesbians. I could introduce you to a lot of stubborn, brittle little Southern lesbians who just were adamant that they were not going to grow up to be the kind of romantics they watched their mothers be.

MR: How many of them escaped?

Allison: I can list at least five. Very few got away, very few. I can list a whole lot more who didn't. There was a point in my life when I started trying to just track what had really happened, and where people had gone, and it just about broke my heart realizing how many of them were dead. You know, there are a whole lot of ways to kill yourself in this society. And a lot of the women I found as a young person are gone. Bad enough that we had liquor, but drugs on top of it, plus fast cars and crazy, crazy adventures.

MR: Are we discussing the underside of the American dream?

Allison: Oh, hell, I think it's the *backbone* of the American dream! It makes everything else possible. I absolutely believe that we are the grease that turns the wheels of this society.

MR: *We,* being queers, or *we*—as in your case—being Southerners?

Allison: *We* being the people who destroy ourselves, and that's both queers and Southerners. And women. I've watched it happen over and over. There has to be a way to stop it, because I also don't believe that it's necessary. I think it's like slavery in the South—at the time, they convinced themselves that it was economically the only way to run their culture. It isn't. And chewing up the major part of the population in order to have a few people who believe themselves to be special to lead a special life, isn't necessary.

MR: Do you put a lot of distance between yourself and all that now? Your life is very different now. You've gone to California, and you're raising your child with your lover. There must be a degree of satisfaction in that.

Allison: Yes, and guilt, too.

MR: Guilt? Guilt over what? Why would you feel guilty?

Allison: Of course, guilt. I was raised a Southern Baptist. I have written extensively about being a romantic masochist. Romantic masochists are consumed by guilt. I wouldn't do so much if I wasn't trying to make up to the world what I feel I owe it.

MR: Is that one of the functions of your work? Are you giving the world what you think you owe it with your writing?

Allison: Absolutely. It's the tithing. It's what I owe the world.

MR: Do you feel that the tithing is being received now? Do you feel that the debt is being paid? Or are you looking perpetually for something you need to give?

Allison: I'm the one who has the debt. And I don't think the debt is paid. It's a lifetime thing, and I am occasionally astonished by how well my work has been received in the last couple of years. And then, every once in a while, they just bring me up short and shake me hard to remind me that I'm still an outlaw. So that's useful.

MR: But you've embraced your outlaw status.

Allison: Shit, yes! It's the source of all the energy. This is the most absurd thing in the world: this pretense that it's not an advantage to be an outlaw. It is an advantage.

MR: Perhaps the disadvantage is in allowing people to think that it's an advantage. Outlaws make people uncomfortable.

And people don't want more people around them making them feel uncomfortable.

Allison: Yes, you've got the idea. The other thing is all that real simple stuff about the energy provided by not lying. The energy that is provided by telling the truth and having a purpose in your life. That's something that the outlaws of this society have stated, and there's the beauty, the advantage of not being inside. You can see a whole lot farther if you don't have those big walls around you.

MR: There are a many elements in erotic writing and pornography that are truth telling—you tell the truth about people's desires. We are a culture of denial. I wonder if you'd like to touch on that: the issue of truth telling in a culture that doesn't particularly want "the truth" about sex and sexuality?

Allison: Sexually, I have a fetish about truth telling. It does help in my work. I find it profoundly arousing to watch somebody struggle to articulate their desires. One of the things my girlfriend and I say together, around this whole thing, is that you can have anything you want if you have the courage to ask for it. But having that courage to ask for it, wow! So we set up situations where you can have anything, honey—you just have to be able to ask for it.

MR: Does it ever get easier to ask?

Allison: Oh, it does and it doesn't. Because you are always pushing further into the level of complexity of what you are asking for. Not physically, so much. For me, it's about emotional questions. I took enormous physical risks with myself in my twenties and early thirties.

MR: What sort of risks?

Allison: Oh, finding lovers who would deliver to me every adventure I could manage.

MR: There is a great deal in your work dealing with your attraction to SM, and the whole arena of sexual power politics. Can you expand on that for me? What is the attraction?

Allison: Maybe because it's scary, because it's forbidden, and because I think masochists are the ultimate reason for society. Those of us who are willing to sweat and bleed with such fervor are extremely valuable. I believe people know it.

MR: You've written about your attraction to tough, butch, in-control women. What is the origin of that attraction? What role did that archetype play in your life?

Allison: I don't think anyone actually knows. The "why" question is always the most fascinating question for outsiders, and it's of no interest at all when you are actually doing it. I had lots of really tough female archetypes around in this society, but you know—Sal Mineo, James Dean—what else do you need? I believe it's an American thing, an American cultural archetype.

MR: I suppose that the question frequently becomes how we, as gay men and lesbians, interpret what is known as "Americana." How we interpret so many of the all-American symbols and totems that we all grow up with, which have become so much a part of the fabric of our erotic consciousness.

Allison: People are always pretending that us queers, we imagined it. Or that we had some pivotal experience in our cribs that led us to go after these kinky desires. No honey, we are as American as we can get. (*laughs*)

MR: Does it travel, in your opinion? Does the all-American ethic still hold up as an erotic standard, outside of America?

Allison: Well, I've been to Europe and I've known European queers, and it's a variation. The American ideal is extremely homoerotic. Extraordinarily so. And—is there a word?— lesboerotic. Yes, it's extremely lesboerotic.

MR: What part does religion—good old American Christianity —play in this fabric? "One Nation under God," "In God We Trust"—that's a pretty basic tenet of what we call the "all-American" ethic.

Allison: I'm a student of gay male ethnic culture—I find it less fascinating than I did a few years ago, because I've been distracted. Maybe it's still the best thing I studied of all time—but this whole thing of "Daddy's boys," and the military model, it's so *Christian!* It's so about taking the youth and perfecting him. I just adore it. And I want to see more of it in lesbian culture. If someone had come along and wanted to be my mean momma, I'd have run off with her in an instant. Especially if I could have run off to San Francisco and worn nifty clothes and ridden motorcycles and spit in the eye of America. Yes. Why shouldn't it be romantic?

MR: There are many women who would disagree with you and, in fact, view lesbians, and women in general who indulge in SM behavior, or even idealize the gay male military-SM culture, as traitors and patriarchists.

Allison: They don't know what they are talking about, and a lot of it is about fear, about a culture they don't understand. Of course, the other part of it is, that same impulse which produces that incredibly nurturing environment also produces a militarist model with an incredibly antifemale destructiveness, in this society. So you know where the anger, resentment, and fear come from. The problem is that you have to be able to make distinctions about what is positive and what is negative. And we don't want to do that. We want nice simple hard lines of sexuality.

MR: Isn't that all-American too? Buying wholesale? You can buy package vacations, package-insurance deals. Why not a package religious or political ideology?

Allison: I think it's lazy. I don't know if it's American. I think it's just "I'm too busy, too overworked. I don't want to think too much. Give me an ideal." It's not admirable. It's all so really, really destructive. It's been a major problem in feminist hysteria in the last decade. Even the people who don't agree with my politics would agree that it certainly has screwed everything up. But then again, most conservative retrograde movements do screw things up.

MR: So your articulated desires—the sadomasochistic ones, the "queer" or "deviant" ones—these don't conflict at all with your views of yourself as a feminist, regardless of the fact that they conflict with the views of the feminist establishment?

Allison: I'm a feminist, honey, and I've been told I was not a feminist. But I'm still here, and I'm still fighting for the right to use the word, and make it a word that we could be proud of and hang on to, instead of being ashamed of. Or having to throw all these little corollaries onto it. I am a feminist—leave it alone and accept it.

MR: How has your attraction to the butch-femme model— about which you've written fairly extensively—played, within the women's community?

Allison: Sexually it's not a problem. It's kind of acceptable. But it's acceptable only as long as I put it in historical terms, and also as long as I am attracted to the same kinds of butches as the majority of the lesbian community. No, honey, the big thing that got me into lots of trouble was talking about child sexual desire. And talking about incest in the way that I was. Because I think this culture eroticizes incest in such a way that a lot of simple solutions to it—which to the antiporn movement means rigid control of male sexuality, as if the male sexuality was the whole root of the problem—just don't work. Saying that in public, talking about how complicated sexuality really is, or how I perceive it to be, is what got me in trouble.

MR: You've drawn a great deal of harsh, excoriating anger down upon yourself within the lesbian and feminist communities by holding—and sharing—ideas like those.

Allison: What year is it? (*laughs*) Let's see: first you get run out, you get pilloried, you get assaulted—

MR: How did you feel when these things were happening?

Allison: I was destroyed completely. I can only now begin to acknowledge how much damage it did. I am more or less deep into the process of recovering from it. If I ever will recover from it.

MR: Growing up the way you did, you looked for strength in yourself and in those around you. You've written extensively about this, but even in the preface of *Trash,* you talk about discovering the women's movement as though they were family. A tribe. "I threw myself into the women's community, fell in love every third day, and started trying to be serious about writing —poems and essays and the beginnings of stories. I even helped edit a feminist magazine." Did you feel betrayed when the condemnation came down? Because you'd put in—pardon the sexist jargon—a lot of man-hours.

Allison: I felt betrayed. I felt robbed. I felt used. And mostly, brokenhearted. That was the biggie. It just completely broke my heart. And then I felt like I didn't have a nation, and that was really hard.

MR: Like your childhood in the South all over again?

Allison: Yes, exactly. And you know, the amazing thing is, my stepfather couldn't kill me—what made *them* think they could? Get real! But it's much more deep and painful when people you have thought were your family, or a safe place, or your nation, turns and goes after you. That's why I had to redefine them as not being part of my nation.

MR: What specifically was it about your work that upset them?

Allison: Well the curious thing is, I think it's what is strongest about my work: that fearlessness about examining truth and being forthright about sexuality. Particularly in the early eighties, sexuality and the feminist-lesbian community got redlined. They were subjects you were not to discuss. I knew lots and lots of masochist women in the antiporn movement who were adamant that this was the subject not to be brought up. The only thing you were supposed to do was cure yourself, which essentially meant, you know, the same thing they told me in Baptist Sunday school: don't jerk off, and don't think about it. Deny it's going on, deny that you have these impulses or, if you do acknowledge them, apologize completely, and kiss the floor like a good nun.

MR: And you were not prepared to do that?

Allison: Oh, honey, I was prepared to kiss the floor. I just wasn't prepared to stop acknowledging! It just doesn't work. This is the thing which has broken it open and changed everything: No one can deny sexual desire permanently. You can wall it up, you can mutate it, you can chain it down; but eventually it will creep out and get you again. Desire is persistent. Boy, my desires have been awfully persistent! It's like having a compass in your soul, and you can always look back at it and see where it's pointing. Now, it might not be pointing at a place that you really want to go, but you can't pretend that it's not moving in that direction.

MR: What was the most painful aspect of the repercussions?

Allison: The most painful part of it was being called a pimp for the pornographic-incest society—for the very work that was basically saving my life! The early stuff that I was publishing, sections of *Bastard out of Carolina*, "Private Rituals"—the short story that I wrote while working on *Bastard*. These people totally flipped out about that, probably because I was acknowledging that this little girl, who is a victim of sexual abuse, also had sexual desire. And that her desire is profoundly masochistic. It completely upset them.

MR: What is it about child sexuality that upsets North American society so much?

Allison: Oh, because they want to pretend it doesn't happen.

MR: But why?

Allison: I think because it's anarchy, and probably more perverse because it's raw. Because it's romantic, and because it's queer. I don't think children make the categorical distinctions that adults make. My son runs around waving his dick at anything. Of course, he's only two, and I don't put any limits. (*laughs*) No, I don't think we understand sexuality, and we're constantly trying to categorize it, limit it, and control it.

MR: For a society which professes to have such a hard time with sexuality, we certainly spend a great deal of time thinking about it.

Allison: Well, exactly. And we're not willing to let it be what it is. That's the thing that's astonishing to me. Now, *that* seems to be profoundly American: We must get it labeled, and pinned down, and controlled. What is most powerful about sexuality is that it *can't* be controlled. Transcendence, enlightenment—all those things that some of us go to sex for—I think that a lot of Americans, particularly, transmute sexual need, sexual hunger, into other things. A drive for success, for acquisition, for some kind of spiritual satisfaction—anything except sexuality itself. I mean, to pretend that sexuality is not profoundly spiritual is a completely American concept. To reduce it to the *base physical* and not—don't you just love that word "base," as if physical could be base?—oh, Lord it's sad, if you really think about it.

MR: Where do groups like NAMBLA fit into this sexual-cultural landscape?

Allison: Well, that's a problem, a serious problem because all of my—

MR: The question is a problem? Or NAMBLA is a problem?

Allison: NAMBLA is a problem, and it's not a problem that I see as being easily—I don't see a solution. Because, theoretically, I could be persuaded to agree with a lot of NAMBLA's proposals. I was reading all this wonderful stuff about childhood sexuality, and I met Dan Zang and I liked him a lot. And then I started meeting men in New York City who were part of NAMBLA, and I hated them. They had that same kind of emotional affect that my stepfather had. A lot of them were liars and abusers, and it just completely screwed up my ability to theoretically agree with them.

MR: How does being a mother also influence your view of groups like NAMBLA?

Allison: Oh, as a mother, I have days when all I want to do is kick butt. I absolutely believe that children have sexual desires, and that they should be honored. And I have real discomfort with the concept of "protection" because I know that protection is about control. But I wouldn't let any of those people near my son. I wouldn't let them near anybody's.

MR: That's the bottom line, isn't it? The maternal animal coming out?

Allison: It's just awful. It's like, I'm as American as anybody. I'd like to have a nice, clean, simple category that would explain all the ways that I think about NAMBLA. But there isn't one. At the same time, what's not talked about are friends of mine, lesbians, who have a profound erotic fascination with young girls. That messed me up for a few years. It's not something that I emotionally or physically can understand, so I had to really work to get it. And that is really much more complicated for me than talking to the kind of men I met in New York who were picking up Puerto Rican boys on 42nd Street, and paying them way too little money, and way too many drugs.

MR: When I was fourteen or fifteen, if some twenty-five-year-old had come to me and had addressed my specific sexual desires, and said, "Here, let me initiate you into this," I would have been all for it.

Allison: Hell, yes.

MR: But by the same token, what I would have been at fourteen maybe isn't what someone else would have been; and that's where, for me, the blurriness comes with things like NAMBLA. I mean, what is the actual age?

Allison: I don't know whether we are going to talk about emotional maturity or what, but there are a whole lot of people in this society who will take advantage of your need and abuse you. And we just don't give enough information about that. I mean, that's one of the things that I like about the existence of the lesbian SM community. It's about sharing information. Some of that information is about who the abusers are, and what they will come to you for, and some of it is about why you would want to do this, and what you think about, before you do it.

MR: Which leads seamlessly into my next question: As a survivor of abuse yourself, and with an attraction to SM, you must be aware of the fact that people frequently place SM and abuse in the same category, as though everyone who is into SM has been abusive, or is inherently sadistic or masochistic, in a self-destructive way. What do you think about that?

Allison: Oh, basically I ignore it. It puts me in an untenable place. For years I was caught in this trap of not being able to write about sexuality, or not being able to write about my actual *lived* sexual experience, because I was a survivor, and that's not possible. I can't deny half of my life for either of those reasons. Also, I think it's dangerous for all the other people like me, and there are a lot of other people like me. Now, I can also introduce you to my girlfriend, who had no childhood sexual abuse, and has a very similar sexual desire to mine—just different enough for us to be attracted to each other. So I know it's not as simple as the world would like to paint it. But the way to figure out how complicated it really is, and learn something about it, is for people like me to be able to talk. If you set these walls up, we don't get the real information.

MR: Well, perhaps in the kind of society we were talking about earlier—where we want everything neatly and pleasantly categorized—we are prepared to accept any atrocity, in the name of maintaining the fiction that we are an antiseptically civilized Ivory soap society. In a society like that, the idea of eroticizing dominance and submission is untenable.

Allison: Well, wait a minute. What's impossible for people to stand is *acknowledging* it! I don't think that anybody had to have my stepfather to grow up to be a masochist. We are watching American television—growing up in the fifties and sixties, for Christ's sake! If you watched *Wild, Wild West,* you knew that the jerk-off point in the hour was when Robert Conrad was going to get tied up and get his shirt ripped off. We all knew what that was about. Or *The Man From U.N.C.L.E.* I can't tell you how many times I watched Illya Kuryakin get tied up by some gorgeous woman, talked to badly, and slapped a couple of times. And I go in the bathroom and jerk off. For goodness' sakes, it's American. It's romantic! If they really want to eliminate SM fantasies from this culture, they should take a good hard look at how extensive it is.

MR: I'm not really sure that people actually want to eliminate them because I think that people actually enjoy them. They just don't like having attention called to them.

Allison: You've got it. (*laughs*) They would like to do what marvelous Baptist ministers are so talented at: they can actually come to orgasm without ever touching their genitals, or acknowledging that they have made a stain in their pants.

MR: Pat Califia quoted you in her book, *Macho Sluts*, as having said that most lesbian porn doesn't pass "the wet test." What's wrong with lesbian pornography?

Allison: It's boring. It's not just lesbian pornography. Most pornography—more than half of it—is really boring.

MR: My specific question had to do with the idea that sex between women always had to be loving and sweet, and there's an awful lot of herbaceous language—a lot of *flowering* and *blooming* and *petals* and *rosebuds*—why do you suppose that is?

Allison: The ads in the back of the *Bay Guardian*—"Wanted: woman who can listen to good music and walk on the beach in the moonlight." I grew up on the beach in the moonlight. That's fine, but it's not sex. The thing that we don't acknowledge is that a lot of porn is about taste and fetish, and we don't acknowledge either one of those factors much. Stuff that I would find really...effective...is specific to my nature. To the nature of my desire. We try to keep homogenizing, and we keep trying to come up with something that will affect everybody the same way, and I don't think there is much that does that. Do you know "The Carol Vance One-Third Rule?"

MR: No, I don't.

Allison: Carol Vance is one of the women who helped organize The Scholar and The Feminist series. She's an anthropologist. She used to say that in any sexual experience, one third of your audience is going to be titillated, one-third of your audience is going to be appalled, and one-third is going to be bored. And until you acknowledge that dynamic, you are going to be in trouble. Because you're never going to know what's really going on. You are going to listen to the people who are screaming at you, "Oh, how appalling!" because they are going to be loud. And the people who are getting off from it are going to be squirming in their seats and not making too much trouble. And the bored people are going to be heading for the door. If we had the kind of wide-open society that I'm working for, that I want to exist, we would allow those thirds to get along with each other. I wouldn't have to get off on your gossamer "walking-in-the-moonlight porn," or we would acknowledge that you're not writing it for me. It would just be there, and people could look on the shelves and it would be on the third shelf down—"Walking-in-the-Moonlight Porn"—you'd go get it and you'd be happy. Four doors down, probably behind a locked grille, would be the stuff that I would like to read.

MR: We're not exactly a tolerant society, are we? Even within the outlaw culture? It almost seems that when you come out, you have spent a lifetime living within a heterosexist ideal. And then the queer community hands you a whole new list of rules and regulations.

Allison: Now, wait a minute. We do it to ourselves. When I moved to New York, in 1979, I went into the commercial SM community, the female-dominant SM community, with a vengeance.

MR: You were a dom?

Allison: No, I did that once. I wasn't even good at it. I worked one day in a house, just to see what the whole thing was about. But I basically did my anthropology degree interviewing female dominants. I worked as a coat-check girl at the club, and did this shit all because I had to figure it out. I had to understand it. The thing that astonished me was watching myself and all the people around me, even though we were complete outlaws—and we were acknowledging that we were outlaws—here we were, really on the edge of society sexually. And we were still trying to set up categories to make ourselves safe! The most astonishing thing in the world to me was the number of people I would interview about their particular sexual deviance—that was the nature of the work I was doing—and they would tell me about, oh, foot fetishes, and how the perfect toe was just—and they would go into rhapsodies about it. And somewhere in the midst of these rhapsodies, they would have to make a catty, mean comment about that guy over there, whose fetish was hats. I couldn't believe it! I never interviewed one deviant who didn't have two scandalous deviants he wanted to talk about. "I like to put my dick in boots and wrap it in barbed wire and jump up and down, but you know, that guy over there who's wrapping ribbons on his, he's really sick!"

MR: Is it about a desire to "belong," do you suppose? Especially since deviants and outlaws, by definition, don't belong?

Allison: Well, maybe a desire to belong, but also a desire to say "I'm not as bad as that one." And I found myself doing it. The ones who got me—really astonished me—were the transvestites. I was just appalled by them.

MR: What was it about them that appalled you?

Allison: Oh, my Lord, they were dressing like my aunts!

MR: Your aunts dressed like drag queens?

Allison: Exactly! Overdone makeup and frilly dresses. *(laughs)* Support hose! And I'm looking at these guys and thinking, *Yuck!* I was offended because I felt that they were making fun of people I love, and all my feminist stuff came up, and that lesbian stuff. I was just totally disgusted. And one night I was actually working, and this transvestite sat down by me and was telling me all about how his straight roommate and his straight roommate's girlfriend had spanked him before he came to this club. And he went into this whole long, detailed story, which turned out to be very hot. I realized it was a complete fantasy—that the whole thing was about telling me this, and I just made myself sit there and be polite like I was in Sunday school in North Carolina, nodding and smiling at him like he was one of the blue-haired ladies in my Sunday school, which is what he looked like. I gradually realized that I had been making him into this kind of *demon,* and then, on the whole, he was just trying to get off in his own way.

MR: What did you learn from that experience?

Allison: It took me years to work that stuff through. The impulse to categorize is really deep. I still feel it. It's just that now, I see it more often. It doesn't sneak up on me. I think that in American culture, a lot of stuff sneaks up on us. We don't know why we are so appalled. We just go with it.

MR: The piece I enjoyed most in your essay collection *Skin: Talking About Sex, Class, and Literature* was the essay about the lesbian writer Bertha Harris, whom you met in 1975 when you took a writing class with her at Sagaris, the feminist institute. You've written, "When Bertha Harris talked about literature, it was like listening to Billy Graham talk about God." From a Southerner, that's not to be taken lightly.

Allison: I think Bertha Harris was astonishingly brave. She was a fearless lesbian iconoclast at a time when that was more rare than you could possibly imagine. And dangerous—I mean, she really got reamed for it. She got ground down, and she basically walked away for a decade. She's just come out from the woodwork again in the last year or so and is writing a new book, but at the time, she was a lifesaver. She saved my life. And at the time I didn't really know enough to realize how important she was. She just didn't obey the rules. And it reminded me, yet again, that I set out to be a rule breaker instead of a foot soldier in the feminist movement, which is what I had become.

MR: Do you still find yourself in conflict with people?

Allison: Yes. Oh, yes.

MR: Fresh conflict? Or the same old conflict?

Allison: Oh, it's the same old stuff, it's just in new guises.

MR: Did the National Book Award nomination for *Bastard out of Carolina* change anything? You still consider yourself to be an outlaw, but the fact that your work has been welcomed into the mainstream is undeniable.

Allison: I know, I know. Well, it did complicate matters for about a year. I must have done something wrong with my mantra for about a year there, especially in the months following the National Book Award. All of my assumptions were about surviving a life in which I would never be given any recognition, any approval, and I would do what I was doing anyway. And when somebody throws approval at you, it just takes the ground out from under you. It was complicated for a while. Fortunately, the world has reverted to type, and I have reverted to type. The timing is really interesting; because by the time the National Book Award came along, I had gotten past wanting any of that, or caring much about it.

MR: What did you think of Madonna's book, *Sex*?

Allison: Boring.

MR: What was boring about it?

Allison: Other people's fantasies often are. Look, the thing that most fascinated me when I really started looking closely at sexuality, particularly classical categories of deviant sexuality, is how much of it can be reduced to the same six or seven scenarios. I mean, how repetitive they are. How tedious they can be, without great skills. This is the thing that gets left out. It's like the early days of the women's movement, when we thought every woman's story was equally valuable. Well, every person's sexual fantasy is equally valuable, but most of them are going to bore the shit out of you if the delivery doesn't have some talent behind it.

MR: I take it, then, that Miss Ciccone's sexual fantasies don't pass "the wet test"?

Allison: Madonna has genuine sexual fantasy, but that book is tedious. The best part of it was where the shaven-headed lesbian has tied her to the chair. I thought that was really cute. If I got off on photographic porno, I would have enjoyed it more.

MR: What do you think of the mainstreaming of porn? One could argue that that's what Madonna has done with her book.

Allison: I think it's a trick. I think it glides on the surface, for the most part, and I don't think it's any new thing.

MR: You don't think that outlaw sexuality is threatened by this kind of thing?

Allison: Well, the fringe is moving all the time, honey, which is the virtue of it. I think if there's going to continue to be a fringe, it has to move all the time. By the time Madonna puts it in a book, and sells so many copies of it, it's no longer the fringe. It's only the acceptable shadow of the fringe.

MR: So the fringe is essentially kept intact?

Allison: You know, the stuff is personal. I'm sure there are a whole lot of people who have actually stained that metal cover with various juices, but I didn't. I have it as an interesting arti-fact. I find a lot of commercial porn even more boring than the romance porn because it is so calculated. And a lot of Madonna's stuff is calculated. Where she is genuine it's fascinating.

MR: Has porn changed over the last decade or so?

Allison: I don't think actually that porn has changed that much, except good stuff has gotten even harder to find. I think it's one of the great myths of our society that there used to be a time when it was all hotter. That's a lie. It's the same. You just have to find it. There are always passionate people making it.

MR: What arouses you personally?

Allison: Oh, honey, I have a two-year-old son. When my girl-friend gets home early from work, and he's late at day care, I can instantly get hard. It's wonderful. But that's desperate need.

MR: Has motherhood changed the way you view sexuality?

Allison: It's made it a whole lot more precious, and a whole lot more rare.

MR: I think that's something even ladies who read *Good Housekeeping* could understand.

Allison: Oh, Lord, I'm so terrible. It really appalls me that I am so predictable, and I'm doing the same thing everybody else has done. My sisters laugh at me. Yes, you don't have sex for five or six years. (*laughs*)

MR: How long have you and your lover been together now?

Allison: Oh, my God, it's six years. Coming up on seven. It's appalling.

MR: Has your sexuality changed as you've gotten older?

Allison: Yes. I'm menopausal. And it's appalling. (*laughs*) You don't have any predictable cycles anymore. I get bitchy as hell, and to me, that means I get horny. So it's changed dramati-cally. It hasn't lessened. The only thing that's lessened is the time in which I get to do it. You should be very glad you're a man.

MR: When you put it in that context, I am. Immensely.

Allison: But you know, people just need to lighten up and enjoy sexuality. It's given to us as a gift, not as a cross to bear.

MR: Spoken once again like a true Baptist Sunday-school girl.

Allison: Honey, I can never escape that old-time religion. I put it to different uses than they intended.

Laura
ANTONIOU

When people get over the idea that every story has to be about Dick and Jane, I want Dick to be female to male, and Jane to be male to female. I want them to have noncongruent genitalia, and I want their stories told. As long as there are writers who are willing to go that step further, erotica will keep getting more interesting and more complex....

Still in her early thirties, Queens-born Laura Antoniou is heiress presumptive to some of the erotic territory staked out by Pat Califia and John Preston, two writers whose work has inspired and shaped her vision of sexuality and erotic fiction. Antoniou's writing moves with assurance between genders and sexual orientations, relentlessly exploring the dark side of sexuality: male and female, gay, straight, and bisexual. From her early sense of the erotic power inherent in switching gender identification at will, to her full acknowledgment of herself as a sadomasochist, Antoniou insists that SM, like hot erotic writing itself, moves beyond the constraints of even conventional gay and lesbian sexual mores. "There is nothing I have ever created in my life that did not have some aspect of dominance or submission to it," she says.

As Sara Adamson, she has written *The Catalyst*, *The Marketplace*, *The Slave*, and *The Trainer*. As Laura Antoniou, she has edited the anthologies *Leatherwomen*, *Leatherwomen 2*, *Some Women*, *By Her Subdued*, *No Other Tribute*, and *Looking for Mr. Preston*, a memorial anthology to honor John Preston.

Michael Rowe: There's a great deal in your writing to suggest an affinity with male characters. What was your father like?

Laura Antoniou: My father was an immigrant to this country. He was a racist, sexist, homophobic bigot. That is the way to describe him. He was the classic male head of the household. My mother, although she was—boy, this is tough—my mother didn't know any better. (*laughs*) She gave me a lot of guidance, away from his bigotry, and did it in a very subtle way. Luckily her influence won.

MR: Did you have brothers or sisters?

Antoniou: I was the oldest child. I was adopted, and I have a younger brother. When I was very young—I don't know how I ever got the idea—I felt it was better to be a boy. Of course, my father thought it was better to be a boy, too, which is where it might have come from. I always felt a little bit ticked that, no matter how good I was, I still didn't have what I perceived to be the social privileges of being a boy.

MR: How were you in school?

Antoniou: Very, very good. Mostly A's. The only subjects I didn't do well in were the ones I didn't care about. But since I was such a precocious reader, and very bold in the classroom, and didn't mind speaking up whenever I felt like it, I got generally high grades.

MR: Did you treat school as a way of not dealing with your home situation?

Antoniou: It was very easy to escape in books because people in books were always having wonderful adventures, and also it got me what little praise I had. I could always be assured that in any mixed company, someone would at least say, "Oh, Laurie is always reading." So that was the attention I got.

MR: Were you a social child? Did you have many friends?

Antoniou: I was very into Dungeons and Dragons, and I was definitely the ringleader. I went out and bought the Dungeonmaster's guide to sort out how to play the games, and I actually played with groups of girls for years before I found out that the majority of the players were boys. I always wondered why all the characters and the modules they sold for the games seemed to be men.

MR: The essence of Dungeons and Dragons is, of course, role-playing. Were you interested, even then, in the politics of dominance and submission, at least inasmuch as they pertained to the games you played with your friends?

Antoniou: Always. There was nothing I ever created in my life that did not have some aspect of dominance or submission in it. When I was writing in junior high school, there were elements of fetish and power and control in my stories. When I started playing Dungeons and Dragons, I included the same elements, the things that turned me on—the power, the uniforms, the military fetishes—and structures where people would belong to other people, and would go through formal signs of obeying. I would work them into my games and be able to tell stories to other people to get them to behave how I wanted.

MR: Were you still identifying with male characters at that time, or had you begun to incorporate female characters as well?

Antoniou: No. By that time, I had shifted my identity to try to incorporate female heroes, as idols or victims, depending on what my head space was.

MR: What attributes did you ascribe to the female characters?

Antoniou: I created very masculine women. I created a pack of the butchest women you ever saw in your life. When I look at the pictures that I had drawn of the characters I made up for books and stories, or games, they all kind of look like Jamie Lee Curtis.

MR: You had a significant lesbian relationship with an older woman while you were in college. Tell me about that.

Antoniou: It was at St. John's University, in Queens. I developed a crush on a woman in college who was a senior, and we played roles in *Twelfth Night*. I was her maid, Maria. She took it on herself to, as she put it, corrupt me. It was a very powerful experience—my first relationship with a woman. I had always had friends before, but nothing as a formal relationship. She taught me a lot of things. I completely surrendered to her.

MR: And did she consciously assume that control?

Antoniou: I believe she did consciously, but not erotically. She got off on controlling other people in a more general sense rather than a fetishistic way. This was not SM. There was no ritual around it. It was just that if she wanted to go someplace, that's where we went. And when we got there, she would order. She always knew what we were going to do.

MR: Did that appeal to you?

Antoniou: Yes, it did. I really needed that kind of control for a while—my life had been very messed up at that point, and she was perhaps the most stable person I knew.

MR: How did this relationship end?

Antoniou: It really ended when she left school, when she didn't return. I don't even remember whether or not she graduated. I remember she wasn't coming back to school, and I made a conscious decision not to go back, either. And very, very quickly, we lost contact with each other. In a way, I had wanted it at that time, I had wanted us to break apart because it was getting too entangling. I knew that she would eventually find a man and get married, which she did. At the same time, I was too scared to actually go to her and tell her what I wanted.

MR: Did you model any of your characters on her?

Antoniou: When I write about her, I go to extremes very quickly. I once tried to include her in a story, and when I reread the pages, she sounded like a cold, calculating, Machiavellian character.

MR: Oh, dear. Funny how the subconscious works, isn't it?

Antoniou: She really wasn't that way when I was there, so I just kind of put that on the side.

MR: Did you leave school to write?

Antoniou: No, I left school to go to another school. Queens College.

MR: What did you study this time around?

Antoniou: Anything. I was a very sloppy student. I didn't care what I was there for.

MR: Now I find that interesting, considering you were such a highly disciplined academic beforehand, and I am wondering if your emerging sexuality didn't confound the issue with school?

Antoniou: I think it was the energy I was expending staying in the closet which really affected how I behaved at school.

MR: What did you look like at this time?

Antoniou: Short, fat dyke with glasses. (*laughs*) I'm such a type, actually. When I went to Power Surge for the first time—

MR: Power Surge?

Antoniou: The lesbian SM conference held in Seattle. I went there for the inaugural conference two years ago, and I had to arrange for housing because I was broke that year. So these nice women who put me up for the weekend called me up, to arrange to pick me up at the airport. They said, "How will we recognize you?" and I described myself: short, fat, short dark hair and glasses, and I'll be wearing a leather jacket with a button on it. Wouldn't you know, there was another woman on the plane going to Power Surge, and we were staring at each other. And at the airport in Seattle, we just started laughing.

MR: My question about your appearance wasn't a complete non sequitur—I was curious about whether or not you had a particular "look" to help you stay in the closet. But it sounds like you didn't.

Antoniou: Well, actually, it's really funny. I was doing the exact opposite. I was wearing men's ties and vests, and I was never out of jeans. I didn't start wearing dresses and suits until I worked for McGraw-Hill, the publishing company, and even then it was only under duress.

MR: What did you do for McGraw-Hill?

Antoniou: I bought computers. I was a computer and software buyer. I went to McGraw-Hill with the specific intention of taking the job only for the short term. What I really wanted was to be inside this big publishing company, and maybe an editorial-assistant job would open up. Like at *Business Week*. Could you imagine? I would be so unhappy working for *Business Week*.

MR: I think there would have been some intriguing articles about office politics, and keeping discipline in the workplace.

Antoniou: Actually, I just went back to McGraw-Hill the other day because I still do my banking with them, and I ran into the only other gay staff member from the time. We reminisced for a while. Yes, in college I dressed pretty butch, but I didn't really talk about being gay. In fact I got myself a nice young faggot boyfriend, and we kind of—ha! ha!—bearded each other for about three years.

MR: Hmmm. The mind boggles trying to envision it.

Antoniou: Well, it was very upsetting for a lot of people around us.

MR: I bet it was. Talk about gender fucking.

Antoniou: He was Haitian.

MR: Oh, you weren't just *gender fucking,* you were being perceived as polymorphously perverse. You were pushing all the buttons on the elevator panel.

Antoniou: *His* parents disapproved. My mother was *scandalized*.

MR: If only they had known what else they could have been disapproving of and scandalized by.

Antoniou: I know. This handsome young man and I shared a bed for so many years, and, well, didn't—umm—do what they all thought we were doing.

MR: All right. Enough of this pansexual remote-control sordidness, Laura. We can thank God you didn't get hired on *Business Week*. How did you begin writing seriously?

Antoniou: I actually started writing when I was eleven or twelve. I kept huge notebooks, loose-leaf notebooks with all of these handwritten stories on loose-leaf paper. And it was mostly because I was getting sick and tired of all the adventure books I was reading that were about boys. In fact, I remember complaining quite bitterly to librarians that they'd better find me some books about girls that didn't involve going to parties and finding boyfriends.

MR: What was the librarians' response?

Antoniou: Nancy Drew.

MR: Can you remember how old you were when you first read a piece of fiction that drew an erotic response from you?

Antoniou: I had found a book at the public library, and the title of it was *Greek Slave Boy*. It was a story of a boy who was sold in a slave market in ancient Rome and purchased by a Roman family. The book had at least one flogging scene, where the mistress of the house intervened in order to show him mercy.

MR: What was it about the scene that you found erotic?

Antoniou: All of it. The helplessness of the situation, the fact that there were people who could abuse him at will. I think part of what attracted me was that he did, in fact, gain allies in the household. The mistress was fond of him, or at least merciful, so there was the element of being a slave but being loved at the same time. I remember thinking that was very odd. Whatever rational mind I had at that early age told me that I would be very unhappy if someone took me away from my parents and sold me off. And yet, in that horrible situation, there were these highly stimulating stories and images that I just couldn't ignore. At the same time, I felt that I couldn't discuss them with other people.

MR: Did you identify with the slave boy?

Antoniou: Yes, I did.

MR: How did you begin writing pornography?

Antoniou: I got involved writing pornography because of an ad in *The Sandmutopia Guardian*. It's this wonderful pansexual SM magazine which has no fiction in it, only fact. The editor had mentioned that Masquerade Books was publishing all these wonderful trashy novels about nonconsensual SM behavior, and mentioned a couple of titles. The only title I remember was *The Lustful Turk*. The editor thought this was delightful, recommended them highly, and also mentioned that Masquerade was looking for writers who could write formula fiction like this. At the time I was working for the PWA coalition, and I was also a volunteer in a lot of local organizations, but I thought it would be fun to try my hand at writing a pseudo-Victorian SM novel. I wrote a letter to the publisher explaining who I was—my publishing background at that time had been entirely nonfiction. I had done a newsletter for my local SM organization, which I had helped found. So I mentioned all this stuff, and within three days I got a call back from the publisher, and he invited me out to lunch. He said he would have to see samples of my writing, and I asked him, "Well, what formula?" He said, "Why don't you write about people doing SM for the first time?" So on my way out of the city that night, when I was sitting in the tunnel traffic, I came up with an idea for a book made up of short stories all concerning a group of people who had seen the same movie and then gone home to try out doing it. I called it *The Catalyst*, wrote my outline, wrote three chapters in about a month, and within days of submitting them, I got my first book contract.

MR: How did you feel?

Antoniou: I was so happy. I was bounding up and down all over the place. I called all my friends. I said, "I'm going to write a book! I'm going to write a book!" It was very exciting.

MR: You've written three books so far—*The Catalyst, The Marketplace,* and *The Slave*—under the pseudonym Sara Adamson. How did the pseudonym come into being?

Antoniou: When I left Queens College to take the job at McGraw-Hill, I suddenly had a lot of time on my hands, and I didn't have a lot of teenage friends hanging out at my apartment anymore. So I started going into the city, and I joined a local SM club. I started going out to the clubs and I started doing phone sex. One night, while cruising for women on the phone-sex line, I ran into an old instructor of mine and we ended up meeting, having dinner a couple of times. He was a man—a significantly older man—and I was really fascinated by him. We played together a few times. It didn't really work out, though, but he was the one who suggested the name Sara as a pseudonym for the phone-sex line, so I wouldn't have to use my real name. Now this is the type of paranoia that pisses me off, now that I am out of the closet and a public figure, but I actually believed that I should not tell anyone my real name. Because if anyone out there in the SM world knew my real name, they would somehow track me down and visit me at home, or blackmail me.

MR: Were you still living at home with your parents?

Antoniou: No. I was living in an apartment, but I just believed that if everybody else was using a pseudonym, maybe I should too, so for a while, as I came out of the scene in New York, I was known as Sara. And just to be perverse, I spelled it S–A–R–A, instead of with the H. And that was it. Now the Adamson comes from my really important relationship with a person of the other gender—I have a very good friend named Mitch Kessler, a whip maker, who is my leather daddy. For a year and a day, I was in submission to him. Mitch has a professional name, because he's a whipmaker—his business is called Adam's Sensual Whips. So when it came time to make up a pseudonym for the book, I used Sara Adamson, dig, dig. But that style of relationship ended and what has evolved is more of a daddy/boy relation-ship.

MR: Did you live with him?

Antoniou: No. In fact the only reason I think our relationship has worked is that I live a significant distance from him and we are not very intrusive parts of each other's lives.

MR: Isn't that unusual for a lesbian?

Antoniou: To have a relationship with a man? Yes.

MR: Did you not catch a lot of flak for that?

Antoniou: I was told to my face at Power Surge that I wasn't welcome there.

MR: Did you bring him with you to Power Surge?

Antoniou: Oh, of course not. I would never try to take a man into women's space. I absolutely respect women's space and, in fact, encourage it. But at the same time, I happen to know that while it's no majority, there is a significant number of women who identify as lesbians who do have sexual relationships with men. Now I've heard rationalizations, explanations—in fact, on the cover of the *Guardian* last year, they had a cover story on cross-orientation play. With gay men and lesbians, which I thought was a really roundabout way of saying bisexual.

MR: Is he gay?

Antoniou: Mitch is bisexual.

MR: That can be listed as out of the realm of the expected. That's a whole different thing, isn't it?

Antoniou: Absolutely. My dream, as a young girl, was that I would grow up to be the Greek Slave Boy. It happened. And the way I relate to this man is as though I were a young gay man. Mitch is a mentor figure. And that's really why I kept the name after the first book came out.

MR: You've written about this relationship in *Leatherwomen*, haven't you? Under another one of your pseudonyms, "Lady Sara"?

Antoniou: What a surprise! (*laughs*) Is that so?

MR: Don't you be coy with me, missy!

Antoniou: Well, it's actually not specifically about the relationship, because "Sir" is a very forbidding figure, and Mitch is much nicer. But yes, I do write about my relationship with this man because it's easier for me to. There's not as much pain involved in this, as opposed to my past relationships.

MR: Does writing come easily for you, or is it difficult?

Antoniou: Writing can be so easy for me. Right now it's very hard. I'm in a state of writer's block that has lasted for about three months. But sometimes, when I'm on a roll, I can write for eight or nine hours at a shot.

MR: Tell me about *The Slave* and *The Marketplace*.

Antoniou: They are my answer, in a way, to Anne Rice's *Beauty* books, and *Exit to Eden*, and also, in a small way, to John Preston's *Master* series. He, of course, created The Network. I have The Marketplace. It deals with some elements of the underground SM slave markets that other people have written about, but mine has my own touches. It's an homage, and it's also an answer.

MR: Do you find that the points you make in your books, about sexual politics, lesbians and gay men, SM, all these things—do the books follow you out into your private life? Do you find that people make judgments about you based on what you've written?

Antoniou: I wouldn't know because not many people have discussed my books with me. In fact, the hardest thing about writing erotica is the isolation. Your mainstream writer friends don't feel it's appropriate to critique a sex book, and that's even assuming they'll read it. You don't get much contact with strangers who have read the books, and my friends, at least, are very reluctant to discuss my books with me. I don't know whether they are afraid that if they criticize them I'll hit them, or whether they don't have much to say.

MR: Is there any danger of erotica, moving forward as a genre, becoming too mainstream?

Antoniou: Not as long as there are writers like Carol Queen around, who will keep pushing and not stopping at what is safe and comfortable. The minute people get used to having books about people who use leather and whips and chains, I want books about people who use knives.

MR: Now, there's a heretical thought. You're going to catch flak on that one.

Antoniou: Who cares? When people get over the idea that every story has to be about Dick and Jane, I want Dick to be female to male, and Jane to be male to female. I want them to have noncongruent genitalia, and I want their stories told. As long as there are writers who are willing to go that step further, erotica will keep getting more interesting and more complex and, of course, it can't help leading people the same way.

MR: What else?

Antoniou: I think erotica needs more heroes. I think we need more characters like the romantic Master in Preston's books. And I think that we need to not only start writing about the sex and the emotions realistically, but stop creating our nineties archetypes and have people grappling with real issues, and winning over impossible odds.

MR: But you do feel that the genre is growing? "Growing up," as it were?

Antoniou: Definitely. The childhood literature that was *Trucker Boys in Bondage* gives way to *I Once Had a Master*, which gives way to this new breed of writers who are literally starting out with entire novels about human characters having human interactions.

MR: You've said that if you identified yourself in terms of your sexual orientation, you'd identify yourself as a sadomasochist.

Antoniou: Yes.

MR: Is this a lifestyle that you live, twenty-four hours a day?

Antoniou: It's the filter I see the world through. I can't meet another person without assessing how they will react when they find out I'm a sadomasochist. Will they be interested? Can I possibly bring them into this world? I can't even contemplate a close relationship with someone who doesn't absolutely accept sadomasochism as an alternative sexual identity, or at least lifestyle. And that really adds an interesting color to one's acquaintances.

MR: Could you imagine yourself writing non-SM material?

Antoniou: Oh, yes, it's on the back burner. The trouble is, I keep getting contracts for more erotic material. On the other hand, SM just seems to sneak into the things I want to do on the side. For instance, I want to write a murder mystery, but a murder mystery which takes place at a leather conference. So I don't know. There isn't anything one hundred percent mainstream in my near future.

MR: What do you think about the argument that pornography —and especially explicitly sadomasochistic fiction—degrades women?

Antoniou: I find it very difficult for the printed word to become an instrument of degradation.
    I am an absolute believer in the concept of free press and free speech. I just got a check—a rather large check—for some work I did. One of the first things I did after paying my bills was to rejoin the ACLU. And I believe that the printed word cannot

harm. It's only what people do with the concepts they've read. So it's not that SM, or porn, degrades women, it's how people perceive what is written. Or what they view, and then act on.

MR: But if it wasn't written down, they wouldn't have anything to act upon.

Antoniou: There's no way of proving that. I had fantasies before I read anything, and certainly there are entire societies of nonliterate people who *do* degrade others, and who *do* cause abuse and suffering. And they are not driven to do this because they have a copy of *Hustler.* There are people who will harm other people. There are people who take a genuine pathological pleasure out of harming or degrading other people, and they will use anything as an excuse. They will take anything and allow it to be the trigger for this antisocial behavior.

MR: Ted Bundy, of course, being the first case that springs to mind.

Antoniou: And we don't believe him at all when he talks about how women led him on, or how his mother was cruel to him; but when he says it's *pornography* that drove him to rape and slaughter, suddenly everyone believes him! John Wayne Gacy, who is happily in hell, I suppose, also tried to talk sympathetically about what was happening to "the family" when confronted with the fact that so many of his victims had run away from home, or were hustlers, and he started lamenting what was happening to "the American family."

This moral high ground is the last refuge of a different kind of scoundrel, who needs a convenient target. We don't want to think there is a killer—or an abuser—hiding behind the average person, so we have to come up with these magical reasons why they are evil. They have to be Hannibal Lecter, or they have to be triggered by something else.

MR: There is even dissension within the ranks of gays and lesbians on the issue of pornography and SM. Bruce Bawer, for instance, made the point several times in his book *A Place at the Table* that leatherpeople are an embarrassment to what he calls "mainstream gays," and that they put a scary face on homosexuality as it is perceived by the average heterosexual.

Antoniou: Oh, God, that one!

MR: And pornographers are an embarrassment as well, for that matter.

Antoniou: Well, I would say that pornographers are an embarrassment to the heterosexual community because many of them are heterosexual. The vast majority, in fact—including the vast majority who are writing supposedly gay and lesbian erotica. So that puts that one out. I usually like to say that the sadomasochists, and the drag queens, and the radical faeries, are to the gay community what the Mardi Gras participants are to the heterosexual community. Every once in a while, we put on our costumes, and we parade down the street, and supposedly a democracy is a social system where it is safe to be unpopular.

MR: That's as much a perception as a reality, though, isn't it?

Antoniou: America has consistently pulled toward the notion that unpopular groups somehow have to earn the right to be safe. It's that mind-set which has leaked into the mainstream gay and lesbian community, causing them to believe that if only they excised the leather queens and the drag queens, and got the Dykes on Bikes to cover their tits, we would be accepted by everyone in the country. But of course that's such a false paradise, and it's so difficult, really. I sympathize with the gay and lesbian leaders. They rise to the top of the pack; and then, before you know it, the rest of the pack is already starting to gnaw at their heels. I think it's very tempting to say, "Well, for crying out loud, leave the titclamps at home, and we'll get you your civil rights!" But civil rights are supposedly universal. They are not granted by a majority to a deserving minority!

MR: Don't hold back on my account.

Antoniou: I have just so much patience for that argument. Then I get pissed off and become even less popular.

MR: You mentioned to me earlier that you had run into conflicts with other SM women about your involvement with men?

Antoniou: With that one man.

MR: Why has that particular relationship caused so much grief?

Antoniou: Because it means so much to me. A lot of women who do SM with men and women identify as "lesbians." It's easy to drop into the lesbian community and just forget about the guy. He's not there, you don't have to talk about him, and so, fine— you're with lesbians, you're a lesbian. When I was at Power Surge, I walked outside one of the afternoons to get lunch, and there was a woman sitting on the stairs crying. I didn't know her, but I gave her my hankie, and sat with her for a while and asked what was wrong. She said that during the entire weekend she had been attending workshops along with everyone else, and talking about her SM experiences with her daddy. And that she had changed the gender of her daddy from a man to a woman, pretending that this was a lesbian daddy she had back wherever she came from. She felt horrible about this. She felt she had betrayed her relationship, that she had acted as though she were ashamed of it. She didn't want to go back inside the conference, and neither did she want to go back home, because she couldn't bear to tell this man she had repudiated his existence. I can't think of a worse thing for a women's organization to do than to make a woman lie about her lover. After all the centuries that women have been taught to lie about themselves and their feelings, to not question, and just be good girls and do what they are told—for women to make other women feel afraid to tell the truth is such a horrible thing.

MR: So you *are* a troublemaker. How did you handle this particular situation?

Antoniou: I stood up at the next seminar I went to, and decried the antibisexual attitude of the conference which was causing women who were attending such pain. I also said that I would never deny that I had had a powerful, empowering relationship with a man, regardless of the company I was in.

MR: What was their response?

Antoniou: A couple of women were very upset, and told me in no uncertain terms that it was so vital for them to have "lesbian space" which was not affected by masculine power. But listen, like I said before, I support women's space. I support men's space. But when people start defining what sexual orientation is, when so many people are so fluid in their sexual behavior and orientation, that's when I begin to get a little suspicious. When someone tells me they want lesbian-only space but they are going to welcome lesbian women who trick with men, I want to know what "lesbian" means. Does that mean I'm not one? What does that mean to a political lesbian? And believe me, there were a lot of "weekend lesbians" at Power Surge and I'm sure there are going to be a lot of weekend lesbians this year.

MR: Earlier you said your orientation was sadomasochism. Do you identify yourself primarily as a lesbian or primarily as an SM person?

Antoniou: Primarily as an SM person. Politically, I'm a dyke. I have erotic and romantic yearnings toward women, and if I were ever to settle down with someone, it would be a woman. But whenever people tell me they need "pure space"—that is, without the essence of the other gender—assuming there are two genders, but we won't go into that—I need to remind them that by saying this, they are telling me that the other gender, whether male or female, is so powerful that any woman who has ever come into contact with a man affects an entire gathering of women. And that attributes to men such power that it's amazing, and *absolutely* unfeminist. (*laughs*)

MR: What about women in men-only space?

Antoniou: Whenever gay men get up in my face about *We can't have women in the leather bar!* I say, "What's the matter? Will your spears break?"

MR: What do you think about the concept of "outlaws"? You've heard it all already—SM as "outlaw sexuality," pornography as an "outlaw literary genre." What about it? Are you an "outlaw"?

Antoniou: Now that I think about it, "outlaw" is very much the way I feel. Not so much an evil one, but self-made loner, just always a little bit outside the accepted.

MR: Are you lonely in that place?

Antoniou: No, remarkably. I used to feel I needed a community around me, lots of people to assure me I was doing the right thing and this is good stuff and I was okay, but I found that a lot of the back-patting in community organizations, both gay lesbian and SM related, is really very desperate. Everyone is assuring each other that they are okay so that we all feel we are okay together. And in fact, I make fun of a lot of that with leather titleholders. The speech consists mostly of leather-together-forever. (*laughs*)

MR: One wonders why, if we are so fond of outlaw sexuality, are we so eager to bring it into brightly lit spaces, and make it mainstream?

Antoniou: Right! I mean, there is a scene somewhere with 5,000 leathermen at a convention being worked up to a frenzy by a speaker who shouts that we are all individuals. And then, all the identically dressed men shout out, "Yes, we are all individuals!" So, in a way, I cherish my identity as an outlaw. When everyone else is wearing black, I will wear purple.

Michael
BRONSKI

I'd argue that the lifestyle being sold by the magazines was a sexual lifestyle. If Blueboy *was about having nice clean sheets and picking up a doctor,* Drummer *was about picking up a mechanic, being tied up in the basement, and having him fuck you.*

"But I'm not an erotic writer," Michael Bronski demurred when I contacted him in Cambridge, Massachusetts, in the spring of 1994 about adding his observations to this collection. I will concede Bronski's point: he may not be an erotic writer, but as the author of *Culture Clash: The Making of Gay Sensibility*, as well as numerous articles and essays in reviews and anthologies, he remains one of America's most authoritative gay historians and culture critics. His insights into the growth and development of erotica as a genre of American fiction are indispensable to any serious examination of sexual writing. From the pre–World War II hand-copied pornography passed clandestinely among friends, to the homoerotic "physique" pictorials and pulp-fiction paper-backs that proliferated after the war, to the glossy "lifestyle" pornography magazines of the 1970s and 1980s, to the main-stream erotic novels and anthologies of today, Michael Bronski discusses and traces the parallel growth of the genre of pornography as the earliest gay-positive fiction, and gay liberation itself.

Michael Rowe: As a gay historian and culture critic, can you give me an overview on the development of what we, today, define as pornography?

Michael Bronski: Pornography is a reflection of how we actually think and live our lives. It's one of the exact reflections. And it's important to keep in mind that pornography, for the most part, is not social realism. It functions differently. The other thing which I think is important to keep in mind is that pornography is in fact based on a market economy, and on a consumer economy. For the most part, in many ways, it is a manifestation of gay men's lives and sexuality. It is also frequently not published by gay people.

MR: Has this always been the case?

Bronski: I think there was probably a point in the 1940s or 1950s where people really did write their own things, and passed them on to their friends. And that may still happen, but clearly not as much. You know, at some point you find things are being published. I mean, you can actually trace gay male erotic writing as far back as *Teleny*, supposedly written partially by Oscar Wilde. It's clearly Victorian pornography. And even that was published on a consumer basis. So I think you begin seeing pornography coming out first in this country with some early things, like *The Scarlet Pansy*. Then you get into the mass-market paperback stuff, probably in the early 1960s. And I think the pornography industry—the gay stuff—is not run by gay people.

MR: Is that because of the economic power of gay people, or the lack of it?

Bronski: Well, no. I think it was a specific industry that catered to what they saw as an emergent market. Gay people are at many disadvantages in the culture, but I don't think money is one of them.

MR: But the criticism that has frequently been leveled at gay society is that it has not tended to support its own writers. It has tended not to be in an economic position to publish them.

Bronski: Of course. I think the other thing too is that there are plenty of gay publishers who are not *out*. When we say gay people, we basically mean *out* gay people. There are two categories of gay people. If you look at pornography paperbacks, the paperback industry blossomed after the war, in the 1950s. And then, as laws relaxed, there was more pornography coming out. From about 1963 forward, you have gay written pornography aimed at the gay male market.

MR: It seems that pre-Stonewall, especially in written pornography, the representational object of gay male desire was not frequently other gay men, but hard-edged street boys and sailors.

Bronski: Before Stonewall, the object of gay male desire was more often represented by somebody who was not a gay man. It was young straight "trade."

MR: Do you see that as being a reflection of internalized homophobia or self-loathing?

Bronski: Sure. In the pre-Stonewall stuff, of course. That is completely true. The other interesting phenomenon you have back then, in both written and visual pornography—in magazines like *Grecian Quarterly*—you have posed photographs, but you also have a lot of line drawings. If you look at the line drawings, they are quite amazing, because from the waist down, from the hip down, the men are very flighty, fairylike, wispy men. And on the top, they have these huge muscles. It's almost as though the old stereotype of the wistful little queen is being grafted onto the macho male fantasy.

MR: Is the grafting of one image onto another tied into a shift in the cultural perception—or self-perception—of an emerging gay identity?

Bronski: Sure. I think what was happening was that gay men were beginning to get more of a sense of themselves and beginning to see themselves more as men.

MR: Post-Stonewall, that wispy, dewy look became almost obsolete, did it not? Replaced by the image of the self-identified gay men as "hot" and macho?

Bronski: I think it was longer in coming than right after Stonewall. I mean, if you look at the immediate pornography after Stonewall—I'm thinking more at this point of visual pornography—it's still the young boys. It's of a "groovy guy." I think that to really appreciate the shocking changing image, look at the old *Advocate*. Up until about 1971–72, they had a cartoon, a single-panel cartoon running in every issue, called "Miss Thing." He was a would-be queen, with bell-bottoms and sort of limp wrists. At some point in 1972, it changes to "Big Dick," who is this big butch guy. It just flips right over. "Big Dick" is "Miss Thing," after Stonewall.

MR: Following Stonewall, we also saw the launch of an armada of gay porn magazines, notably *Blueboy*, which were expensively and lushly produced, with pictorials and fiction.

Bronski: There were *Blueboy* and *Playguy*, as well as three or four others. I actually have runs of them in the other room.

MR: How did the stories that appeared in these early magazines differ from the ones that were written in the years before?

Bronski: First of all, it was a whole new venue. You really didn't have short stories like these before. What you had was very sentimental stuff in *Mattachine*. There was a spate of gay porno novels of the mid-1950s and early 1960s which were sort of like, Young Boy Comes to New York, Meets People in the Theater, Gets Fucked Over, and Then Commits Suicide.

MR: You had to be punished for being gay?

Bronski: Right. Then there was a change—Young Boy Comes Down and Fucks Around and Has a Good Time. Because *Blueboy* was essentially patterned on *Playboy*, it was not a simple morality show. They don't live happily ever after, and they don't have to kill themselves, but they live. The other thing that I think is important is that the magazine doesn't exist to give you sexuality, it exists to sell you stuff. So *Playboy* magazine existed to sell the *Playboy* philosophy to the man of the 1950s. *Blueboy* didn't exist to sell you gay liberation, it existed to sell you a gay lifestyle, as defined in urban centers by advertisers.

MR: Is it an obvious statement to make, that the point at which they were selling us a gay lifestyle would be the point where there was essentially a vacuum, without anyone knowing exactly what a "gay lifestyle" was? Or is that an oversimplification?

Bronski: I think that's an oversimplification because people are real people with real lives.

MR: They didn't pretend to sell us real lives.

Bronski: Right. I think that it was being discovered, issue by issue. *Mandate* was interesting because it had lots of entertainment stuff in it, and it was essentially an openly gay continuation of a magazine called *After Dark*, which was a very closeted—but very gay—entertainment magazine. Every month they had cowboys, leather guys, butch men, whatever. John Preston would talk about how this meant that people all over America, in smaller cities, would have something to model themselves on, which is true to some degree. I took issue with John over this point. My counter to that was that it was actually *taking away* people's imaginations and giving them a package that they had to live up to. I mean, did every woman in the 1950s really want to look like Marilyn Monroe?

MR: What part did erotic fiction play in the formation of this identity?

Bronski: I think that's a little bit tricky because I think it was a situation where, clearly, these magazines had to have something in them besides advertising. So what they had were photos and stories.

MR: The erotic written word supported the erotic pictorials?

Bronski: Completely. I think it makes more sense to look at those stories as totally supporting what the image of the magazine was. I think, also, that if you looked at the stories in *Blueboy*, you would find that most of the stories dealt with upwardly mobile men with nice apartments, who went out to the theater. If you read *Playguy* they dealt with fucking with the plumber. They were actually selling you whatever the image was.

MR: Do you think, then, that perhaps the appearance of an occasionally brilliant and literary story—which also happened to get you off—was more accidental than not?

Bronski: I think it depended on the editor. I mean, although I said all these magazines were owned by straight people, they were generally edited by gay people. So I think a magazine like *Blueboy*, like *Playboy*, tended to go for better stuff. I think *Playguy* tended to go for junkier stuff, but that was merely because of what was more important.

MR: Let's move forward to the late 1970s, and the emergence of magazines like *Drummer* and *Macho*. Those magazines had very specific requirements, and I wonder if it's just personal preference when I say that those stories in these magazines, which catered to the leather-SM lifestyle, were perhaps more specifically erotic because they had to cater to a very specific facet of sexuality?

Bronski: That's one way of looking at it. That may be partially true. I'd argue that the lifestyle being sold by the magazines was a sexual lifestyle. If *Blueboy* was about picking up a doctor, *Drummer* was about picking up a mechanic, being tied up in the basement, and having him fuck you. So the stories were, in fact, more erotic. More centered on a certain type of sex, and more sexual, because what they were selling you was a *sexual* lifestyle, not an upwardly mobile lifestyle.

MR: Are there any particular stories that come to mind from that particular time which struck you as particularly brilliant?

Bronski: The later stories of Steven Saylor, writing as Aaron Travis.

MR: How much later?

Bronski: "Blue Light" was first published in 1980. Robert Payne had some good stuff.

MR: Did the authors have name value at that time among their own readers? Would people read these magazines and look for a particular author's story?

Bronski: I think that there was some name recognition, but not a whole lot of it. I think the lack of recognition really speaks of the disposability with which the magazines treated much of the fiction. Whether they were good or not, the magazine treated them as disposable.

MR: Moving into the late 1970s and early 1980s, we come upon the earliest appearance of AIDS. There were quite a number of years when the disease was not actually identified, and business was pretty much as usual in large pockets of the country. Was there any kind of flourishing, at this time, of erotic books, as opposed to magazines? Had the book-publishing field enjoyed a commensurate growth with the magazines?

Bronski: No, because from the 1960s on, you had Greenleaf Classics, and then there were five or six companies which were all publishing crappy paperbacks. Throughout all of that time— the 1970s and 1980s—you had lots and lots of little junky $2.95 paperback books coming out.

MR: To your knowledge, did the characters in the magazine stories shift, or did their appearance or their way of carrying themselves change around this time, between the 1970s and early 1980s?

Bronski: I think that two things began to happen. One was, all of these magazines were driven by demographics. What you had in the gay world was that people who had been between eighteen and twenty-two were now becoming thirty-five. So we had the blossoming of the baby boomers. I would argue that if there were two messages we received after gay liberation happened, one message was that it was okay to get fucked, which was not true before.

MR: Because it made you less of a man.

Bronski: Right. And the second one was that you could actually love yourself. You didn't have to go after straight "trade." You could go after another gay man. So this was actually a manifestation of self-love, which meant that, as everyone was getting to between thirty-five and thirty-eight, the images were actually changing. The men were a little bit older, a little bit butcher, a little bit hairier, a little bit bigger.

MR: And now, in the mid-1990s, for the first time since gay liberation began in the early 1970s, we actually have a generation gap which was not there before.

Bronski: I don't think that's true.

MR: Well, let me see if I can explain what I am saying, and then you can tell me if you think it's not true. A lot of the gay men who were middle-aged in the 1940s and 1950s were closeted and had fled into the woodwork by the time gay liberation happened. By the mid to late 1970s, many men of this particular generation were no longer represented demographically. The gay-liberation generation of Stonewall is now in its forties and hasn't lost any of its ability to articulate its political concerns.

But these kids today—the twenty-somethings—have political concerns of their own. What I am hearing quite a bit is "You seventies guys, you guys in your forties!" It's almost a father-son thing now.

Bronski: Well, to go back to where you began, when I was in gay liberation, after Stonewall, there were men my age who were in Mattachine. So, in terms of a generation gap, I was twenty when Stonewall happened. There were men at twenty-three who were leading New York Mattachine.

MR: Did you run into a conflict with them?

Bronski: Everyone hated one another. I mean, the Mattachine people hated the gay-liberation people, and we hated the Mattachine people, so you would immediately have a generation gap. Which, interestingly, is not actually an age gap, but truly a cultural generation gap.

MR: So the twenty-somethings are actually third generation?

Bronski: Or fourth. Gay life generations run five years, as opposed to the straight twenty. Kids who are twenty today are fourth generation after Stonewall.

MR: Has the militant sexuality—the Queer Nation, hard-muscled, in-your-face ethic—taken on an erotic edge of its own that is distinct and separate from your generation's?

Bronski: No. It's an exact replication of it. You know, this has all been brought back to me since I went to the GLS reunion in New York. One of the main tenets of gay liberation was to have sex. That sexuality was good. That the personal was the political. It's different from what we had in the 1970s, but the message is the same.

MR: I interviewed a young gay male writer yesterday, and during the course of our discussion, we were talking about the generational difference in erotic writing between the 1970s and the 1990s. One of the things we discussed was that much of the work from that era was very slam-bam-thank-you-sir stuff. If you got a good story out of it, great. Today much of the eroticism is wrapped in some really fine, well-paced writing. I'm not saying that the writers are better, necessarily. It's just that today, they seem to be able to take their time. Much of the social and political ground has been broken already. They are not coming into as hostile a world as your generation did.

Bronski: That's somewhat true, although keep in mind that I came out into a world which, after Stonewall and gay liberation, was a wonderful thing.

MR: We were talking about *this* generation—these kids being able to take more time. I'm wondering whether you feel that the more reflective tone is reflected in the written erotica.

Bronski: There are three or four things here. The first thing is, I'm not sure people *do* think they have more time now. I'm not sure that AIDS hasn't created a situation where people think they have to write faster—and more quickly—to get it all out before they die, whether they are sick or not. I think we had a much longer and better sense of time back in the sixties and seventies. Because you felt you had your entire life.

MR: And your second point?

Bronski: My second point is, that type of writing was new then. There was a freshness to it, you know? I think people now have more of a sense of history. There is more of a history now. Whether people draw upon it or not is up to them. So I think there is a different cultural context coming in.

MR: Is it more sophisticated?

Bronski: I think that it's more complicated. I think "sophisticated" is a tricky word. But it goes into my next point, which is that—and this is my vulgar Marxism coming out—writing in our culture does not exist without a venue. So my question is, what are you comparing, then and now? If you are comparing stories that were in the early issues of *Playguy* with things that will be printed in *Flesh and the Word 3*, it's eminently more sophisticated, because John Preston picked out good stories.

MR: But John Preston was also able to find a publisher that was willing to publish them. I can't really see the old E. P. Dutton publishing the work.

Bronski: No, you're completely right. And it doesn't mean the stories are better now than they were, it merely means that there is a venue that will publish better-written fiction. Now, as somebody who still looks through a lot of porno magazines, believe me, there is as much bad porno being written now as there was back in 1973. It's just now we have a different venue because Dutton has decided they can make money. I'm not against people making money. I'm sort of a vulgar Marxist, not a strict one. I just think it's really informative to actually look at gay porn. One way to look at it is through the lens of what it means—the consumer product. But if it means that Dutton can publish a book and make a lot of money with it, yes, they are going to publish a better book than the junky stuff.

MR: Do you think that writing of this caliber was potentially available back in 1973? And simply was not written because the venue was not there?

Bronski: I think it was maybe written differently. Here's a leap of the imagination—imagine that Tennessee Williams and James Purdy were twenty-two today. Where would they be writing? So it's not that it was not being written, it's just being written differently today. There was great gay writing back in the fifties, sixties and seventies. It was not particularly erotic writing, because there was no venue for it.

MR: Do you think pornography has become more bourgeois now?

Bronski: What do you mean, bourgeois?

MR: I mean—

Bronski: I'm a vulgar Marxist, but I'm not just going to trade in terms of that question.

MR: Damn. I thought I could trick you into a tirade. My point is, do you think that pornography is more on the coffee table now, and less on the nightstand?

Bronski: I think the entire society has changed over the past thirty years, and descriptions of sexuality are far more acceptable now than they were. Don't forget, the early sixties had magazines like *Avant Garde* and *Evergreen Review*, which were essentially classy erotic magazines meant for coffee tables. So, no.

MR: It's all in the packaging, then?

Bronski: It's in the packaging. It's also I think in the fact that you can do more, you know? I mean, for years my lover Walta and I would watch TV and we would see these things. And Walta would just say, "Can you believe that when you were ten years old, in 1959, that you'd actually see lesbians on TV?" There are any number of things that we see on TV that we take for granted now. And I think that is true of publishing as well.

MR: Do you feel that there is some sort of a social responsibility for porn writers to come up with new scenarios?

Bronski: No. I think it is the social responsibility of porn writers to be as completely authentic to their own sexual desires and interests as they can be.

MR: But isn't one of the strengths of pornography the fact that it brings you away from average everyday life?

Bronski: Just because something is clandestine doesn't mean that it can't be honest. You are talking about pornography as always functioning as an alternative to—as the darker side of—life.

MR: Like an infidelity, involving only yourself and the image you pull from the writing.

Bronski: But it doesn't mean it can't be honest. I keep going back to Steven Saylor. But you know, Steven's stories are what Steve really finds hot.

MR: What you are saying is that formula sex writing, with fantasies that the author doesn't even believe, is not only dishonest but ultimately destructive?

Bronski: Destructive, yes. I would say that. And it's destructive because it gives people fake scenarios, no different from most TV and most movies.

MR: In your opinion, do the visibility and the quality of the work improve our chances for succeeding?

Bronski: No.

MR: What about the cosmetic appearance of the books? The packaging?

Bronski: In terms of packaging, no. We are dealing with a political ideology, and it cuts in different ways. In the Colorado and Oregon campaigns, we've seen gay people attacked because they were perceived to have more money. So I'm not sure that presenting something as though we *have* more money, and it's more upscale, is going to be in our favor.

MR: You're describing a fairly bleak, no-win situation for erotic writing, then, because if one presents the work as being well packaged and well produced, then one is accused of having too much money. And if it's seedy back-alley mimeographed porn, it's seen as dirty and pernicious.

Bronski: But that's the point. The point is that they hate homosexuals, not that they'll like nice homosexuals more. That's always been a myth. The other thing that we didn't talk about, which I would just mention, harkens back to the early 1980s. I hate to keep arguing with people who have died, but Preston would always say that he wrote *Mr. Benson*, and it struck such a chord that people started showing up with *Mr. Benson* T-shirts. Well, you know, John never mentions that he and *Drummer* magazine marketed those. (*laughs*) It was not a grassroots movement. It was a marketing ploy by the magazine.

MR: Which is not necessarily the worst thing in the world.

Bronski: I'm not saying it is. I'm just saying, let's call it a marketing ploy. I'd argue that maybe it's not a good thing. Because maybe we all have very inventive minds, and we don't need to be actually looking for Mr. Benson. And that in fact what consumer capitalism pornography does is actually limit our imagination by presenting us with prepackaged, predigested homogenized sexual images, and that we would be better off, not without pornography, but with a pornography that perhaps encouraged us to have our own imagination. Or that really worked at extending our imagination. What is always so shocking about Steven Saylor's Aaron Travis work is that it pushes your imagination.

MR: Do you think that written pornography pushes imagination more than visual?

Bronski: Generally, I would think so, because I think people respond to it differently. Let me say this: good written pornography, yes.

MR: Does the reading public make the distinction? Between good and bad? And do they do so now more than they did before?

Bronski: I think some people do, some people don't, and it's dependent on a variety of things. One thing is the accessibility of pornography. If you only have access to very little, because you're a teenage kid who lives in the suburbs and you only can steal a copy of *Blueboy* once a month...well, you don't become a Shakespearean scholar because you read *Hamlet*. You become a Shakespearean scholar because you've read all thirty-two plays. You have to have a broad range of pornographic reading experiences to be able to become discriminating. I think that there were people back then who read everything, and were discriminating.

MR: Are they more discriminating now as porn becomes more mainstream? Or less? Will an anthology series like *Flesh and the Word*, which presents authors very clearly identified, with biographies, create a following that did not exist before?

Bronski: I think, yes. But I think what you are actually getting is that the people who are reading *Flesh and the Word 1*, *2*, and *3* are the people who have bought *Men on Men 1*, *2*, and *3*. I think that the average person who runs into Glad Day and picks up *Stroke*, *Thrust*, and *Drummer* does not necessarily pick up *Flesh and the Word 3*.

MR: Do you think it's a class thing?

Bronski: No, I don't think it's a class thing. I think it's an interest thing. I think if you are interested in looking at porno magazines, you may not be interested in reading good literary pornography. I think good literary pornography like *Flesh and the Word* is, in fact, an extension of the market created by mainstream publishing for gay fiction.

MR: Do you think it's providing a safe hiding place for literati who want to whack off, but couldn't even bring themselves to buy those magazines? Is *Flesh and the Word* the backroom of the literary community?

Bronski: No, not really. I think there are plenty of those people who can actually go out and buy *Thrust* and *Stroke*.

MR: How do you feel the emergence of the New Right has changed the landscape of sexual writing?

Bronski: On a very concrete level, it's actually created a situation where things are not going to get published. Clearly, in Canada, you cannot publish certain things. In Canada, *Playboy* and all the porno magazines submit their blues to Customs so they know what they can get into the country. There are several states in which they actually have laws that you cannot publish even a fictional description of man/boy sex. Not pictures, but a written narrative.

MR: Do you see this getting worse?

Bronski: I see it being a contested battle on a number of fronts. I'm not sure that it will get worse.

MR: Is that too trite—"better or worse"?

Bronski: I think it's misleading. I think it sets up a duality that doesn't really exist. I mean, we went to see Suzy Bright at Harvard a few years ago. She had a beautiful evening coat. She slipped it off, and underneath was a very sexy dress. She said she was here to tell us that the sex wars are over, and we've won. It may not seem that way, but we have. Actually I saw her years ago, on Johnny Carson. Gloria Steinem and Joan Rivers were on, and before they began, Gloria said, "Joan, I want to thank you." Somehow it had been set up for Gloria and Joan to fight, and Gloria said, "I just want to thank you. I see you on TV. You're telling condom jokes, you're telling tampon jokes. You know, any progress that's been made can be fought over, but we never lose it. You've made such strides in talking about things which are important to women, from a woman's point of view, there is no way the New Right is going to win. We've broken all this ground." So I feel that on some levels we have really broken all this ground. And we can fight over the incidents where it's going to be presented, but essentially we have won the battle. Because once you present people—gay people and straight people—with the possibility of having more pleasure, people don't want to give it up. The culture doesn't want to give it up.

Pat
CALIFIA

In a better society, there would be a lot more Amazons.

Pat Califia is the undisputed queen of her own erotic domain, and she has crowned herself precisely by not giving a damn about what anyone else thought about it. Controversy is an unavoidable by-product of writing honestly and fearlessly about needs and desires that polite society wishes would just stay in the dark where they belong. Strong women, dangerous women, SM women, gender-bending women—Pat Califia revels in what her "respectable" colleagues dismiss prissily as unworthy topics for genteel literature. Instead of "genteel" literature, we have *Macho Sluts, The Advocate Adviser, Doc and Fluff, Sensuous Magic, Doing It for Daddy*, and *Public Sex: The Culture of Radical Sex*, as well as hundreds of thoughtful—and thought-provoking—articles, essays, and reviews.

Not surprisingly, her literary reputation continues to be made in spite of, or perhaps because of, that same refusal to lie down and write politically correct, ladylike erotica. "Califia," says the *San Francisco Sentinel*, "seeks to build a constructive alternative to a feminist utopia that offers, at best, a hushed silence on female erotic exploration."

This interview was conducted in the summer months before the Little Sister's bookstore trial in Vancouver, where, in October, Pat Califia would be an articulate, impassioned witness for free expression, and against prior restraint. During the course of our conversation, Califia outlined her life and work—from growing up as the daughter of a Mormon family through her eventual move to San Francisco, and the emergence of the powerful "Amazon" writer, whose work excites fear and anger in her detractors, and fascination, exhilaration, and dizzying freedom in her readers.

Fierce, brilliant, and articulate, there is only one Pat Califia.

Michael Rowe: Going on the premise that who we eventually become is rooted in the place where we have come from, and the people we have come from, I'm curious about who and what went into the creation of Pat Califia. Can you tell me a little bit about your childhood? Where did you grow up?

Pat Califia: During my early childhood, we lived mostly in the western states, and we also lived briefly in the South. Basically, the way it worked was, whenever my father finished a building project, we would move. So I had a very mobile childhood, with a lot of skipping around to different parts of the country. My family is—or at least my mother is—very religious. My mother is a very devout Mormon and, in fact, her family goes way back to the beginning of the church. My great-grandfather was a polygamist, and so that religious affiliation colored a lot of my early experiences.

MR: One of my favorite sections of Edmund White's *States of Desire* deals with Utah, and what he found there. For some reason, it seems, the Church of Latter Day Saints produces an inordinate number of homosexuals.

Califia: (*laughs*) It certainly does, doesn't it? You'd think they would wonder about that. In some ways, growing up Mormon was very good for me. If you grow up in a Christian religion that is not fundamentalist, there may be a liberal gloss put on their attitude toward people of other races, toward women or gay people. But in Mormonism, they just say it straight out: if you're queer, you may as well be a murderer, and women are supposed to be quiet and submissive, and have kids. They talk to their husbands, and their husbands talk to God, and that kind of lets you know right up front what your status is. Either you can deal with it, or you can't. The other part of Mormonism that has been useful to me is that it's an extremely unconventional and bizarre set of beliefs that people espouse with a lot of fervency and a lot of sincerity. And there's a real strong precept in the religion that if you know what the truth is, you have a moral obligation to say it, no matter what the consequences are, and no matter how deeply people will hold your ideas in contempt.

MR: It doesn't sound as though it's designed to produce the kind of rebellion that you've espoused.

Califia: Absolutely it is. All the people on the fringe of the Mormon church who have been way out there—there were a lot of early feminists in the early Mormon church—these were women who often left their husbands and families to follow a charismatic prophet who spoke in tongues, to go live in a godforsaken part of the country, to build a religious utopia. They were willing to live in plural marriages; they were willing to put up with husbands who were gone most of the year because they were out on missions. These women suffered incredible hardship in order to have a life that was consistent with their deepest principles, and that's the part of Mormonism that's been very helpful to me. I mean, a lot of times I think I am sort of a little leather missionary. I also got a lot of training in public speaking that has come in really handy.

MR: It's frequently difficult enough to discover you are gay or lesbian in more forgiving religions, but in a religion that is so intolerant, and, in fact has, as you've said, a very out-front rule for both women and gays—I'm curious as to how that affected you.

Califia: Well, I was always very angry about it. From a very early age, I basically was telling people that I was not ever going to get married, and that I thought it was a crock, and that I was never going to have kids.

MR: How were these pronouncements received?

Califia: I got a lot of hostility and a lot of physical violence.

MR: Physical violence?

Califia: Yes.

MR: At home, or outside the home?

Califia: Both. And I think that it's also complicated by the fact that my sexuality, as a child or as a young person, wasn't really about being *gay*. It was about being a *pervert*. I mean, I knew from the time I was really little that I was fascinated with pain, and with bondage, and that those things were really sexually exciting for me. That was the area my attention was focused on. I mean, I think I have chosen to live as a dyke in the society because that is the niche that is the most comfortable for me as woman who wants to be independent, and as a woman who's sexually interested in other women. But that is not, in some ways, the core of my sexual identity. In a lot of ways, the core of my sexual identity is that I am a sadomasochist.

MR: How did this manifest itself in your early years?

Califia: I was sort of this little collector of any kind of sexual information I could find. I would keep lists of sex terms and try to figure out what they meant. I read voraciously in quest of any kind of information or titillation. I jacked off a lot. I was always looking for opportunities to do things that I knew I wasn't supposed to do. I have this memory of being five, and opening the door to my parents' bedroom. They had lain down for an afternoon nap, or to fuck or something. My father came to the door. He was naked. He yelled at me and said, "What are you doing standing staring at me? Don't you know that little girls shouldn't look at their fathers when they are naked?" And I stopped, and I thought about it, and I realized that I didn't know that. (*laughs*) In fact, I didn't see anything wrong with it, and I was in big trouble. Because there were these really big rules out there, things I wasn't supposed to do, or believe, or think, that made other people very angry. And I couldn't trust my own intuition to navigate my way through that. So, after that, I basically led a sort of split life, where I did the things I had to do to keep the outside looking as normal as possible so that people wouldn't harass me.

MR: For instance?

Califia: Like go to church. Give my little talks at Sunday school. Go to school, make straight A's, all that crap.

MR: You were a good girl?

Califia: I don't know if I'd say that. I was smart. I was intelligent. I don't think I ever made people very comfortable. I think they always knew that there was something else going on. I was too sharp, too critical of adult authority. I also was too prone to go off and do wild and bizarre things that people could not figure out.

MR: What, for instance?

Califia: For one thing, I tied up all of our baby-sitters. When I was about seven, I had my first baby-sitter. We had an agreement that she could watch anything she wanted on television, as long as I got to tie her up. At first it started with just her sitting in the chair holding on to one end of the rope while I ran around and around her chair, to kind of wrap her up. Then it got a little more elaborate. And I was perpetually tying up neighbors' kids.

MR: Did anyone guess the origin of this fetish?

Califia: No.

MR: When did you start writing?

Califia: I've always written. I wrote my first poem when I was eight years old, and I published newspaper articles when I was in junior high school. I've written ever since I learned my alphabet, basically.

MR: Had you always wanted to be a writer?

Califia: Yes.

MR: How did you get from wanting to be a writer to wanting to be an erotic writer?

Califia: I was in my early twenties. I was living in San Francisco because I'd finally managed to get from Salt Lake City to the Bay Area, which saved my life. I was living with a woman who was very rigid. She was a stone butch. She had major gender issues. She didn't want to have sex with me, but she also insisted that we be monogamous. And that we were going to be with each other for the rest of our lives.

MR: How did you feel about this kind of relationship?

Califia: I was not having a very happy time with her. I was at a place in my writing where I would write poems, and I would write stories; and the minute that they were done, I would rip them up and burn them. And I was having a lot of trouble with self-loathing. I was trying to figure out what I could write that would be important, or significant, or literature.

MR: What were the criteria, as you saw them?

Califia: The criteria were not clear. I mean, this was like the mid-1970s, and you know, lesbian literature barely existed. But certainly lesbian literature did not include the kind of things that I thought about when I closed my eyes. And so, what I decided at that point was, I was not going to worry about the literary canon, and who was a genius, and who I was going to emulate. I was just going to write a story about something that was very important to me, and really scary, and I would never publish it. But I would write it, and the fact that I made a bargain with myself that I wouldn't publish it meant that it could be true. So that was when I sat down and wrote the story "Jessie." It got reprinted in *Macho Sluts*.

MR: Was that a turning point for you?

Califia: That story opened the floodgates to a bunch of writing of sex that went in a whole new direction for me. I mean, I wrote that story before I ever did any SM, before I ever met any other women who did it, or who felt okay about it, or could even talk about it.

MR: What was it about lesbian SM that made it so radical at that time?

Califia: The line then—about dykes—was that lesbians do not do SM. It was something some gay men did, but we did not do that, especially in the wake of the women's movement.

MR: What time frame are we talking about here?

Califia: Mid-1970s—1973 or 1974.

MR: A very tumultuous time politically, even for progressive politics.

Califia: It was just really crazy. And in San Francisco, the women's community was very separatist, very antibutch, very anti-any kind of expression of sexuality. You could have people not speak to you for years just because you turned up in public and showed cleavage. It was a time when lesbians were really mean to each other.

MR: Why was that?

Califia: In some ways, I still don't quite understand why we found it necessary, and why we thought that would fight the patriarchy. I just think that misogyny is so deeply entrenched in society, and it's so much a part of our indoctrination, that even as women who love other women, we find it really fucking difficult to turn it loose to do anything different.

MR: Were you always attracted to the butch-femme model?

Califia: Well, I don't know that I *am* attracted to it.

MR: I'm just getting this from your writing, actually.

Califia: The community that I came out in, in Salt Lake City, was a very old-fashioned 1950s-style butch-femme community. I didn't have a lot of acceptance among those thugs because I was a hippie, and I was a minor, and I did drugs, and I was a feminist, and they all thought that was just completely bizarre. So it's taken me quite a long struggle with that system to figure out ways that I can sometimes use it to give myself—or my partners— pleasure. And it certainly is something that I honor as part of lesbian history. But when I do butch-femme, it's basically something I *do*. It's not something that I *am*. What has mattered the most for me, in terms of my own mental and sexual health, is that I have really strong male and female components which are pretty evenly balanced.

MR: Which is fairly unusual, really, because most people are in full flight from the other gender as it manifests itself in them.

Califia: Oh, God, no! I mean, the male that is my guiding counselor and inner self has gotten me out of more shit! I mean, I am really grateful for the characteristics I have that society would label male. I think that it's inevitable in a world where the man has most of the money and mobility and privilege, that when women try to liberate themselves, the first thing we get accused of doing is trying to be men. And I say, "Cool. Let women try to be men; let men try to be women." And out of that, surely, we will reach a place that is more sane. And less hateful.

MR: What is it about male identity that attracts you so much and enables you to write in a male voice so authoritatively? You've written some very hot gay male porn.

Califia: Oh, good. I'm glad you thought so.

MR: Even your female-to-female porn has elements in it that are very attractive to gay male readers. This has not seemed to be the traditional province of writers whose work is revered and adored by women and the women's movement.

Califia: No, no, it's not. Well, I've been very fortunate in my life to have many friends and lovers who were gay men. When I came out into the SM community in San Francisco, in 1977–78, there wasn't really a lesbian SM community. The group that I helped to start was the first lesbian SM support group in the world. So most of the people I hung out with were a group of leathermen here. A lot of whom were into fisting, and pretty heavily into drugs and wild sex, and I think their take on life was that they had done it all, so women were not really a big deal. I mean, they'd had sex with 15,000 men. So an occasional woman was not, like, really a threat to their identity. And they were curious. They were a kind of gay man that AIDS really has made disappear.

MR: What kind of gay man is that?

Califia: The most important thing in their lives was sex. They had really been really fiercely dedicated to it. They were often really nasty to each other in their pursuit of it, and in their dedication to developing a homoerotic standard of masculine beauty. They were also totally twisted fucks. They were willing to do anything that might get them off. So I was really fortunate to be able to be on the fringes of that scene, and see that if you were insatiable, and had a lot of curiosity, and you were really bold, you could make things happen that nobody in their right mind would ever think of. These erotic adventures could really come true. But you had to go out there and push it, and be willing to put your ass on the line. You had to *ask*. You had to be pushy; you had to say what you wanted; you had to be the one to initiate and get it off the ground. I've always found that style a lot more appealing than waiting. Because if you wait, nothing happens. I don't want to be eighty-five and lying in bed, and thinking that there was something I wanted that I didn't have the balls to go out and say, *How can this be? Let's bring it into the world.* I feel like I have a pretty strong male gender identity. A lot of the fucking I do, the SM play that I do, is from a male headspace in a male persona. And certainly, having a female body, I can never really understand what it's like to be inside that male body, but I have gone out of my way to acquire as much secondhand information about that as I can.

MR: You pursue this in your writing as well, this same sort of fearlessness. It's rather an understatement to suggest that you aren't concerned about offending because you seem to take a delight in it, saying, "This is me—take it or leave it." And people have actually taken it. Was there a time when it was hard to sell the persona in print?

Califia: Oh, it's always difficult. Especially post-AIDS. I'm totally a not-respectable commodity. I'm very lucky to have been able to have made a living as a writer. I'm very deeply grateful to my readers and to the people who have made that possible for me. I've been lucky to have a few editors who were really brave, and if it wasn't for people like Robert MacLean, who published my early stuff in *The Advocate*, and Sasha Alyson at Alyson Publications, there would not be any such thing as die-cast SM literature. Most recently, the women at Cleis Press have been really cool and have taken on the job of publishing a book of my essays. And of course, people like Richard Kasak have happened along now, and I find it interesting that kind in the wake of AIDS, I'm actually finding it easier to get published in the straight press than I am in the gay press. Magazines like *Skin Two*, which is a straight fetish magazine out of England, and Kasak's Masquerade Books, are actually more willing to take a chance on sex and do things that are blunt, to challenge the status quo, than magazines like *The Advocate* or mainstream gay publishing houses.

MR: I wonder what you think the impact of AIDS has been on erotic literature. I've been looking at the way different writers perceive trends, and it seems that in the 1970s and 1980s, just before the major AIDS eruption, sex was celebratory and it was not furtive. But today, it's almost like there is an anger powering sex. As though we feel we have been cruelly punished for being sexual, and we are going to take back the sexuality.

Califia: Yes.

MR: It's almost athletic, isn't it?

Califia: It is athletic, and I think what AIDS did was up the ante. It really did. It raised the cost of being known as a sexual outlaw, and it also made it more important in a lot of ways. As though now, if you want to save your sexuality and live it out in a kind of adventurous way, you have to be really smart. You have to take care of yourself. You have to protect your partners, and you need a lot of chutzpah to be able to label yourself in public because most people's response to AIDS has been to increase their sexual shame. To pretend that what we are all looking for are these monogamous relationships that are just the most tedious, shallow imitations of heterosexual marriage possible. I find that really morally bankrupt and disturbing. That's what our movement seems to be encouraging us to do now. It doesn't work, and statistics *show* it doesn't work.

MR: And yet, the exact same climate seems to be making stars out of pornographers.

Califia: Well, yes, partly because people want to read about stuff that they are not doing. I think there is also a new generation of folks who are really curious about what the golden era of gay sexual excess was like prior to AIDS. And it's also a memorial. I mean, one of the things that was true for me was the *Doing It for Daddy* book, which is dedicated to a gay male friend of mine. He died of AIDS. And in all of the books where I write about sex, I'm celebrating the lives of those people who are gone. And trying to find a way to perpetuate their legacy, and make sure that the values and progress they achieved aren't just totally lost into the mist of history.

MR: You don't seem to have a very optimistic view of the gay movement at the moment.

Califia: I think it's really sad to watch the gay movement become a single-issue crusade for an AIDS cure, maybe with a little ancillary coda that we like to stay in the military, and have domestic partnerships. How fucking boring. I did not become a queer so that I could get married and be a soldier. That is not at all what this is about for me.

MR: How do you see the direction the gay movement has taken today, in the context of the vision that the post-Stonewall liberationists saw for gay liberation?

Califia: I think that the early revolutionary potential of the gay movement was that we would transform all social institutions and that we would transform people's relationships to their own bodies. That we would create new social forms that would honor pleasure and would honor human freedom. And that there would be an end to some of those institutions that made it so very, very fucking difficult for us to come out: basic marriage, the family, the church, the institution of childhood itself.

MR: What does it mean to you as a writer, being a historian before your time? Being left behind, with all of these people who have passed on? Are you a historian now?

Califia: Yes, I think so. And it gives me a lot of grief that's hard to deal with, that sometimes makes it hard to work. And I often feel that I am trying to express things that would have been said better by the people who lived it directly. In the book I just put together for Cleis Press, which is called *Public Sex: The Culture of Radical Sex*, I have an introduction to one of the chapters where I talk about the bathhouses. I've written a chapter on the same topic for Mark Thompson's gay history book, which is like gay history through the eyes of *The Advocate*. It's ironic to me that as a woman and a lesbian, I'm defending the baths, and the whole culture that surrounded them, and talking about what was positive and what we should salvage from that era, when the people who should be talking about this are all the men I knew who went there, who loved it, who found that it made their lives a lot easier and happy. I don't think there would have been a gay liberation movement without the baths. And so, sometimes I have that kind of cognitive dissonance where I am thinking, okay, am I entitled to say this? Am I the appropriate person to be left with this job? But it just is my job; so whether or not I am appropriate, I have to do the best I can with it, and not fuck it up.

MR: Has anyone challenged your right to do this?

Califia: Oh, repeatedly.

MR: For instance?

Califia: There are men who are offended that I write an advice column for *Advocate Classified*, or get upset that I write gay male pornography. From time to time, I get nasty letters from readers who are upset about it.

MR: "How do you know? What do you know about our problems?" That sort of thing?

Califia: "What do you know about our problems? I hate women! I don't want to read anything a woman writes!" You know, that kind of stuff. Really hateful, misogynist stuff.

MR: Are we talking about a male societal construct that lends itself to an aversion to women answering men's questions about their sexuality? Or are we talking about something as simple as misogyny on the part of gay men?

Califia: Well, no, I think there is—okay, yes and no. Part of what happens here is that in our culture, as much as I love women, women are mostly a force for sexual conservatism; and women who are feminists or women who choose to challenge the sexual status quo are really in the minority. I think that it's all very well and good to talk about how horrible the patriarchy is, and yes, it is horrible, and I don't like it, either. However, the fact is that the gender system we have, and the homophobic system of hierarchy we have, result in some sexual practices being valorized, and others being oppressed. Hierarchy is not a simple matter of victims and oppressors. We all hold it up in one way or another, and women get certain things for their position in the society that they are not usually prepared to give up. So women are, in fact, a lot of times the people who control children's sexuality, who make them afraid of their own bodies—especially little boys. I think the abuse directed at little boys is drastically underestimated. I think a lot of it comes from their mothers. I think, in fact, a lot of homophobia and fear of other boys' and men's sexuality does come from female caretakers who don't like the idea that there might be any competition for a male's attention from another male.

MR: As a woman in SM who interacts with leathermen, you would have a keen awareness of male-only space, in bars and clubs. And yet you have shared in the history of those places, some of which no longer exist. What is your take on the presence of women in those spaces?

Califia: I think men have an absolute right to be in spaces and institutions where they can be only with each other. I think it's very important for gay men—and for other men—to be able to be with each other and not worry about having women judge them or interfere with their process, or otherwise get in the way. So I have mixed feelings about it. It's like when I used to go to leather bars South of Market in the late 1970s. I knew that my presence in some of those bars really fucked with some of those men, and ruined their evening, because the whole point for them was that they were going to be in an all-male environment, hanging out with other men. And to see a woman there, even if she was wearing leather and obviously into the scene, changed the dynamic. I didn't like that part of it. The problem for me was that there was no place else to go. At that point in history, if you went into a dyke bar in a leather jacket, chances were real good they wouldn't serve you.

MR: Do you feel comfortable writing about straight men?

Califia: Yes.

MR: Do you feel any particular connection to heterosexuality? Or the power politics in the traditional heterosexual model?

Califia: My interest in that whole arena is mostly in ways to subvert it, and ways to separate out some of the fucked-up power dynamics from what's erotic and what's salvageable. I think it's kind of funny that everybody says butch-femme is just an imitation of heterosexuality. I think in some ways it's the other way around. A lot of the polarized ways in which men and women behave and dress have to do with creating erotic tension between each other, and it winds up going so global that it governs every other sphere of life. I think that long after male privilege bites the dust and ceases to exist on the planet, they are still going to have some of that peacock behavior that has to do with emphasizing differences, because it's more erotic than to come together. I think that without the impetus of encountering the stranger, sex loses some of its mysticism.

MR: It doesn't sound like androgyny has much appeal for you.

Califia: No.

MR: In your introduction for *Doing It for Daddy*, you've suggested that "masculinity" is something that can be taken out of the male context and exist in and of itself. Do you want to elaborate on that?

Califia: Well, I think that when you look at the positive aspects of masculinity, the reason why it's so durable is because the qualities are things that society needs. There are honorable, good things about masculinity. What's wrong with it is trying to connect it automatically to a gross amount of privilege, or connect it to the right to abuse other people who are not masculine. Or to engage in such combative and hostile competition with other masculine people that you wind up damaging each other. I think that the path of masculinity is a really valid, spiritual choice to make. I mean, I like men. I have always had trouble with the idea that because I like to sleep with women, I automatically have to hate men. I hate a lot of the things that men do—there are certainly specific individual men that I could gladly chop into dog food. But as a general rule, I sometimes am more fond of men than I am of women.

MR: Is femininity an equally valid path?

Califia: Absolutely.

MR: For either gender?

Califia: Absolutely, yes.

MR: What is your take on the hostility toward effeminate men, within some segments of the gay community, for instance?

Califia: I think it's very strange. It's interesting to me that the aboveground man of the SM community is a butch one, and that there is hardly any kind of aboveground acknowledgment of leather drag queens. And yet they are certainly there. And they've always been part of the scene.

MR: Gay male SM is perceived widely as being the turf of—at least in theory—the very masculine.

Califia: It's about being hypermasculine. I think also that most gay men have gotten beaten up a lot for being sissies, and that in some ways, it takes more guts to put on a dress.

MR: Conversely, is it more courageous for women to adapt masculine attire and attitudes?

Califia: You can't just reverse it and have it be true. Male and female stuff is not always a mirror. I think that the risks are different. I think that when women put on feminine attire, what they often do is run the risk of being labeled sexually available, and the fact that it certainly increases the amount of attention you get makes it more scary to be out in public. So, I think that for both men and women, part of what happens in being associated with feminine signifiers is an assumption that you are vulnerable, that you are available, that you are looking for attention. And that you basically deserve whatever attention you get, no matter how rough or misdirected it might be. There's a really good reason why drag queens and femme dykes are really mean. Most of the bar fights that I have seen have been started by femmes. And finished by them, more often than not. I think that for women who put on male attire, if you pass, you are in a double bind because you find yourself in a world where you have to live according to male expectations. Which include the expectation that if you are challenged physically, you will respond in kind. And if you don't pass, then you enter a world where there's an incredible amount of hostility and violence.

MR: What is the root of that?

Califia: It's not actually all that different from gay men who wear uniforms or leather. I think people pick up on the idea that there might be an element of parody there, and they get real angry with that. They feel that their icons are being fucked with. We really live in a society where people want to believe that identity and behavior and desire are all determined. That you don't have any space to make an individual choice. You are born with these chromosomes which mean you will put on pants, or you will put on a dress. Or you'll have short hair or you'll have long hair. Or you will or won't play with dolls.

MR: You enter very violent territory when you fuck with society's expectations of gender roles. As a man, I have always believed that the harshest punishments of heterosexual men toward homosexual men are meted out when there is a perception that the homosexual men have given up their male prerogatives by being receptive, rather than invasive. It's as though gay men—especially effeminate ones—have "let the team down." The team, of course, being the tribe of heterosexual masculinity.

Califia: And that is all connected. There is no flexibility in that system, and no room for anything to change or be put together in a different way. And what we gender outlaws do is make it clear that there is a choice. You can put it together any fucking way you want. And that makes people very angry; partly, I think, because most conventionally masculine men and conventionally feminine women who are heterosexual are not very happy. They are deeply frustrated. They are real resentful, and they are pissed off. I think the thing that most pisses them off about gay people is the idea that we are out there having more fun than they are. I mean, you can just hear it, these querulous tones they use when they talk about sexual life and decadence in the gay community. It's like, "Well, honey..."

MR: The trappings of SM and leather have certainly been dragged out before the great vanilla heterosexual public, and have been adopted as a fashion trend.

Califia: Yes. It's true.

MR: What do you think is going to happen to that? Do you

think that they are just going to get tired and move on to something else?

Califia: Oh, sure, of course.

MR: Is that good news?

Califia: I don't know, I have mixed feelings about it. I mean, on the one hand, it ticks me off that Madonna can make millions of dollars with her Time-Warner book [*Sex*] when I know that there are people in my community who are dying of AIDS, and you know, we could really use that money in our community to help protect ourselves and make our public space larger and more secure. And that also ticks me off because I think that whenever the mass media uses parts of our community, or our art, or fashion, or culture, they always get it wrong. I don't think Madonna knows anything more about SM than Andrea Dworkin does, although I'd probably rather be misunderstood by Madonna than by anybody else in the world.

On the other hand, as much as those images are exploited and distorted, it's certainly better than not having any imagery out there at all. It's kind of like those horrible lesbian porno novels in the 1950s. When I read most of them today, I just kind of gag because of all the misinformation about lesbians. But when I talk to women who have read those books, a lot of times what I hear from them is not that the misinformation didn't really sink in: what sunk in was the information that if you went to New York, to Greenwich Village, you would find women who were lesbians. And I think that MTV has some of the same functions for the leather community, and that there are going to be an awful lot of folks coming out as a result of that.

MR: There are people who would say that they cherish their status as outlaws, and that the mainstreaming of pornography—for instance, having it published by mainstream houses or being espoused by mainstream writers—is a dangerous thing, and a bad thing. When someone like Anne Rice publishes the *Beauty* books, does it move SM out of the outlaw and into the limelight?

Califia: Well, first of all, I don't think it's fair to interpret Anne Rice's work, or the *Flesh and the Word* anthologies, or Suzy Bright's *Best American Erotica*, in that particular way. I think that we are facing a lot more opposition than that, and the fact that somebody might own one of Anne Rice's books doesn't mean that the cops are going to stop hassling leather bars. It would be nice if that was the world we lived in, but we don't. I think that it's really important for books to go out that once again say *there are sexual choices*. And there are people who do the stuff, who tie each other up, or who get spanked, or who have a fetish, and aren't maniacs. They are not murderers, they don't commit suicide, and they don't need to go into therapy for five years to be able to live with themselves. I just think that's invaluable. I think it saves lives. It keeps people from wasting years on self-destructive behavior and denial that they could spend establishing identities as adult, mature, responsible, happy perverts. So I'm really glad to see mainstream publishing houses touch SM erotica and put it out there. I mean, part of why I decided to be a writer, more than a political activist, is because books go places where political actions don't, and they last longer. I think books carry subversive ideas in great sweeping currents around the world. I've gotten fan letters from Japan, from Russia, from Saudi Arabia. How the hell *Macho Sluts* went into Saudi Arabia, I have no fucking idea.

MR: Which brings us back to the issue of the need for lesbian porn. You've taken some pretty sharp shots at lesbian pornography in the past.

Califia: I have?

MR: You have.

Califia: What do you mean?

MR: "...many lesbian pornographers just aren't brave enough. I suspect that many of us aren't writing about what really gets us wet. We're writing about what we think should get us wet.

Or we're writing about what we did last weekend, which might have been very nice then, thank you, but doesn't stretch the imagination. Journal entries make lousy fiction." That's from *Macho Sluts*.

Califia: That's true. I did write that. (*laughs*)

MR: I wonder if you would elaborate on that for me. Why is it that so much of women's porn has been criticized by women as being very boring?

Califia: Well, maybe because we're bored with it.

MR: What is it about it that bores you?

Califia: That's a really huge question. At this point, there is so much material. Certainly not everybody is writing boring stuff. The kind of writing that I get annoyed with is the kind of—okay, there are a couple of things that happen a lot when women write about sex that piss me off. One is when they are not really writing about sex. They pretend they are going to, but then they stop short of being explicit. I really don't like it when it's soft-focus, and we kind of pull the camera away at the last minute. I don't like it when women's porn has a political agenda, and in fact the agenda is not to turn people on, or to write about lesbian desire honestly, but to prove some political point about lesbians being better than other people, or more politically aware, or more victimized, or whatever the hell you want. I don't like it when the agenda is to create an apology or justification or rationalization for being a dyke. I don't like it when there is censorship, when it's real obvious that the writer feels like only certain activities, or certain types of people doing those activities, can be portrayed. There's also just a lot of bad writing, very amateurish, where there are poor characters, poor plots, not enough description, not enough challenge to the reader. It can get really predictable, and very tedious. Those are the generic things I have found irritating.

MR: What is the impulse behind that kind of self-censorship? I can guess what it is, but I'd like to hear what you have to say.

Califia: I think it's really hard not to do. I think most writers do it, whether they are lesbians or straight men. If anything, straight male writers who want to be recognized by the *New York Times Book Review* as being "serious artists" with something to say, do it even more than we do. Which is interesting, because since they occupy a safer place in society, you'd think that they would speak more freely. I think women are terrified of being too outspoken about sexuality, because we are afraid that inappropriate people will see it, that we'll be exposed to criticism or to ostracism by our own community. And also, it's hard to write pornography if you are not writing from a place of experience. Women are sometimes really afraid to go out and have enough of the experiences that they need to have in order to be able to describe what certain acts were like. Imagination will take you a long way, but it won't take you all the way.

MR: I find it particularly fascinating to watch the Religious Right and the antiporn feminist movement thrash about in bed together on this issue of pornography and censorship. Because these are two groups that actually truly *despise* one another. What are we to make of this unnatural coupling?

Califia: I've been trying to point out for a very long time that the moral agendas of the antiporn feminists and the Religious Right dovetail, and I find it very scary when people like Andrea Dworkin or Catharine MacKinnon call for us to work with right-wing women. That the issue of pornography is so overwhelming, and so important, that it's something we can build a coalition around. It's very frustrating because I don't understand how anybody who cares about women's civil rights can espouse that as a strategy. What about abortion? What about equal pay for equal work? What about gay rights? It's such a stupid suggestion on every single level that I'm really baffled and perplexed about why these people have any authority left. I'm really puzzled about that.

MR: You are open to the charge that your work, by virtue of its very essence—the eroticizing of the politics of dominance and submission, and sometimes violence—is in and of itself violent, and inciting of violence. How do you propose to address this?

Califia: I think one of the issues that comes up a lot with writing about SM, or writing about sex, is the issue of violence. My work has been criticized a fair amount for including violent scenes, or implications of violence, or graphic descriptions of violence. I've never really gotten a chance to talk about that in an interview, and I don't know if that is an issue which occurs to you.

MR: Yes, it does actually. I'm very interested in that, because you still hear things, even today, in 1994, like "Don't go home with that guy in leather because he'll beat the shit out of you!" The whole idea of the mutual respect—and the mutual space—is not something that people are very fond of acknowledging.

Califia: Well, I certainly have done my share of writing about how SM is not the same thing as violence. Talking about the negotiation process and consent. But the issue of violence in fiction, I think, is a really interesting one. And that in fact, in some ways, violence is as controversial as sex. Certainly, on television, it's much more permissible to show a car crash than to just show people fucking, which I think is very bizarre. As a woman writer, I feel that there are two main taboos that can obstruct you from really being a grown-up and writing about your whole life. One of them is the taboo that says "nice girls don't talk about sex." But another really major taboo is that women don't talk about violence. Or, if they do, they talk about it in a certain prescribed way which has to do with being a victim of male violence. As in, it's not okay to talk at all about the violence that we perpetrate upon each other, it's not okay to talk about women who abuse their kids, and it's also not okay to talk about women responding to violence in anything other than a victim way.

MR: Have you addressed this specific issue of violence in any particular piece?

Califia: When I wrote *Doc and Fluff*, I had a real agenda around dealing with violence in a way that was real new and different in women's writing. Which is, first of all, to describe it as graphically as I described the sex. Because I live in a really violent world, and the stuff that has happened to me and my friends is, if anything, more horrible than anything I can ever put in any book. And so, if I live in a society where that's permitted to go on, I want to be able to talk about it in my writing.

The other thing I wanted to do was talk about women defending themselves against violence, and being vengeful, and being mean, and creating some images of women who are physically powerful, not just morally superior—not just politically more astute, or more loving, or more nurturing. I'm really tired of that shit. I'm tired of sitting around waiting for things to be different. And I think it is good and healthy for women, and it's time for us to think about asserting ourselves more in the physical arena, defending ourselves, defending our community and making sure that when people fuck with us they pay.

MR: That's a fairly Amazonian perspective.

Califia: I think that in a better society, there would be a lot more Amazons.

MR: Where does that leave someone like you politically, in terms of being part of political affiliation?

Califia: What do you mean?

MR: Well, it would be difficult—if not impossible—for someone who writes the kind of things you do, and believes the kinds of things you do, to find themselves embraced wholeheartedly by most feminists.

Califia: That's not actually true. I think there are plenty of feminists who are not sex negative. There's a group in New York called Feminists for Free Expression that does a lot of lobbying against stupid legislation put forward by the New Right, and by antiporn feminists, and they are just a hiss and a byword among those people. I mean, you can just kiss good-bye to getting tenure in a women's-studies department if you've done that kind of work. But, in fact, I think that some of the more brilliant minds and theorists know that this is a very important issue, and they do not agree with the Catharine MacKinnon strategy.

MR: How do you interpret the recent emergence, and "acceptance"—for lack of a better word—of new high-quality written pornography, and the simultaneous decline of memorable filmed pornography?

Califia: I think that law enforcement in this country has focused almost exclusively on photographs and videos, so the quality of that work has declined seriously in the last ten years. But I think the written word—partly because it hasn't suffered so much from law enforcement and so people are pouring more creative energy into it because it's a relatively safe venue—has actually increased.

MR: Do you see it as remaining safe? Or is it as susceptible to censorship as the visual medium?

Califia: No. I think the government will do whatever it thinks it can get away with. I think we are really lucky we have a First Amendment, but already the trend in other English-speaking countries is toward banning.

MR: Like my own, for instance? Like Canada?

Califia: Right. Banning SM and exploration of SM issues, whether it's in print or visual media. No, I don't think we can take for granted that it will always be available. It is of grave concern to me that my work is banned in Canada, and to some extent in England, and I do feel politically isolated on that issue. It makes me really angry that even folks in the women's movement who are anticensorship can't seem to bring themselves to actively defend the material that is most threatened right now, which is stuff like mine. I do feel politically isolated. I feel really helpless in this situation, and it really makes me angry. It makes me crazy, as a writer, to know that my books get burned and other women think that's okay. Especially considering that I have given up a lot in my life to concentrate on producing work that is basically for a women's audience. And is written from a feminist perspective, whether it's one the mainstream would recognize as such, or not. My work is very much focused on women and on exploring issues that have to do with what it would take to make the world be a better place for us.

MR: You have a new generation of erotic writers crowding up behind you now, many of whom have been influenced by your work. Do you enjoy that?

Califia: Well, I'm forty, and it's sort of nice to know that a few perks go with just being a bit older and not going away. I know there are certainly a lot of people who wish I would shut up and go away. And that's just too fucking bad. They can just experience what it feels like to want. I'm going to take a fucking word processor to the old folks' home with me.

MR: You're in graduate school at the moment. Where and what are you studying?

Califia: I'm getting a master's in counseling psychology at the University of San Francisco, which is a Jesuit college. I can't seem to get away from the religious.

MR: The Jesuits must love you.

Califia: Actually, they do. (*laughs*) But I think they are kind of the perverts of the church.

MR: There's a strong erotic element to religion.

Califia: Oh, God, yes, absolutely.

MR: Was there nothing about Mormonism that turned you on *at all*?

Califia: No.

MR: There was nothing for you there at all?

Califia: I can't imagine. I have a nun's habit, and I've had a lot of fun in it. I cannot imagine doing anything remotely connected with Mormonism. It's a really boring and strange kind of tradition that doesn't seem to generate any fetishes in my life.

MR: Not even tying up Marie Osmond?

Califia: Ooh, it would be really scary for me to have to be in the same room with Marie Osmond. I don't know. That sounds like a threat.

Lars
EIGHNER

There's a lot of stuff happening on the street. The second day out of Austin, I turned a trick on the road. When I got to La Puente, there was a young gentleman across the street who would come over in the daytime. Usually, by the time I got to a typewriter, there would be enough little scraps in my head that had been saved up. There wasn't any trouble cobbling them together.

By the time Lars Eighner wrote *Travels with Lizbeth*, the critically acclaimed memoir of life as a homeless man traveling across America with his dog (an essay from which was selected for the 1992 edition of *The Pushcart Prize Anthology*), he had long since made his name as a practitioner of a very American brand of gay male erotic fiction. His three collections of short stories, *Bayou Boy, BMOC*, and *American Prelude,* deal with some of the classic all-American icons whose enduring appeal continues to etch the parameters of the American erotic landscape. Eighner's evocative use of language and keen ear for dialogue, which would eventually attract praise to his mainstream writing, published in such diverse media as *The Threepenny Review*, *Harper's*, and *Utne Reader*, is already present in his earlier erotic work. By his own admission, he always approached the writing of pornography as a craft, deserving of the same care and skill as any other literary genre worth doing well. "The erotic scene was 'the picture,'" Eighner explains, "and I probably put an inordinate amount of work into 'the frame.'"

At the time of this interview, Austin was sweltering beneath a heat wave. In the evening, grown only slightly cooler, Eighner talked about the years prior to his first publication in *Blueboy*, his odyssey across America as a homeless pornographer, and his subsequent acclaim as a social historian who never strayed far from his roots.

Michael Rowe: Where were you born?

Lars Eighner: I was born in Corpus Christi, Texas, on Thanksgiving Day in 1948.

MR: Did you grow up there?

Eighner: Early in my life, my parents moved to the region of my father's home in the Midwest, and remained there for two and a half years, until they were divorced. Then my mother and I moved to Houston, where her parents were. I remained in Houston until college.

MR: Did you have any kind of religious upbringing?

Eighner: My parents were Presbyterian—in fact, they met at a little Presbyterian college in Arkansas. It's not a very serious religion. I did learn the shorter Westminster catechism. By the time I was in confirmation classes, it was pretty much that my rich aunt was supposedly coercing us. However, once I left home, my younger brother became a Baptist missionary, the family relocated to Tulsa, and evidently their religion took a sharp turn to the right.
It was very strange, because I don't remember it being like that when I was growing up.

MR: Do you remember your first crush?

Eighner: I do. His name was Bobby Lumberg. I was in fourth grade, and of course he didn't know I was alive. But that probably goes with crushes.

MR: Your work deals so much with the sexuality of all-American youth. Were you one yourself?

Eighner: Oh, no! Not by any stretch of the imagination. I was quite fat as a child, and actually I've been in good shape only for three or four years of my life—between ages thirty and thirty-four. I would go to the baths on day passes, and I would use the weight machines. I think I was the only person using them. I'd come back in two days, and the pegs would be where I'd left them. All anybody ever used them for was to pump up before they went to the orgy room. But they closed the baths pretty early on in the AIDS epidemic, even before there was really much evidence as to what it was. Also, Houston was not the kind of town where it would occur to anybody to use the baths for education. People run right back to their fundamentalism in times of crisis.

MR: How odd to think of the baths as a center for health and fitness.

Eighner: I just don't feel comfortable working out in big gyms, or really, working out with anyone else around. I'm hoping to get myself a Universal Gym for the house when I make some money.

MR: Youth, and the pursuit of sex by youth, is a recurring theme in your erotic writing. Were you sexually precocious as a young person?

Eighner: I don't know if you have access to *Bayou Boy*, but the early chapters of "The Houston Streets" are very thinly veiled autobiography. The character grows away from me as he gets older; and by the end of the story cycle, he doesn't resemble me at all. But the first two or three chapters are fairly close. I suppose the earliest things I remember are tearoom things. I remember going to the tearoom at the movies, and at the University of Houston.

MR: How old were you at the time?

Eighner: I was probably seven or eight, but I was very tall as a child. I was six-one before I was eleven. I'm sure nobody thought I was eighteen or twenty-one, but I'm pretty sure that no one knew I was as young as I was. There was a neighborhood boy whose name was Virgil Forrest, but he was called "Keepie" because his middle name was Keep. That was the first actual lying-down-in-bed sexual thing that I did. It was pretty abusive on his part. My experience from that early time was that I would be treated well by the much older people I went with, and I would have less pleasant experiences with people who were my own age.

MR: How did your emerging homosexuality feel to you as you discovered it? Did it seem natural, or were you conflicted? And how were you treated by your peers?

Eighner: Well, I was obese, you know. Kids who are in any way "different" are often not treated well by other kids. It's difficult for me to distinguish now how much of the stuff I went through—"You're queer!"—had to do with the fact that I was "different," and how much of it was really perceptive on the part of the other kids. Anybody who wore glasses, or wasn't particularly skinny, would be called the same thing. Internally, I was never really very conflicted about it. My mother had taken all kinds of psychology courses, and had saved all of the textbooks. I read all the adolescent psychology and all the abnormal psychology I could. This stuff was printed in the early 1950s and mid-1950s—Kinsey was still hot news then. So at least the basic demographic facts were available, and people were beginning to realize that gay people weren't all lunatics in the asylum, and criminals.

MR: How did you begin writing?

Eighner: Actually, it had been assumed from an early age that I would be a writer. My grandmother was a minor Texas poet, and

I had been to workshops since I was a child. So all my life I had been doing some writing. When I got to college, I wrote term papers for money throughout the Vietnam War, because there were so many guys in college who really had no business being there, except to dodge the draft. One day I realized I was into my thirties and hadn't started. If I was going to write anything, now was the time to do it. So I wrote a piece of semi-fiction for a local underground publication. I was dating somebody at the time who worked at the printer's, and he was freaked out because, of course, he was pretty clearly in the piece. He was afraid that all his lesbian friends in the production department would recognize him. He broke off the relationship almost immediately after that happened. I was irritated at that, and I said, "I'll show him," and I started sending things off to *Blueboy*, which at that time had been the preeminent national gay magazine. You can judge that by the fact that they were paying between $200 and $300 per piece of fiction.

MR: Had you written or published anything prior to the *Blueboy* debut? And by that, I suppose I mean solid short fiction or articles?

Eighner: I had written gay stuff for the underground papers here, under a pseudonym.

MR: Why the pseudonym?

Eighner: We were pretty much terribly isolated here in Austin. I started writing this stuff just as I'd heard of Stonewall. So I really had no guide as to what was politically correct—there were no gay publications. There was just an underground hippie publication, and some of those people were really sexist.

MR: The idea that hippies were homophobic is not something that would occur naturally to someone of my generation, although, of course, there is ample evidence today to suggest that they were.

Eighner: Long hair and beads was just a way of getting laid. We still have much the same thing here today—we have the "organic" people who are really suspicious of gay sex because it's "not organic." They have an idealized concept of nature, which gay sex doesn't fit into.

MR: But specifically, why the pseudonym?

Eighner: The pseudonym came about because, in early 1969, I had been involved with a Red splinter group, the SDS [Students for a Democratic Society]. They were very antisexual on a broad front, and I had been with them for a couple of years. I decided that it was time for me to come out of the closet to them and confront the issue of gay rights. At one time, for political reasons, my family had the idea to have me committed. For political reasons. "Larry Nadir" was the name I adopted when I had to leave town.

MR: *Committed?*

Eighner: In the winter of 1968, I had stopped by my parents' home on the way to the SDS national conference in Ann Arbor. My parents went through my luggage and they found the *Little Red Book*, and all that. They decided that I was crazy. As soon as I was back in Austin, I called them one evening and they weren't home. I browbeat my brother until he told me that my parents were on their way to Austin, unannounced. As near as we can figure, having me committed was what they had in mind. So I was put on the underground railroad to a Columbia dormitory, and I stayed there for a couple of weeks till I was settled in New York. Anyway, when I came out to the group I was with and wanted to confront the issue of gay rights, they said, "Oh, no, homosexuality is a bourgeois disorder. Maybe you can do something for us if you stay in the closet, but you can't advance in the party under these circumstances. We're not going to deal with it." That was exactly the time that I started writing for the underground paper. So I carried over the name I been using politically—Larry Nadir—and it became my pseudonym.

MR: But between the underground-paper writing and the *Blueboy* erotic fiction, there was something like a ten-year period where you didn't write much of anything. What were you doing?

Eighner: I met somebody and we moved to his hometown, which was very small. He was strikingly beautiful, as many of my companions have been, and we just couldn't hit it off in his hometown. First of all, it was *his* job, and *his* family and *his* friends who would show up at our house, unmistakably with the attitude, directed at me, that I had turned him queer. And when we made contact with the "gay community" there, which consisted of *the* gay hairdresser, *the* gay interior decorator, and *the* gay house restorer, we kept getting these invitations, like "Gee, we'd like you to come over for cocktails late Saturday night, and by the way, please leave Lars at home, if you would."

MR: How perfectly ghastly.

Eighner: You have to realize that when a community is that size, and is also about ten years behind the rest of the country, it puts a new light on things like *The Boys in the Band.* You see where the catty-bitch stereotype comes from. Often when my companions have been very attractive—which has happened an inordinate number of times—they're really not interested in anybody else. The attraction, for them, seems to be on some other level. And people who approach superficial beauty in a superficial way aren't offering them anything they couldn't already have. My companions over the years have always known where they could find other stuff if they wanted it.

MR: But in this case, clearly, your relationship in his small hometown ended for reasons other than a wandering eye on his part. What did you do then? Did you return to Austin?

Eighner: Yes. For a period of time, I got involved with a drug crisis and counseling service. This was a semivolunteer agency. Sometimes I was paid $55 per month.

MR: Is that where you began to write the erotic fiction, or did the drug-counseling work occupy you to a point where you were unable to do anything else?

Eighner: It wasn't so much that I was ignoring everything else, but anyone who's done that kind of work will tell you that it takes over your life. Unfortunately, I had enough stamina not to burn out, and it ate away three or four years of my life. I did virtually nothing else. And then I got the job at the state hospital, and started writing fiction. The first piece was called "Hunter's Moon"—I don't know what it's called in *Bayou Boy*, because all of the titles were changed. The story came about when I was hitchhiking.

MR: Did you approach pornography in a different way than you would have approached any other kind of writing? You've said that you had always intended to be a writer, but had reached the point where it was essentially now or never.

Eighner: I was always going to be a writer. This was what I was going to write—the genre I was going to work in. Although the theoretical development of what I was doing was worked out over years of correspondence with John Preston and Steven Saylor and others, I really felt innately that this was *the* form for gay literature. I don't know whether it was Preston or me who first called pornography "gay men's vernacular literature."

MR: "Gay writing," as such, would have been practically nonexistent. Was there any sort of a protectionist feeling for what little nonpornographic material there was available? Was there any sense that the whole "gay men's vernacular literature" concept was a radical notion?

Eighner: Actually, that's what made it *not* a radical thought. If you looked at anything that was gay-positive in those days, it was porn. I had read the pulp-porn novels from the adult bookstores, but there virtually was nothing else. There was no such thing as a real gay mystery story. At the same time, it was important for me that pornography could be co-opted. I realized from the first that, probably, most readers wouldn't notice anything but the erotic scenes; but I felt like the depth, the detail, and the quality had to be there for my sake. And it *was* there, in case you wanted to look for it. But I didn't expect anyone to look for it. The erotic scene was the "picture," and I probably put an inordinate amount of work into the "frame." It struck me that the way to approach writing porn was to treat it as a craft.

MR: Did your marketplace show a marked preference for a specific type of writing from you?

Eighner: Steven Saylor, who was an editor at that time, really liked the stories I did which were more commercial—the college stories, for instance—and I'm not particularly proud of them. A number of people have liked them, so I've continued to do them throughout the years. I could take my time on those early stories, because I was otherwise employed.

MR: How did you connect with Steven Saylor?

Eighner: I had a story which was originally called "Blood and Guts," and is now one of the "Houston Streets" stories [in *Bayou Boy*,] the one set in the hospital. My editor at *Blueboy* or *Torso*, whoever I was dealing with at that time, wouldn't take it because he thought it was too gruesome. I finally sent it to *Drummer*, and Steven bought it for *Mach*, which is one of their magazines. The rates were terrible. But Steven had been to college here, and he was interested in me because I was from Austin, and his family lives not too far from here. So we kept up a correspondence. He put me in touch with the other people— John Preston, Tim Barrus, and all of us who had absolutely no connection with anyone who'd ever had any thought of writing for *Christopher Street*. I kept trying to think of stuff to write for Steven, but they were paying $25 or $50; and even when I was otherwise employed, I couldn't often afford to send him pieces. When he and Rowberry started doing *Inches*, and their rates were up to standard, though still not very high, I figured I might as well be writing for him as anyone else. He was buying large volumes of my work, everything I could turn out. Once he started working for *Inches*, there were only two or three stories that weren't appropriate.

MR: Where did your fantasies come from—the ones that became the basis for the stories?

Eighner: I really insisted that the stories reflect, in some way or other, something that had happened. The sexual stories were based on things that were real. Characters were put together from composites. Some of the story lines were derived from newspapers. As for the college stories, I lived in several fairly flaky dormitories in the late 1960s and early 1970s, and things *were* pretty loose. Not everything that seems to be fantasy is fantasy. Now, of course, I do allow myself to invent stuff, but where it comes from, I don't know. I've tried to cover the waterfront— I do write scenes that don't particularly appeal to me. A typical example was—I just came back from Stonewall, where I was invited to read for the leatherpeople. I read a piece called "Super Tad," which I wrote as satire. It was purely parody on my part. I was truly shocked to get fan mail on it from people who thought it was the hottest thing they'd ever read. I was rolling on the floor the whole time I was writing it. I can't read "Super Tad" without cracking a smile. But there are people who think it's hot sex.

MR: But that's the function of erotic fiction, isn't it? To strike a sexual nerve? To get an erotic response? How do you feel when that occurs?

Eighner: I'm usually a little astonished. I'm really a little slow. In *You Can't Go Home Again*, Thomas Wolfe says he had the experience of people thinking that he'd been spying on them in *Look Homeward Angel*, that he'd revealed their innermost secrets. But Wolfe said he thought he was putting down the most obvious stuff. And that's how I think—to me, what I write is the most obvious—what anybody else in the world would trip over. I don't think I'm really sharp, and I don't think I've got a penetrating insight into other people's scenes. But, to a certain extent, the work itself has a life of its own when it gets beyond a certain point. And there's an internal logic to it. I think the work knows things that I don't know—there are realities contained in the work I couldn't otherwise know were there unless someone told me. Also, a lot of my stuff is really sketchy. I'm deliberately short on physical descriptions in a lot of places, my theory being that the reader can fill in the details as they best suit his or her tastes. I believe in giving the reader room to imagine and contribute to the work, instead of tying everything down so there's no room for the reader's interpretation. Something I did a lot of, in the early stories, was to write in voices. This was one of the problems I had in New York recently. The fact that I can capture voices and dialects on paper doesn't mean that I can speak them, or read them out loud, the way they should be read.

MR: But that's one of the strengths of your writing, though. The realistic verbal intercourse between the characters.

Eighner: I have an ear for people's voices. I think I'm able to reproduce stuff on paper that I couldn't do myself. I don't suppose that a composer can actually play every instrument that he writes a line for.

MR: *Travels with Lizbeth* details your life on the road as a homeless man traveling across America with your dog. The reality of how homelessness actually comes about is frequently less obvious than the result. How did it come about in your case?

Eighner: I had never reconciled myself to the differences one has to reconcile to in order to work in a bureaucratic institution like the mental-health system in Texas. There are the published humane policies of the institution, and then there are the way things really work, and the way people really think. I was constantly in trouble. The straw that broke the camel's back was that I was working on a ward, and we had a Jehovah's Witness on staff who was proselytizing the patients. This struck me as a really bad idea, because a lot of the patients at an institution already have problems with religious ideas. The Jehovah's Witness ended up striking one of the gay patients, and I reported it. He resigned, which looked like the right outcome—justice had triumphed. But at that point, it was pretty much decided that it was time to get rid of me. So, having won my point, I immediately started getting all the worst assignments: being sent to the medical ward to deal with the vegetables, and stuff like that. They finally wore me down, and I was offered the choice of resigning—or being fired.

MR: What did you discover when you resigned?

Eighner: I didn't realize how bad the Austin economy had become. There was virtually nothing for me. I couldn't write enough to keep myself together. That was a terribly disillusioning thing—the first story I sold to *Blueboy*, I sold for $250, and then I sold some after that for $350. At those rates, I could have made a living, by Austin standards. But in short order, *Blueboy*'s rates plummeted, and everybody's rates stabilized at $100 per story. It was impossible to keep body and soul together on that. Another thing that had happened while I was in state hospital was, although Austin had always had lots of big old houses, which would be subdivided, so you could get a nice big room with a shared bath for $50 per month, they had all been leveled, and replaced with condos during the boom. So when the bust came, there just wasn't any low-cost housing. I hadn't realized that. In any event, my savings just went, and I wasn't able to replace it by writing, or any other kind of work.

MR: You then followed up a lead for an assistant-editor position and hitchhiked to California.

Eighner: That was for *In Touch*. I discovered that they run this ad in their own magazine, and sometimes they run it in other magazines, particularly the slightly-better-than-bar-rag weeklies they have out there in California. Evidently, the ad doesn't ever actually represent any real editorial opening.

MR: Why would they run it, then?

Eighner: I don't know why they run it. I also figured that with my hospital and crisis experience, I might get a job working with PWAs. But everything didn't work out in California.

MR: There was one particularly moving scene in *Travels with Lizbeth* where you tried to trade stamps for money in a book-store, in order to get tar off your dog's back. You saw magazines with your stories behind the counter, but were not able to afford them. Other people had access to your work, and you didn't even have access to money to buy it yourself.

Eighner: It was kind of strange, but in a situation like that one, your whole perspective changes. You don't deal with the more cosmic questions, or the greater ironies. You have so many present problems that you deal with them. When you're done with that, you go to sleep. That's the one saving grace of living that kind of life—you just don't have time to look at the long picture, or to stand back. You always have something that has to be immediately dealt with. And also, much of it is possible. If you were taking the grander view, you might be thinking about things that were not possible. Even later on, when I was sleeping on the streets, the thing was to get up, find food for the day, and "secure the camp" as much as possible. There is a routine for survival that takes up every waking minute.

MR: And you kept on writing throughout that entire trip? What kind of work did you do, and how did you do it?

Eighner: There were many long letters to Steven, and many to other people, but I don't believe other people saved them. I wasn't really writing stories when I was hitchhiking. Whenever I got to a typewriter, I'd turn out something, and most of it sold, eventually. There would be checks following me. But I knew that without being able to type stories, there was hardly any point to writing them longhand. Nobody would read longhand stuff for publication. Besides, I've always composed on a typewriter. Although my handwriting is quite good, longhand doesn't really look right to me.

MR: Did you have any trouble keeping yourself in an erotic state of mind to write the stories, once you got to the type-writer? If you were concerned about basic survival so much of the time, what did you draw on?

Eighner: That really wasn't a problem. By my second stay in Hollywood, I wasn't actually living a monkish lifestyle. There's a lot of stuff happening on the street. The second day out of Austin, I turned a trick on the road. When I got to La Puente, there was a young gentleman across the street who would come over in the daytime. So it wasn't entirely impossible to imagine these things happening. Usually, by the time I got to a typewriter, there would be enough little scraps in my head that had been saved up. There wasn't any trouble cobbling them together.

MR: It sounds as though you are in a perpetual state of erotic imagining, Lars.

Eighner: I compose in my head almost constantly. I know people who run a little sound track for their lives in their heads. I compose my thoughts, then I go back and revise them. It's peculiar, but it works for me.

MR: You are unquestionably also a regional writer, and you are known for having staked out Texas as your territory.

Eighner: Part of the problem was that I was cast that way. Stan Leventhal was one editor who insisted that he wanted regional stuff.

MR: But it's so strong.

Eighner: It's just a matter of being exposed to the characters. I think that I would catch what was around me, wherever I was. There's some significant deviation from that kind of stuff where I've been exposed to other people. But the dialogue and stuff is really easy, because I've been exposed to the language all my life. I'm not really sure if sometimes readers don't put a lot of that into these stories themselves. Preston's favorite story was "A Cowboy Christmas." You can read that story a hundred times and you'll have a great deal of difficulty finding any dominance and submission, or bondage, or leather, or any SM of any kind, in that story. It's a sweet little romance. But invariably, leatherpeople love that story. This is really perplexing to me. There's not much in the way of butt slapping or tit torture, but leatherpeople love it. I don't know why. It's a mystery.

MR: What is it about Texas men that strikes such a universal sexual rapport with readers?

Eighner: I'm not sure. There aren't really many cowboys in my stories, or in Texas anymore, for that matter. There's a kind of independence that people do have here. So I think there's a lot more crossover sex. It's partly the Latin influence, which says that any man can be a top without compromising his heterosexuality, because the sex of your partner is less of a key issue than who's "sticking it in."

MR: And "the man" is—

Eighner: The man is somebody who sticks it in. It doesn't really matter what he sticks into. The Latin influence has a lot to do with the way things worked out around here. Also, something I wrote in *Lavender Blue* is that if you've written that somebody is a cowboy, or a roughneck, or a biker, you create such an indelible impression on the reader that you can characterize counter to type all through the rest of the story. And people who still want to see the cowboy will see the cowboy, and people who are prepared to deal with something counter to type will find what they are looking for. In fact, I really try to write counter to type, because the "type" guys have been done to death.

MR: Even by you?

Eighner: Well, it was hard, once stories got down to 3,000 words or less, to do any "rounding" of the characters. At 5,000 and 6,000 words, you had some room to work. But at 3,000 words, you had to get right to the sex, and the characters just don't have much chance to be very full.

MR: One of the other comments about your work is that it is very American, with all-American icons, like frat boys, college jocks, and football players. What's your take on the appeal of straight men to gay readers?

Eighner: I'm not sure, except that it has something to do with the ability of even people who are fairly narrow otherwise to say "fuck you" to the world and go ahead and do whatever feels good at the moment. I owe not only a lot of literary inspiration to that sort of attitude, but also a substantial portion of my sex life. The truth of the matter is, I don't suppose I've ever had many close friends who were comfortably self-identified gay men. I used to feel really bad about that, but then it seemed to me that not everybody had to do that—be identified.

MR: How do you feel about androgyny, which is notably absent from your work?

Eighner: I have a great deal of respect for drag queens and nelly people, who have actually done a great deal more for the movement than hundreds of clones you could mention. When local organizers say, *"Let's keep the queens out of the parade!"* I'm the first person to squawk about it, but I don't find it very attractive personally. I can do without the androgyny.

MR: The core fantasy of so much erotic writing in the past has been the idea that the hottest sex is with men who are "gay only for the sex" and otherwise straight.

Eighner: As something of an expert in the species, the supposedly "straight" males who have gay sex, or even the straight males in general, have taken a terrible bashing on this business of being sexual machines who are unconnected. For lots of them, sex really *does* come first, but very few of them are really completely capable of detaching sex from everything else. After a while, they begin to realize that there's something going on. In a way, it seems almost spiritual to me, this going across the grain of what their sexuality is. Which is why it's a terrible injustice for the politically active types to be defining people in terms of preference. This is definitely an issue that started in the 1970s. The only way you can observe preference is subjectively—there is no objective measure of preference. In a way, politically correct people paint themselves into a corner that way. If they would go at it as what people actually do, instead of what they say they'd prefer to do, we'd all be better off.

MR: What type attracts you, personally?

Eighner: I love youngish muscular types. I end up with so many of them. Or maybe they aren't finding anyone else receptive to them as anything but that. I thought a fifteen-year-old athlete was my sexual ideal for many years, and then I turned fourteen. So I guess now it's a twenty-one to late-twenties type that I'm most interested in. Usually fairly smooth and muscular.

MR: The kind you write about.

Eighner: Curiously, they've all been fairly short. A recurring fantasy of mine is to have a fairly tall lover because I'm something like six-three myself. I'm instantly attracted to tall men with dark hair and blue eyes, but somehow I always end up with short men with blond hair and blue eyes.

MR: *Travels with Lizbeth* catapulted you into something very much resembling celebrity. Your story was available to everyone—even the readers of *People* magazine—who might not have been familiar with your sexual fiction. How did it feel to go from being a homeless gay pornographer to being published in hardcover by St. Martin's Press, and lionized as "The Thoreau of the Dumpsters," as Phillip Lopate described you?

Eighner: The first thing was, the publicity stuff just paralyzed our lives. We were living in a very tiny efficiency apartment. Two photo sessions or major interviews a week just threw our lives into chaos.

MR: Where else did you get coverage?

Eighner: It started with *Texas Monthly*, and they turned out to be surprisingly influential. They gave us some leads on selling the movie rights. Then there was the *New York Times* cover, and the *People* thing, and then we spent some time making a documentary which eventually ended up on PBS. At the time, it seemed like there was something big every week. Television and radio interviews were frequently done from the house. The local press in Dallas flew a major reporter down here. I had scheduled the *Dallas Morning News* for Thursday afternoon and the *Fort Worth Star-Telegram* for the following Monday. I'm terribly naïve—it didn't occur to me that the *Dallas Morning News* wasn't flying a reporter down here and picking me up in a big red car to take me out to cappuccino and then have photographs made, just for a book-page piece. It turned out to be a Sunday front page. And then the guy from the *Fort Worth Star-Telegram* never called back because now they were in a competitive situation. I'm sure that he thought I was setting him up to be following his competition. The *People* people had been scheduled to come for several days, and suddenly the *CBS Sunday Morning News* wanted to come at the same time. They cleared it with *People*, and spent time covering *People* covering me. But the *People* piece didn't come out for two months. The first thing you learn when you deal with the media is that no one ever gets everything one hundred percent right. But between the trips to New York and people coming here, I didn't get any work done.

MR: What did all that attention do to your self-perception. Did it turn your head?

Eighner: Not really. I suppose I'm sort of detached. The same sort of impulse that insulated me from feeling hopeless and worthless when I was on the streets insulated me from taking any of the publicity stuff too seriously. I gathered that good things were happening, but we were still *desperately* poor (*laughs*), so my eye was on the bottom line the whole time. In fact, we're surprisingly short of money right now. (*laughs*)

MR: Nobody ever said money and fame had to go hand in hand.

Eighner: It comes in waves. It'll be August before I get my hands on a substantial chunk of money at one time. I think I'm on my third or fourth advance from St. Martin's. My first royalty statement just covered the period to the thirty-first of October. Well, on the thirty-first of October, there were only 13,000 copies in print, and only 6,000 sold, and none of the subsidiary rights had come in.

MR: How has the cross-country wreck-an-author tour been for you? Do you like traveling?

Eighner: I don't like traveling. As far as I'm concerned, I'm a business traveler. This last trip to New York was the first time I'd ever traveled in tourist season. *God, I hate tourists!* Next month, I'm taking off for London. In a way, this whole thing is exciting and thrilling, but I know it's going to be a grind. I'll be heavily scheduled, going from one place I don't where I am, dealing with people I've never heard of, to the next.

MR: How does it feel to see all your old work in print in your various anthologies?

Eighner: There are three collections in print now, and Steven has gone through his files and found another one-and-a-half. I'm going to be splitting a volume of science-fiction and weird stories with Clay Caldwell. We both have sci-fi fantasy stories, but neither of us has enough to make a volume on our own, so we're going to split one. A new edition of *Lavender Blue* is coming out, and I'm trying to finish this book of essays, *Gay Cosmos*, and a screenplay.

MR: We haven't actually discussed the issue of censorship, or how hard it is to publish gay erotica in the United States or Canada. We should talk about the fact that much of your work involves characters who are under what would be viewed legally as the age of consent. But first, do you feel that gay publishers are supportive of gay erotica?

Eighner: The idea that you can't publish a piece of gay erotica with any gay press in the country is very depressing. The situation seems to be changing. And, of course, Kasak, which is not a gay press, knows how to sell books, which is something that lots of gay publishers don't know how to do. Virtually all of the Badboy titles had been issued before, by someone who didn't find it worth their while to keep them in print. That is really depressing. And there's no erotic category for the Lambda Literary Awards.

MR: What about censorship by religious and antiporn feminist-influenced government?

Eighner: I think it's a really bad idea for the gay community to accept—uncritically—all this stuff that comes from the feminists. Like that case, wherever it was, which said that somebody at a firehouse, on a twenty-four-hour shift, can't sit and quietly read *Playboy* because the woman sitting on the next sofa might be offended by his reading it. We're not talking about displaying the centerfold—we're talking about a ruling prohibiting him from *reading* it. There has to be a time where either the gay movement will distinguish themselves from the feminists on this issue, or the gay movement won't be worth having.

MR: What about depictions of underage people in print? And

by underage, I'm not necessarily referring to children, just people under eighteen or twenty-one.

Eighner: I'm extremely irate that you can't have underage people in print having sex, at least with any of the publishers I know of. You don't have to have minors involved in the production of the work. I can understand that with explicitly sexual photos of models who are actually young, society might have an interest in preventing that sort of thing from happening. But you don't have to have kids to make a print book. Badboy's version of *Bayou Boy* has been edited very heavily to remove the obvious reference to ages, although I think that anyone with intelligence will realize that these guys are quite young. But I don't think that any of that could be mistaken for something that caters to chicken-hawk fantasies. This is not about picking up little boys in the pinball parlor and doing weird things to them. The story is almost never from the adult's viewpoint, anyway. But that means that if you want to write even nonerotic fiction, you must have these characters who suddenly become sexual at the age of eighteen, and they don't have any memories of sexual fantasy.

MR: Very realistic.

Eighner: Nothing sexual has happened to them before they were eighteen! And that's one of the reasons why I have never undertaken a major novel, because it's just impossible to develop a character—a whole human being—who essentially has no sexual history before the age of eighteen.

MR: Where does Edmund White's *A Boy's Own Story*, and semi-autobiographical fiction like it, fit into this equation?

Eighner: There's a slightly relaxed standard if you present something as being frankly autobiographical. Boyd MacDonald managed to print stuff about very early sexual experiences, but the excuse was that these were stories about events that had actually happened. But once you assume the veil of fiction, you can't do any of that. It's really distressing to me that this is not a big issue in the gay community as a whole, and that the "respectable" leadership won't even consider it. Since I was fourteen, I never had any interest in people who were underage; but when I was younger, I went with men when *I* was underage. It's very disturbing to me that NAMBLA gets the kind of short shrift it does from the gay community, that the community refuses to have any dialogue with NAMBLA at all. The community simply will not accept the fact that people can be supportive in principle without having an interest in little boys.

MR: In Canada, we recently signed into legislation a very strict law about depictions of any sort of sexuality, written or visual, that portrays anyone under eighteen having sex. Even with other under-eighteens. The law effectively prohibits coming-of-age stories of any sort and has drawn a great deal of criticism from writers and artists of all types.

Eighner: Speaking as an American to a Canadian, I have lived under the thumb of Canadian Customs for years, because virtually all of the magazines I wrote for tried to get imported to Canada. The excuse that writers are always given is "Canadian Customs won't go for it."

MR: You're not going to get a defense of Canadian censorship policy from me, I'm afraid. My national loyalty doesn't extend that far. Let me ask you, rhetorically maybe, if you believe that prior restraint, of any kind, is ever appropriate.

Eighner: I'm one of those people who believe that you have a right to cry *"Fire!"* in a crowded theater. I don't believe in any kind of censorship—before or afterward—at all. I think if you go into a crowded theater, you'd best be prepared to evaluate all cries of *"Fire!"* on the objective evidence.

Nancy
KILPATRICK,
writing as "Amarantha Knight"

Sex and horror are intertwined in that way because they are two taboos in our society. I've always wanted to make the connection with that darkness, or what society calls dark. Dark to me is not bad. Dark is just the other side of the moon, the side you don't see.

Two literary genres, perpetually derided simultaneously as both subversive and trashy, are erotica and horror. We may all look down our collective noses at romantic bodice-rippers of the Harlequin and Silhouette variety, but we don't think of them as dangerous—just ridiculous.

Never mind that the very roots of American literature encompass horror (*Wieland, or The Transformation* written by Charles Brockden Brown in 1798), or that authors, from Henry Miller and Anaïs Nin to Anne Rice have written explicit sexual fiction that is studied in universities and sold today in the best bookstores.

Fundamentalists and antiporn feminists rage at pornography as though it were written by Satan himself for the primary purpose of disintegrating "the family" and/or as an indisputable incitement to violence against women. Academics sniff disdainfully at horror (dismissing it snobbishly as "popular," which is intended to be insulting), rejecting it as a literary cyclamate with no value, except as brain candy.

Having said that, the public is reaching for both erotica and horror with unprecedented enthusiasm. In a Puritan-based society like our North American one, where we are schooled from earliest infancy in the belief that the body and its appetites are "bad," or "dirty," and must be controlled and denied at any cost, the appeal of dazzling supernatural power (embodied, for instance, by the vampire), or complete carnal satiation, is a powerful glamour indeed.

Nancy Kilpatrick, a 1993 finalist and 1994 nominee for the coveted Bram Stoker Award, is making a niche for herself in both fields. As Amarantha Knight, she has written a series of erotic novels based upon such horror classics as *Dracula*, *Frankenstein*, and *Dr. Jekyll and Mr. Hyde*. Under her own name, she has written *Sex and the Single Vampire*. And her mainstream vampire novel, *Near Death*, was published to critical and popular acclaim in late 1994.

In Toronto we discussed what she sees as the connection between horror and erotica. According to Kilpatrick, both fields find themselves attacked and lauded for the same fundamental reasons.

Michael Rowe: Maybe we should start talking about how you began to write erotica because your specific literary background is in horror.

Nancy Kilpatrick: I've always written erotica. To me, much horror is erotic. We live in a society where the body is disconnected. I'm a product of this society, as we all are. I have always tried to make the reconnection.

MR: The reconnection with yourself? Or with other people?

Kilpatrick: Living in the body. In our society, living in the body is considered taboo. All you have to do is look at the number of feminine-hygiene deodorant commercials—everything is geared at getting away from those smells, those tastes. Moving into that physical realm is where I've always wanted to go, and horror is in that realm. Horror is physical, whether you are talking about splatterpunk, psychological horror, supernatural power—

all of it. If it doesn't hit on a physical level, it doesn't mean anything.

MR: As you see it, what is the connection between sex and horror? The two are used synonymously enough, and almost always in deprecating terms.

Kilpatrick: Sex and horror are intertwined in that way because they are two taboos in our society. I've always wanted to make the connection with that darkness, or what society calls dark. Dark to me is not bad. Dark is just the other side of the moon, the side you don't see. To make that reconnection, I like to go into the darkness. A lot of people are scared of the darkness, so they want to stay away, which is why you have reactions when you say you write horror. People read your stuff and they say, "Oh, God, how can you think that? That's practically on the verge of madness! What kind of sick mind is this?" When you get into this, it really is only the other side. And some people, unfortunately, don't give it much play because they are too repressed.

MR: How do you mean, repressed?

Kilpatrick: I mean repression in terms of psychological repression. In an extreme case, if you were to take a two-year-old child and lock him in a closet, slip food under the door, and take that kid out ten years later, you're going to have a lunatic on your hands. That's the way it is. And I think that if you repress the darkness, and don't admit that it's there, and don't deal with it, what you end up with is something very twisted and distorted. That's where you get wars. That's where you get massacres, torture, mayhem, killing, and all this craziness that goes on in the world.

MR: Would you comment on why both of these genres are frequently under attack, often simultaneously?

Kilpatrick: I think those areas are under attack because they are so volatile. They also take you into realms where you don't know where you're going end up. When you step into the sexual arena, or when you step into the horror arena, you don't know where you're going to end up, so control is lost. That goes against ways of thinking that are more rigid. Society basically says, "This is the way it is. Let's not ask any questions or deviate from this. We know the truth." Anybody who says "I know the truth!" you know, you run like hell because you're talking to a maniac.

MR: What is it about moving beyond limitations that is so distressing to people? I mean, it's obviously a question of preaching to the converted on this issue. Anyone working in the erotic or horror field has an answer to this question, but what's yours?

Kilpatrick: You move into another realm, and you change your ways of thinking. Your values might change completely in a lifetime. Several times, even, just because things shift. Horror moves you into a realm where, because you're out of control, you could be different. It's the same with sex and death. That's why those things aren't talked about—because it's really unnerving.
  Horror and sex go together. When you read something horrifying, or when you have a sexual experience, it brings you right into your body. It brings your soul into your body, which is what I think the appeal is. It bypasses all the bullshit up there, so that you're sure you're alive. And a lot of people are not sure they are alive. Sex and horror pull a person right inside their own skin.

MR: Do you see traditional Judeo-Christian morality as being a contributing factor to this? It seems that what you are talking about is cutting off—denying—one's basic appetites. A society of people who are perpetually in denial.

Kilpatrick: Definitely. If you go back to the matriarchal societies, what you end up with are mythologies—theological mythologies—which have incorporated the dark side. In many countries, that's still the case. In India you have Kali. Kali is not bad—Kali is like the other side of life. There is birth, and there is death.

MR: Kali is a dark goddess. We are not a goddess-oriented culture. Judeo-Christianity, and indeed most monotheistic religions, are male oriented. What role does the gender of our religious icons play in our perception of light and dark?

Kilpatrick: We have Christianity, where there is this triangle which is either all-male or genderless. There's no feminine. There are many places in Europe where you find statues of the Black Madonna. We don't have a Black Madonna over here. We have a sort of white, ethereal Madonna, who isn't even given credence.

MR: Like a token?

Kilpatrick: The feminine—and I don't mean women here, I mean the feminine in all humans—is missing. It's the earth, it's the body, it's everything that has to do with the physical. It's the part that's ignored. So, yes: strong emotions, and strong physical sensations—horror and sexuality, for instance—pull the physical right in. That's why a lot of people say, "Oh, that's *horrible*, that's *scary*," or move away from it. It doesn't have anything to do with what the story is about, or what it is you are doing. It has to do with their own fear.

MR: The fear, in effect, of their appetites?

Kilpatrick: Yes. Fear of where will this lead—the way to madness.

MR: Okay, I'll buy that. Our culture is about suppression of the appetites. Horror unleashes that. You write erotic horror, and your specialty is vampire fiction. Vampires are identified closely with sex and sexuality. If you would, please rise above the traditional sexual interpretations of vampire iconography—invasion of the body, corruption of virginity—and tell me what you think it is about vampires that push such strong buttons in people?

Kilpatrick: When you talk about *appetite*, the first thing that comes to mind is that the vampire—whether male or female, gay, straight, or pansexual—has an appetite that supersedes all morality. That appetite has to be sated. Nothing is going to get in the way. I think human beings are envious of that. We have so many societal limitations, with so many rules of behavior, that people can't just go and fulfill their needs very easily.

MR: Attraction to vampires, then, is an attraction to an outlaw ethic? The idea of being outside sexual and moral parameters?

Kilpatrick: Yes. In the gay world, for instance, it's much easier than most other realms. In the gay world, at least for the last thirty years, men have had steam baths. It's the direct approach—if you want to get fucked, you can do it. You just walk in there and grab somebody, and as long as you are mutually agreeable to the situation, you just get the thing that you need. But for most other people, lesbians included, there are not those places. A character, or a situation, where you can just go and get what you want—that's very appealing.

MR: Especially when part of getting the appetite fulfilled involves seduction.

Kilpatrick: Oh yes. Now, the old-style vampires didn't seduce anybody. You know, the pre-1950s vampires—they weren't into seduction. Dracula was probably the closest. I mean even Varney, the first real vampire, didn't seduce. He just snuck into bedrooms when people were asleep. The vampire was an undead thing, a corpse reanimated. It was not a pretty sight. The mythology itself is based on the walking dead. From the grave. In North America, the movie *Near Dark* probably came the closest—vampires who are grungy. They look like they've been wallowing in the dirt. That's more like what vampires always were, and there's not much seduction involved there. No, you don't want to be seduced by anything like this.

MR: What prompted the shift in perception from "walking

dead" to seducer? *Near Dark* and the messy vampires notwith-standing, because that was a fairly recent film.

Kilpatrick: When they cleaned up the vampire in fiction, that did a lot in terms of seduction. You could have a being who basically knew what people wanted, which was intimacy. And who was able to get what he or she—the vampire—wanted, out of the human being, by saying essentially, "I'll give you this if you give me that." Of course, usually, the vampire didn't come through with the other side of the bargain.

MR: That sounds like a metaphor for a disappointing one-night stand.

Kilpatrick: On the other hand, that's also changed. Now you have sexual vampires as well. It kind of works out for everybody.

MR: The intriguing thing about vampire fiction, especially inas-much as it relates to erotic tone, is the relatively recent shift towards bisexuality. In your own vampire fiction, both the erotic and the mainstream, there is tremendous bisexuality. Even pansexuality.

Kilpatrick: I was recently in a city where they had an SM demon-stration, which they have all over the place now, calling it "theater" to make it legit. All these people were doing this and that to each other, the usual kind of stuff. The sort of thing that people are afraid to say—these people were there saying it, and to a packed house of hundreds of people. They had these gorgeous lesbians, and they had these gay men, and they are all saying, "Let us have our fantasies!" This absolutely gorgeous woman was sitting in this chair, and she just oozed sexuality. She was sitting there reading this poem. She had been a lesbian all her life. She had been in a detox center, drying out, and there had been a guy there. He was about ten years younger than her, wearing tight jeans, and she'd had this fantasy about fuck-ing him which she'd written about. She read this, and it was so hot, honest to God. The word "sizzle" comes to mind. There was a packed house of people, and you could have heard pins dropping.

MR: People of all different orientations?

Kilpatrick: Of all different orientations. It was just so erotic. It was dynamite, and it blew everybody away. And basically she was trying to say, "Why do I have to be restricted in what I fantasize because I'm a lesbian?" There were tricklings of this in the 1970s—this was my generation. In the 1970s, people were more experimental. It was not as rigid as now. We are a global village, but why is everybody trying to make each section of the village separate? I can't figure it out. I would prefer to be in a society where people are just open and say, "I am me." That's a very dangerous position to take. That's the kind of openness I hope is in my books. That's what I am trying to convey—that openness—and I guess the thing that bugs me most is when people are not open. I don't want to try to force anyone to be what they are not; but on the other hand, I just think it's so neat when somebody like Marco Vassi goes from being straight to being gay to getting married. The guy—from what you read about him—tried stuff. He was just being where he was at.

MR: And society sees anarchy?

Kilpatrick: Oh, yes. Chaos. Because now this person cannot be categorized. Most people can't handle living like that. I understand that. I don't belittle people for it, but it's a shame. Because we don't know if we have more than one life. We may or may not. I like to think that consciousness continues. I think anyone with a brain knows that matter at least will take another form, and consciousness might as well. But who knows? Who really knows? Nobody has yet come back and told us much of anything.

MR: When we first spoke, and I asked you what your sexual orientation was, you really balked at that.

Kilpatrick: Yes, I have a real resistance to the question because people want to categorize other people. Having been interviewed before, I've seen that it's very easy to be categorized—as a writer, as a woman, as a person. It's very easy to be put into a slot and then have someone say, "Oh, now I know who you are." But you don't know who I am. I can't be reduced to a sound bite. Nobody can. Our whole society is trying to reduce people to sound bites. What I am trying to get down to is that I think it would be great if people were able to just explore who they are, rather than feel they are pressured. And, of course, mainstream society pressures people sexually to be heterosexual, but I think gay and lesbian society also pressures people.

MR: To stay within their own orientations?

Kilpatrick: To stay within their orientations, exactly. I mean, I've seen it. I know.

MR: A lot of horror writing involves the complete annihilation of barriers, because you have to annihilate the barriers before you can tell the story. Perhaps a lot of what you are talking about—exploring sexuality—also involves removing barriers. Is this, perhaps, another of the connections between horror and erotica?

Kilpatrick: Yes, definitely. Both of them push out boundaries; because if it's good horror and good erotica, people are hopefully asked to explore areas that they are unfamiliar with. Of course it's kind of fun to explore the same territory several times, but it's also boring, and people are always trying to find something slightly new and different. Good horror does that because it takes you past where you thought you were afraid. You find that you are actually more afraid than you thought, or there is something else that you didn't know you were afraid of. What's exciting about it is the feeling of danger: can I do this and survive? And people always want to push.

MR: Much of your erotic fiction involves very harsh SM scenarios. The "pushing" of boundaries of pain and pleasure in your pornography has caused your novel, *The Darker Passions: Dracula*, published in the United States, to be detained at the Canadian border, even though you are a Canadian writer—

Kilpatrick: They were stopped, they were read, and then it was determined that they were okay. I was prepared for them not to be admitted, but obviously somebody opened to a page that he felt was okay.

MR: Which is ridiculous, because there is enough in your erotic fiction to have them be banned, at least inasmuch as Canada Customs defines the criteria for book banning.

Kilpatrick: I know. If you read the books, all the things they say they stop books for are in my work, so obviously they missed those. Which is just a human error. (*laughs*) It's a stupid process. As you pointed out before, some of the scenes I write people would not be able to endure. They wouldn't be able to go to the next scene in the book—they'd need four weeks to recover. This aspect of it is fantasy. Which is why the censorship thing is so infuriating. When you get something in book form, the fact of whether people do it in real life or not is irrelevant. In book form it's fantasy. There's a difference between fiction and nonfiction. When people are looking at fiction, they have to be thinking metaphor. If they are not thinking metaphor, they have a problem. They don't have the ability to distinguish because they've closed off their mind to the concept of metaphor. Which our society is not big on, anyway. But that is part of the reason for censorship.

MR: The argument could be made that people who have closed off their minds to metaphor, and to symbolism, and exploration, have no business censoring, because they do not possess the understanding they need in order to make these decisions.

Kilpatrick: Yes. It's like those people on the film-censoring boards—they watch four hundred films a month, then they say they have the ability to judge what is "degrading." I don't think anybody who has even gotten into what they call "degrading" experiences watches four hundred videos a month. The censor boards are obviously not the average viewer, and they've lost the ability to judge. They've been overexposed to stuff that they don't have any tolerance for, anyway. It makes no sense.

MR: Do you find there is a crossover between horror readers and readers of erotica? At lunch we were talking about how the new fiction is very explicit and sexual, and is perhaps reaching an audience that is more willing to explore bisexuality, SM, and any number of permutations of sexuality.

Kilpatrick: It's much more obviously sexual. I think there is an expansive feeling afoot within the new fiction. People are being a little more adventurous, more investigative of what is not necessarily their own straight-and-narrow path, which is good. And the vampire is going to be part and parcel of that. The vampire has changed over the centuries according to the social mores of the day.

MR: And the sexual mores?

Kilpatrick: Yes. The whole image of vampires as being repulsive is gone. Vampires can walk around in daylight. Chelsea Quinn Yarbro has ten or twelve books in a series where the vampire wears his native earth inside his boots so he can walk around in the daylight. The whole mythology on that has changed. Many of them don't need to drink blood, or they can drink it without killing the person.

MR: Do you see this as rejection of antiquated social mores? Being violated by a creature who has just crawled out of the grave, covered with mud and dirt and slime, is a perfect metaphor for a societal perception of sex as dirty and degrading and base. Today you have vampires dressed well, walking around in the daylight. They do what they do, and they like it.

Kilpatrick: That has a lot to do with people being looser about sexuality—certainly more so than they were in Bram Stoker's day.

MR: As a woman writing both horror and erotica, what do you think about the time-honored tradition of the heroine dressed in white and the whole issue of victimization? A lot of that has changed now—many vampires are female, and they kick ass, but I wonder what you think about that tradition of assigning roles based on gender.

Kilpatrick: Well, again, that's part of the reflection of the values of the mainstream of society. But in fiction, I tend to view things less on a gender basis. I tend to view it more as a reflection of certain aspects of a person. Now we can use the terms "masculine" and "feminine," but they get really clouded. There are a lot of women who will read gay vampire stories and they will identify with the male characters, even though they are female.

MR: Why?

Kilpatrick: Because I think we're not talking about gender, we are talking about—I have to use these words because they're all I have—masculine and feminine energy, which have nothing to do with male and female whatsoever. Let's get that straight.

MR: Are you talking about power versus perception of power?

Kilpatrick: Aspects of male energy, as reflected in the gay characters, or aspects of feminine energy as reflected in the gay characters. That's the thing the person is tapping into, not so much the gender. It's that old pansexualism. Readers can do it. People have a harder time in real life doing it.

MR: Anyone who views sexuality as being very rigid—things that "men do" and things that "women do"—is going to have the same trouble with horror as they do with pornography.

Kilpatrick: Yes, definitely. There are an awful lot of ugly attitudes that people have, you know. It gets back to fear. People have a lot of fear. They take these approaches which are very narrow, but in reality they are hurting people by those attitudes.

MR: Specifically, which attitudes?

Kilpatrick: Some of the right-wing stuff—"It's an abomination to God!" You know, two men having sex together or whatever. But it's not just hurting the person that it's aimed at, it is also hurting the person who says it. These energies abound in the universe, and anytime somebody is putting out *this is wrong, this is bad, this has to be cut off or censored*, you can be sure the person is doing it to themselves as well. It's an internal dialogue as well as an external. Both things are happening. When someone is murdering, he is murdering something inside, too. This is soul destruction we are talking about here.

MR: What tone were you going for in the books? The books deal with the Victorian era, and guilt was a strong motivating factor in the sexuality of that era.

Kilpatrick: When I started writing them, I wanted to go for a tone that matched my own—at least, more than what I usually read. Often in erotic writing, people are portrayed as guilt-ridden, tangled up in guilt, tangled up in shame. I was trying to write something that didn't have much of that in it. I know that's kind of a turn-on for some people, but I wanted to really try and find these Victorian characters who—this is part of where the humor hopefully is in the story—are taking sex in such a matter-of-fact way with everybody, anybody, all the time. They kind of tripped into these situations, and so they just experience what they experience. I was trying to get away from that moralistic tone.

MR: How were you raised? Were you raised in a conservative household, or a liberal one?

Kilpatrick: I had a peculiar upbringing, in that I didn't have parents and I went from relative to relative. I won't go into all the details of it, but I was virtually ignored. By being left alone so much, I ended up having a very strong fantasy life. So I was always right-brain, and I didn't have anybody telling me that wasn't okay. That made me different. I was a very "feeling" type of person. I knew that I existed because I was in touch with my own feelings, and there was a lot of sadness and pain in my family.

MR: How did that affect you?

Kilpatrick: Some of it affected me directly because it had to do with me. Some of it was not my own, it was the people around me. People like me tend to carry that for other people. So I was plunged into a lot of unhappy feelings as a kid. I think many writers were. It's kind of across the board. I'm not brilliant by a long shot, but I seemed to be one of those kids—I was very shy when I was young—who would go to school, and I wouldn't do anything that I didn't have to do. I didn't study. I did only the minimum amount of homework, but for some reason I always got by with B's, and A's sometimes. I was bright enough that I could do that. It wasn't a priority to me because at a certain point you hit a level where they aren't teaching you anything you don't know, and what is really of interest is not there.

MR: Did you go to college?

Kilpatrick: I started at Temple, in Philadelphia. I dropped out because there was nothing there for me. I knew I was just going to be wasting my time and I wanted to do other things, so I did. But it's funny, you know? Because I was so shy, I think I was almost invisible as a kid. I was virtually left alone in the school system, too.

MR: How did your "aloneness"—for lack of a better word—affect your interaction with other people?

Kilpatrick: It gave me a lot of difficulty because I was not sure I *could* actually interact with the world very well, because I wasn't accustomed to it. For me, there wasn't much going on outside. I had to create reality, and I did it from an early age.

MR: Did that act as a screen for you? And as a writer, obviously, there are advantages to being able to completely shut out the sounds of the world.

Kilpatrick: Because of that, I didn't get a lot of negativity. I've never had the problem with writer's block that many writers have. I always felt I could just plunge right into my creative, intuitive, fanciful side instantly—anywhere, anytime. And I have. In the last few years, as I have become more established in my field, people are asking me to do stories for particular books, and that is rather limiting.

MR: Does lending yourself to other people's expectations of what you can, or should, write complicate the process for you? You claim that you've never experienced writer's block.

Kilpatrick: I wouldn't say I've had writer's block, but what I've had is difficulty working with other people's reality. It tends to be more difficult. You get writer's guidelines for publications and they are looking for something specific—it would be like writing a *Star Trek* novel or something. You're working within the realm of that world. It's not your own world.

MR: You've written a line of erotic books based on standard horror classics, like *Dracula*. This is obviously an extended commercial project, unlike your novel *Near Death*, which is a mainstream vampire novel. Into which category does your *Darker Passions* series fall? Your own work, or work for hire?

Kilpatrick: Somewhere between the two, because with *Dracula* I started out with the idea that I wanted to really work with these classics and rewrite them. The scenes between the scenes. I tried so hard to stick to the plot, but I had to deviate a little bit in *Dracula*. By the time I got to *Dr. Jekyll and Mr. Hyde*, then *Frankenstein*, I was beyond the point of saying I was going to have to stick to the plot. When I started writing them, I was trying to stick to the stories as I saw them, in terms of the horror element. So the fourth book, *The Fall of the House of Usher*, has more horror to it than the first three. *The Fall of the House of Usher* lends itself more to horror anyway because it has more of that dark gothic stuff we were talking about. There's an insinuation of incest there, the madness that comes about through incest. Someone coming back from the dead. I'm now working on *The Picture of Dorian Gray. Dracula*, however, is not really that horrific.

MR: Nancy! That's heresy!

Kilpatrick: I am sure a lot of people will read it and say, "Oh, my God, this is *scary!*" But I've read it so many times that it's not scary. Frankenstein is also not scary. It's not horror—it's a sad tale of a creature who lives in a society that he can't fit into. He's being misunderstood constantly.

MR: He must be an erotic author.

Will
LEBER

It started as a very brief short story. But what was interesting about it was, there was a woman in the class who said basically that she couldn't say anything about it, because it upset her too much—because it had a gun and sex in it. It was really too much sex, and why would I ever want to do that?

Will Leber, a San Francisco writer, appears as part of this collection of erotic authors on the basis of one extraordinary piece of short fiction—the only writer among the group to be accorded this distinction. His short story, "Sucked In," about a San Francisco AIDS activist who seduces and objectifies the object of his loathing, embodied by a heterosexual, Republican family man, a Secret Service agent whose "muscular shoulders jut up above the throng," whose "blond hair is crew-cut," and whose "tanned skin glistens in the sun." The story echoed like a rifle shot through the pages of *Flesh and the Word 2*, and announced the arrival of a major new talent on the erotic fiction landscape. Leber also appears in *Flesh and the Word 3*.

In "Sucked In," Leber confronts, head-on, the dilemma faced by anyone who finds himself drawn sexually to a symbol—or a person—representing his oppression. How far do political and moral loyalties extend? Too, the undeniable lure of the potential violence, inherent in any sexual interaction between men, is described in writing that is both lean and startlingly pellucid. Last, of course, the story is placed squarely in our times, and deals unsparingly with the eternal question of the degree to which the power of sexual fantasy can override almost any reality, given just the right set of circumstances.

Michael Rowe: Where did you grow up?

Will Leber: I grew up in California, in a very small agricultural community called Dixon. It's about an hour and a half from San Francisco. I went into San Francisco first time in my life probably when I was in high school. I didn't know it was that close.

MR: Can you describe your adolescence?

Leber: Dixon is a very small town, so my high-school class was very small. My adolescence, you know, I did the normal things. I played high-school and junior-high-school sports.

MR: You were a jock?

Leber: Yes, up until the time that I got my shoulder broken playing football.

MR: Playing football?

Leber: And I quit playing football. And as far as like being sexually active with boys, I stopped when I got into high school. I had a boyfriend until high school, sort of, who was more of a regular friend, and then by high school we stopped, just stopped by mutual—I don't know if it was a decision more than just that we knew we were supposed to.

MR: Was that painful?

Leber: Yes, I think so, to some degree. It wasn't like we had an incredible emotional attachment in every way. It was painful in the same way as it is for most young gay people. It's painful in that you don't feel any real connection to anybody if you're not "out" in some sense.

MR: And being out wasn't really much of a question?

Leber: Yes. I didn't know of anyone who was known to be gay, where I grew up. There was speculation about the drama teacher, things like that.

MR: Well, they always say drama is phys ed for gay kids. The choir and the drama group.

Leber: That's right.

MR: So you dated girls during high school?

Leber: I dated very little in high school. I had a girlfriend when I was sixteen, very, very briefly, mostly at her urging.

MR: Had you always known you were gay?

Leber: Just about. I mean, from a very young age, yes.

MR: Do you remember any of your earlier erotic experiences?

Leber: Yes. I was trying to figure out when I was first sexually active, which was with boys, and probably I think I had to be eight or so. If not earlier.

MR: Did you write at that time? Did you keep a journal?

Leber: I wrote a little bit. One of my big influences, the one who really started me writing, was an English teacher at my high school who had gone to Stanford and had actually grown up in Dixon. He was very encouraging, and a very fresh presence in that town, because he was someone young and dynamic in a high school of teachers who had been there a million years, and that sort of thing.

MR: Leigh Rutledge was telling me that when he was an adolescent, when he was starting to write in his teens, and his late teens, he would actually channel his sexual energy into his fiction writing. He would write heterosexual fiction, and make it very sexual. I'm wondering if you sort of sublimated your sexuality, or channeled it in any way at that time.

Leber: No, I didn't really write about sex. I remember writing one story about some very free guy with long hair running around through fields, and ending up on the beach sort of fucking the sand or something, and that was about as far as I got.

MR: You've cut quite a swath since then, judging by your story "Sucked In," from *Flesh and the Word 2*. It's a strong piece of erotic fiction.

Leber: I wrote it in a writing class that was taught by Bo Huston at A Different Light Bookstore.

MR: How old were you when you wrote this?

Leber: I must have been thirty-five.

MR: I ask because it's a very youthful story. The voice is very youthful and contemporary, and the topic is obviously very youthful as well. Were you a member of ACT UP yourself?

Leber: No. I've been to demos, but I'm not a member of ACT UP. It started as a very brief short story. But what was interesting about it was, there was a woman in the class who said basically that she couldn't say *anything* about it, because it upset her too much—because it had a gun and sex in it. It was really too much sex, and why would I ever want to do that?

MR: How bizarre.

Leber: Yes, and she was actually afraid to touch the manuscript.

MR: Seriously?

Leber: It was like, *oh wow, she's that freaked out, this must be something worth pursuing.* But much more sex was added after I sent it to John Preston. It wasn't necessarily that he said it needed more sex, but he had other objections which led to it having more sex.

MR: I'm interested in the correlation between the sex and the violence in the piece. It's very in your face. Was that a deliberate thing, the gun?

Leber: Yes, I think so. You are supposed to explore the relationship between dominance and violence, to some degree, and sex. And the acting out of some of those fantasies that you actually have about sex and violence. And also about retribution, and about wanting power.

MR: Now the object of lust in the story is a clean-cut Republican all-American Secret Service agent, obviously very, very different from the protagonist character, in the demonstration. I wonder whether or not the concept of opposites is attractive to you.

Leber: I think that people have more of a desire for power than for something that's the opposite of them, per se—the desire for the things that perhaps a dominant society puts out as being powerful and glamorous. Those are the things that you want. This character has a struggle, internally and externally, with the forces of the things he wants, versus what he thinks maybe he shouldn't have.

MR: But you eroticize and fetishize the characteristics of the Secret Service agent. This wasn't just *any* Secret Service agent. There was almost a celebration, a reveling in his that antiseptic perfection those people sometimes have.

Leber: I don't know what I would call it. I think that the thing of it is that certain symbols are recognizable within gay subculture, which I think are totems of power—mirrored sunglasses, crew-cut hair—and are part of dominant society. The starched white shirts, that sort of thing. So I think it is partly attraction to those symbols, rather than the person.

MR: Are you a fetish-oriented person?

Leber: Not extremely. I think it is good to fetishize something, get excited about something.

MR: Like what, for instance?

Leber: Like probably some of the things we were just talking about.

MR: Is this an SM story? Would you characterize it as such? It certainly has elements of dominance and submission.

Leber: I would say it's more about dominance and submission than SM per se. Although I don't actually practice SM, I probably find dominance and submission much more interesting. There's so much dominance and submission in vanilla sex that I find very interesting, and I think dominance and submission is a major paradigm of sex in general.

MR: Would you characterize yourself as dominant or submissive?

Leber: Good question! I'd have to say versatile, of course, but I'm often submissive and I'm sometimes dominant. (*laughs*)

MR: You've just said absolutely nothing, but you've done it beautifully. "Sucked In" has a sense of immediacy to it. It's very much in sync with the 1990s. Do you see this decade as a time for change, for upheaval, in the sexual arena?

Leber: I think that generally there has been a larger movement in the 1990s toward more sexual exploration. For instance, sex clubs opening. They're trying to open bathhouses in San Francisco. They have underwear parties. There is a general movement back toward more sexuality in people's lives since the late 1980s.

MR: Why is that, in your opinion?

Leber: In part, demand. People have gotten tired of the "Just Say No" messages of the Republican 1980s.

MR: Do you sense, in the upheaval, a lot of anger against the price that AIDS has extracted? Is a lot of this sexual exploration giving the finger to the disease?

Leber: I think there is definitely an element of people acting out against the general repressed feelings that they have. But that sounds like gay men doing kamikaze missions because they are tired of being repressed, or something like that, and that doesn't sound right to me.

I think that what's going on is very exciting, and hopefully it's going to lead to a renewed discussion about sexual libera-tion; as opposed to what's been going on, which is really not about liberation and hasn't been for a long time. It's more about things like fighting the Right on their playing ground, and stuff like that, rather than establishing our own.

MR: Do you find erotic writing is a release for you? Do you find it a sexual release? Do you work out fantasies in the writ-ing?

Leber: I definitely work out fantasies, yes. I definitely explore fantasies, or explore what I think about sex, through writing.

MR: Can you give me an example of that? In a short story that you've worked on, that we possibly haven't read yet?

Leber: Yes. The short story that's going to be in the *Flesh and the Word 3* is about someone going to a sex club, and he's going to the sex club after the funeral of a close friend who died of AIDS. And so, for me, that was, in a way, an exploration of what it is to have sex in a sex club. It is also about the guy's first time going to one, and what that experience is about, and what motivates someone to take the step to have public sex, and to deal with the potential dangers of having sex in the more public setting—psychological, physical, possible AIDS contact—all those sorts of things. So that's one example.

MR: Is public sex a radical act these days? Has it taken back a little bit of the edge that it had in the 1970s, in the Mineshaft era?

Leber: Yes, I definitely think to some degree it has. I think there are a lot of people opposed to public sex, but they seem to be generally opposed to sex, and are generally looking for a more conformist sexuality than other men.

MR: Are we talking about gay men or straight people?

Leber: I'm talking about both. It is unfortunately the perception of a lot of gay people.

MR: What's behind this kind of thinking?

Leber: I don't know. I think there is a general desire to, as they say, "get our place at the table," and all that stuff. And so, there are a lot of gay people who have had success in getting more integrated, and they are willing to do that at the price of abandoning something for themselves, or for some other group of the gay community.

MR: The flip side of that, of course, could be that one of the benefits of gay liberation should have been the fact that we could, in fact, choose our own lives. Or at least have the wherewithal to pursue the life we want. There is a whole school of thought that suggests that the in-your-face activists of the 1990s are, in fact, as intolerant and hostile to the idea of gay couples adopting children, and legal marriage between same-sex couples, as the Republicans are.

Leber: As a group, or a whole, let's say, I don't think they are opposed to people being in couples, if that's what they want to be.

MR: What is it along those lines that they are opposed to, do you think?

Leber: Well, I think that there's a great need for people to shake up the system and make people realize what they are accepting when they say that what they want is "gay marriage." And if they want that on the same terms as heterosexual marriage, what they are really asking for comes with thousands of years of history of property rights—the property rights being each other's bodies, things like that. I don't think we should necessarily be excited about that.

MR: What do you think about the idea that pornography degrades? Women spring to mind, but I've recently heard that a lot of gay men also feel that it degrades and turns them into sex objects. Is this really the first major barometric reading that gay men are becoming far too bourgeois, far too much like heterosexuals? Or is there something to it?

Leber: No, I certainly don't think that as a whole class of writing pornography degrades people.

MR: Do you think, perhaps, that heterosexual pornography is more degrading to women than gay pornography is to men, based on the idea of equality?

Leber: Well, I think that has to do with the fact that society is degrading to women, and that some pornography is simply reflective of that degradation, more than it has to do with pornography being the cause of the degradation. And I think that gay pornography is on a different playing field, so it has a very different impact. It seems very different for me to read about gay men practicing SM than to read about straight people practicing SM, where a man is dominating a woman. In some ways I would find it probably more acceptable for two men to dominate each other. (*laughs*)

MR: Isn't that kind of a double standard, though?

Leber: Oh, yes, I think it is. It's not that I'm in any way saying heterosexual SM isn't perfectly acceptable, but we are talking about perceptions of degradation and where they come from. And I think that because the general society degrades women so much, the reaction to heterosexual SM, where a man is dominating a woman, is very much amplified by the general society.

MR: When did you start your gay writing?

Leber: Really just recently. I guess the dominant force was just that I wanted to do gay writing, basically, and that was always something I had wanted to do. And I was getting older.

MR: The great mid-life shift.

Leber: Yes, whatever.

MR: Have you written a lot of porn?

Leber: I haven't written a lot of porn, no.

MR: How do you feel about the word "porn"?

Leber: I don't have any problem with the word "porn," per se. It sort of makes me think about being a pornographer and having that label, and that kind of thing, which at one time, I thought, well, maybe what I do isn't *pornography*, maybe I'm not a *pornographer*, maybe I'm a "sex writer," because prostitutes call themselves sex workers, or something. I don't think it made any difference to think of it in that way, really, although I wasn't ready to label the kind of writing I do pornography either. At first I didn't really know that it fit the genre.

MR: What was your take on the genre?

Leber: My take on the genre was that my work would have to have much more sex in it. Well, it's generally what's in a skin magazine. I haven't published in skin magazines because I don't think they would accept my stuff. Mostly because you have to have sex very quickly, up front in the story, and usually without a lot of explanation and that sort of thing.

MR: My question leaned more toward the idea of what you yourself think of the genre of pornography. Most people have some sort of response. They are either very attracted to it, or not.

Leber: Well, there is a lot of very good porn writing and there's a lot of bad porn writing, I guess. It really varies. I think that there are certain writers who are really good.

MR: For instance?

Leber: Lars Eighner, John Preston, Pat Califia, Steven Saylor... who else can I think of? I'm probably leaving out people.

MR: What excites you, personally? What turns you on?

Leber: Let's see. I think I get excited by—I don't know, I get excited by all kinds of things. Sometimes I'm excited by things like men in suits, in terms of sexual excitement. Sometimes I'm excited if I like the guilty feelings of sex. I find those very erotic. You know, then I have the typical list: convertible Jeeps, tool sets, going fishing...

MR: All traditional tokens of masculinity?

Leber: Well, that isn't even necessarily so. My biggest criterion for interest usually is interest from the other participant. If you are talking about cruising another person, I would say that's the major criterion for me, some reciprocity of interest. But in terms of objects, I have a fairly traditional list of objects.

MR: According to your bio, you've had the same lover for, what? Sixteen years?

Leber: Longer than that. Almost nineteen.

MR: What does your partner think about your work?

Leber: He's very supportive of it. He is supportive of porn, he's supportive of gay writing in general. He doesn't really have a problem with it at all. Sometimes he thinks he's found the truth in my writing. It's always the danger of a writer—that people think you live your writing—and so if you are writing pornography, they think it doubly. And if you're writing pornography in the first person, then they are certain of it.

MR: What kind of thing drives you as a writer? Is it curiosity, is it a desire to work out scenarios on paper that you might not have time to experience in your life? What is it that you express when you sit down to write?

Leber: I guess that I'm generally, right now anyway, just interested in what gay urban men are experiencing and what their lives are becoming.

MR: What do you think urban gay men are looking for today?

Leber: I think there are definitely people looking for some sense of community, and trying to figure out what it is that gives meaning to life. And I think part of that has to do with so many friends dying.

MR: Could that possibly be the answer we were looking for in terms of why we have the blossoming of high-caliber erotica right now? Is it possible that since sex has been such a potent issue, and simply because for a lot of people there is not a lot of time, do you think that could be why people would want good stuff now?

Leber: Yes, I think it is part of the answer. That people want answers, people want reasons to explore their sexuality. But just in general, it seems people are again much more interested in sexuality in general, and finding out what value it has for their lives.

Michael
LOWENTHAL

*I couldn't be more appreciative of what my forebears have done
for me, politically, sexually, and culturally, but I do feel that I
am of a distinctly different generation, and things are different. And so if I hear one more forty-something gay man say to
me, "Oh, you young guys have it so tough. If only you knew what
was real, and what sex was like back then..."*

Michael Lowenthal, born a month and a half before Stonewall,
speaks the language of a generation of gay writers who have
yet to impact fully on the culture at large. With no effective
memory of the post-Stonewall struggle for gay liberation, and
having grown up more or less aware of the ever-present reality
of AIDS, their world-view is unencumbered by many of the
social and cultural milestones that have shaped the world-view
of gay men as little as a half-decade older. Their perspectives are
rooted in the immediate present.

Lowenthal, the first-ever openly gay valedictorian of
Dartmouth College, has swiftly begun to make his presence
felt in the arena of American gay writing. An essayist and short-
story writer, his work has appeared in *Men on Men 5*, *Best
American Erotica*, and *Flesh and the Word 2* and *3*. In addition,
he took over the editing of several of John Preston's books
when the late author was in the final stages of AIDS and unable
to work.

Michael Lowenthal's views on the field of erotic writing are
worth noting, especially inasmuch as they represent the perspec-

tives of a young writer who has emerged into a world where writing about gay experience—once considered pornographic by definition—has merely become another literary genre, defined ultimately only by whether or not it is good writing. How much less of a leap of imagination, then, for someone of his generation, to judge pornography by the same objective standard?

Lowenthal accepts the mantle of "pornographer" with equanimity. It doesn't particularly resonate for him, but it doesn't distress him in the least. If he writes about sex, and the reading of it is an erotic experience unsullied by guilt or the feeling of having "gotten away with something," his objective has been achieved.

The sexual fiction of this generation appears as likely to be published between the covers of a mainstream anthology as by a pornographic magazine. The work is not necessarily more upmarket, but the marketplace itself has modified somewhat. And the gay writers of Generation X, like their twenty-something colleagues, are a product of the marketplace. Where an older writer might feel as though he or she had scored a particular victory over the public's perception of "pornographers" by publishing in *Flesh and the Word*, Lowenthal and his age group would see it as merely a prestigious anthology publication.

Is this the voice of the new generation? From Boston, Michael Lowenthal talks about growing up gay, the joy of unconsummated sex, and gay generation gaps.

Michael Rowe: I think we should put this interview with you in a generational context because you are fairly young. How old are you?

Michael Lowenthal: Twenty-five.

MR: Can you tell me something about your growing-up years? What kind of a family did you grow up in?

Lowenthal: I grew up in your better-basic suburban American family, mostly in Chevy Chase, a suburb of Washington, D.C., and with the added twist, I suppose, that we were a textbook third-generation assimilated Jewish family. My father's parents were German immigrants who came over in 1939. My grandfather was a rabbi, and my father was raised in a very observant home. My mother, much less so. In any case, when we grew up, we had kosher food, and I went to a Hebrew school and was bar mitzvahed, but at the same time we had a very suburban Christian-American existence.

MR: Was that a bit schizophrenic? In terms of your cultural development?

Lowenthal: It was what I knew, so it felt normal. I didn't think much about it.

MR: Tell me something about your early sexual experiences. When did you first become aware of the fact that you were gay?

Lowenthal: It's interesting, I just wrote out a version of my very first sexual experience which I hadn't thought about for a while, but Alyson Books was doing a collection called *My First Time*. Anyhow, I thought a little bit about it, and I loved my first sexual memory. The question of when I first became aware of being gay could be answered so many different ways—in terms of a cultural realization, a self-definition, whatnot.

MR: But the self-definition came late. Eighteen, right?

Lowenthal: Yes, well, definition to myself as opposed to self-definition to other people. I can give you all the various stages, but when I back up to give you the most basic answer, I say that I have never been *unaware* of being gay, or having had attractions to other boys or men. I realized only later that other people did not have this orientation, and then I had to rerealize for myself what I was. But I think the first sexual experience I had was with another boy, and I am not exactly sure, but I was certainly not older than seven. I think I was six or seven.

MR: Do you remember what it was about him that attracted you?

Lowenthal: Umm, I can tell you what in the memory stands out as being erotic, but to tell you the truth, I have no idea how we got together or how we got where we were. But I loved the difference in him: he was black, and I just loved the color of his skin, and feel of it, and I just loved that he was a boy, if that makes sense. I mean that was my memory of it, it was just so fun and it was with a boy.

MR: Interracial prepubescent gay sex in the suburbs? That's actually a fairly radical cultural thing for you in Chevy Chase, Maryland.

Lowenthal: This took place before I lived in Chevy Chase, although I think your observation holds. It was in Princeton, New Jersey. And as I said, I don't really remember how we even got there. I would assume that he lived in the apartment complex where we lived. It was kind of faculty and staff housing, and presumably one or both of his parents worked for the university. But looking back, not only our being boys, but the racial thing, was a very unusual cultural move.

MR: What about sex objects closer to home? Did you find your father erotic when you were growing up, at all? Was he the first male presence in your life or was there some other one?

Lowenthal: Yes, I have one semierotic memory of my father which I think I don't particularly care to go into, and I have vague memories of perhaps an erotic attraction, although maybe just a fondness for his Old Spice cologne. But that's really it. No, I was never particularly—he didn't really serve that function in my life.

MR: And what about your mother? Did you identify with her in any way at all?

Lowenthal: The first thing that comes to mind is that I identify with her politically, and have since I was six. I remember very clearly being at an antinuclear-power rally alongside my mother, and feeling like we were soldiers in the struggle together.

MR: Did you start writing when you were a teenager?

Lowenthal: I wrote some as a teenager, and then stopped for a while, and then eventually got back to it. I don't remember... what was I writing? Stupid teenage love poetry.

MR: Did you get it published?

Lowenthal: I actually published a few things in a high-school literary journal.

MR: Did you feel any particular desire to be a writer at that time? Was that your goal?

Lowenthal: Yes, absolutely.

MR: Can you elaborate?

Lowenthal: (*laughs*) I'll go back even further if it's not counterproductive.

MR: Please, feel free.

Lowenthal: My mother has, to this day, the Mother's Day present I gave to her when I was in second grade. We all made books. We bound up paper, and made covers, and created these lovely little books, and then we wrote in them and presented them to our mothers. We wrote about our families, and where we lived, and then we wrote what we wanted to do when we grew up. And I wrote at that time that I wanted to play left field for the Boston Red Sox, and in the off-season half of the year, live on a farm in New England and be a writer.

MR: You knew this in the second grade?

Lowenthal: Yes, and the only thing that has changed is that my hopes have dimmed somewhat about being a left fielder for the Red Sox, although certainly not my desire. And I really always have had in my mind that I would like to be a writer.

MR: That sounds very wholesome and all-American, Michael.

Lowenthal: I was always a little bit too out of it to be an all-American kid. I was always a little bit on the fringes. I didn't do Cub Scouts and Boy Scouts, as many of my friends did. I played some sports. I was on the baseball team for a while, and the basketball team, and soccer team, and football team when I was really very young. But then, as I got into junior high and high school, I dropped out. I got a little bit more geeky, I missed most of the popular culture that happened when I was growing up. I didn't listen to the radio.

MR: Good Lord!

Lowenthal: Call me a traitor.

MR: You're a traitor!

Lowenthal: Thank you.

MR: You mean, like you *never*...

Lowenthal: I mean I listened vaguely for a very short time. I could identify "My Sharona," which I now notice has come back in a new version, which really makes me horrified to think that my childhood is already fodder for nostalgia.

MR: Yes, well that's the thing today. They have Retro Night, where they play Blondie's "Heart of Glass" and that kind of stuff. So, as you cruised, culturally oblivious, through your adolescence, you would obviously have become aware of yourself in a more sexual context. I wonder what sort of young fellows attracted you at that time. It's sort of a broad question because I am also curious about how you would have explored your sexuality at that age.

Lowenthal: I would say the kind of boy who attracted me then was the kind that walked on two legs.

MR: You were an easy lay, then?

Lowenthal: Yes, you could say that.

MR: Did you explore with your friends?

Lowenthal: Yes, I've had lots of little adolescent sex-play moments, the memories of which I cherish to this day. And in some ways I hate the part of me that thinks sex will never be as good again as it was then.

MR: Why is that?

Lowenthal: It was all so—

MR: If you say it was "innocent," I'm going to shoot you.

Lowenthal: Well, no, I wouldn't say that, because that's too horrible. But it was so chaotically energetic, not fraught with emotional or cultural baggage. And so friendly. *Intensely* friendly. It feels like the kind of things I did then had "for real" what the JO clubs in New York and San Francisco try to re-create. Unsuccessfully, to my mind. Although I don't have great experience with those clubs, so I shouldn't really comment.

MR: What sort of imagery attracted you at that time? Did you have any particular fetish objects? Magazines? People? Actors? Did you watch TV?

Lowenthal: I watched *some* TV. I'm trying to think.

MR: You're going to have to turn in your Gen-X card, babe.

Lowenthal: I am.

MR: I think you really are.

Lowenthal: You know, I don't think so. I can barely identify, for example, *people*, like pop culture. I can barely identify people. I'm fluent enough to be able to joke about who was the cutest one of the Brady Bunch—clearly Bobby—but I've always had a markedly nonvisual life and memory.

MR: What about writing? Any particular writing that caught your fancy? At that time?

Lowenthal: Well, then we come up against this fact that I didn't really *read*.

MR: Okay. No radio, no TV, no books, no visual imagery at all? It sounds like you've just sort of spelunked your way through your adolescence.

Lowenthal: I think this is true.

MR: Michael, how do you explain this?

Lowenthal: (*laughs*) I apologize for not being articulate about it, but this has been a continuing black hole in my life.

MR: Did you feel in any way constrained by your homosexuality as an adolescent?

Lowenthal: Absolutely. I wanted to have ultra-sex all the time with boys, and they didn't seem to want to have it back with me. It was terribly frustrating. I think I whitewashed some of my anxious memories. I know that I had some difficulties coming to terms with my being gay; but largely, or at least in retrospect, my problems weren't that I was tortured about being bad or evil, or that I felt this is wrong. It was mostly pain and frustration at the realization that other people didn't feel this way, and how was I going to arrange my life so that I could ever get what I wanted? Because other people didn't seem to understand why I wanted these things.

MR: Were your sexual overtures rebuffed on an ongoing basis?

Lowenthal: I mostly didn't get around to having the guts to make the overtures. Actually, most of the times that I was bold enough to do things, I did get a payoff. But I was a little bit timid.

MR: You certainly lost that in a hurry, didn't you?

Lowenthal: I did! I'm trying to think...I was just remembering the other day, one of my greatest crushes in junior high and high school. I've always had an obsessive crush personality. He was so wonderful, and I was so smitten with him. I also felt that as a person, he was compassionate and secure enough that I could test some things out on him. I actually did.

MR: What was his name?

Lowenthal: Pat. He was a gorgeous, muscular redheaded guy with a wonderful big smile, and I became friends with him in my typical pattern. I think maybe we were in a class together. We didn't really know each other, then one day we actually talked for the first time. And, maybe the next day, he invited me over to his house, and I stayed for four days.

MR: Heavens!

Lowenthal: And for me, it was absolute love, and felt like marriage. I was just hoping beyond hope that he was feeling the same way. It became clear, pretty soon, that he was just being a buddy.

MR: How did you feel about that? Did that devastate you?

Lowenthal: More or less. And this was just a perpetual frustration of part of me, thinking I would just rather have someone hate me, or reject me completely, but I couldn't take this middle ground of someone seeming so interested in me, friendly with me, willing to spend lots of time with me, and absolutely unable to go that last step which seemed so natural. But at the same time, I was so obsessed and crushed that I wouldn't give it up for the world. I still would spend as much time with him as I could, even though it was frustrating every second I was with him. At one point I finally pulled the old *Hey Pat, I have all these feelings, do you think that's normal?* routine, and bless his heart, he said, *Oh, I think that's fine and I think lots of people our age have those kinds of feelings, and I wouldn't worry too much about it.* Which was a wonderful response for somebody who was straight, as Pat was, and, presumably, is.

MR: How did you keep these feelings from your parents? Did you talk to your mother?

Lowenthal: No. Nope, I did not talk to anyone in my family about it. As I got a little bit older, fifteen, sixteen, I talked with my girlfriends about it.

MR: That was safe ground?

Lowenthal: Yes, that was my pattern.

MR: Did you keep a diary at all?

Lowenthal: No. One year, I kept a journal. That was more because I was traveling around the United States and wanted to keep a record of that.

MR: Did these sexual frustrations of yours find manifestation in any writing—early writing—which has since indicated to you that you were dealing with this?

Lowenthal: Yes, I definitely wrote at least one or two things that were directly related to my frustrations. I wish I could remember really what they were or what they were about. I may still have them at my mother's house somewhere, but yes, I clearly remember a couple of things.

MR: According to your bio, you came out at eighteen.

Lowenthal: Yes, I believe that's true. Yes, late eighteen.

MR: Tell me about Dartmouth. College must have been a whole world of wonders for you after high school. College tends to be a lot freer and a lot more exploratory.

Lowenthal: Well, true to form, I kind of missed the boat on college, too. I've been truly horrified recently to realize just how few people I slept with in college. If I were an amputee, I could still count them on one hand. And by the way, I'm not sure you can print that.

MR: Try me.

Lowenthal: I'll give you a little story, and that will lead me in, and get me thinking about it. My mother hates long-distance driving, and almost never does it, but she agreed to drive me up to college, which is about a ten-hour drive from where we lived. It felt like a big deal. It was Mom "giving away the bride." So fine, we did it in two days. We stopped in New Haven, Connecticut, and stayed with a camp friend of mine.

MR: "Camp" as in "summer camp"?

Lowenthal: Right. Dave and I were just buddies, and having gone to the summer camp where open affection between boys and men was actively encouraged, we were—

MR: Goodness, what sort of camp was this?

Lowenthal: Actually, that camp had a big erotic influence. Anyway, Dave and I took a walk together that evening, and because it felt completely natural, we had our arms around each other as we walked down the street in his neighborhood. And it was really nonsexual, but as we were walking, a couple of kids passed us and yelled, *"Hey fags!"* or *"Hey, faggots!"* This was the first time it had ever happened to me, and I felt such a mixed reaction: partly horror, but mainly anger, not that they would call *me* that, but that they were wrong about what was going on. And they were wrong about Dave, who is not gay, and it made me angry that I couldn't just express this affection without it being a *gay thing*. Anyhow, my mom and I finished the drive, and partly because of what had happened the night before, but also partly because it was this big transitional time, it was the first time I remember being absolutely conscious of having this thing between us that I wasn't saying.

MR: You and your mother are so close, it must have felt like dishonesty.

Lowenthal: It was a big issue, and I wanted desperately to tell her, and I couldn't figure out how.

MR: Were you attracted to Dave?

Lowenthal: Yes. But I was kind of beyond that with him, at that point—you know what I mean? That wasn't it. The thing I wanted to express to my mother in general was my gayness. And it was a very painful ride up, and I felt like I arrived with this baggage, in a sense.

MR: What happened when you arrived at Dartmouth?

Lowenthal: I generally didn't deal with anything like sexuality. I just worked. I did schoolwork. So it wasn't that big a deal for me. I just...sex wasn't really a part of my life. So I did that for a while, a year, year and a half.

MR: What were you writing at this time?

Lowenthal: My first term in college, I took a course in reading and writing short stories. A freshman seminar. I wrote half a dozen short stories. They were on various and sundry things, but one of them sticks out in my memory. It involved a lesbian relationship between a waitress at a nightclub and a blues singer who performs there. It was very risqué for that class, and in retrospect, it was a clear attempt to address these issues without putting myself in them.

MR: How was it received?

Lowenthal: With some timidity, but a few expressions of support. It's hard to remember.

MR: Did you publish in college?

Lowenthal: No.

MR: Did you continue to explore your sexuality? We have a few fingers left.

Lowenthal: (*laughs*) In the beginning of my second year, I led an orientation hiking trip for the first-year students. It's a big thing at Dartmouth. I ended up having an affair with one of the students who had been on my trip.

MR: An affair, or a bang? Did it last over a long period of time?

Lowenthal: Between a bang and an affair. A few bangs.

MR: A volley of shots?

Lowenthal: Yes.

MR: Did you feel the need to fall in love, Michael?

Lowenthal: Need? I *always* feel the need to fall in love.

MR: I get a feeling that with you it's not necessarily necessary to have it reciprocated?

Lowenthal: What I feel, frequently, is a fairly erotic mental or emotional response. Not necessarily love. There's no rush greater for me than feeling attracted to every ripple of air created when somebody's body moves the slightest inch, or the way his hair is parted, and something about what he is doing at any given moment of the day, and yes, I get off on that completely. And it's so often not reciprocated that I suppose it's not an important issue.

MR: Is there a wide range of men that attracts you?

Lowenthal: I'm flexible, and I surprise myself, but in general I feel like my ideal tastes are quite narrow at this point. Quirky, but narrow. I find myself attracted to very skinny, waiflike, usually young-looking guys.

MR: You were the openly gay valedictorian of your year. How did you manifest yourself as an openly gay valedictorian?

Lowenthal: At Dartmouth, the valedictorian gives a speech. He or she is the only student speaker, and so I gave a speech, and really, among many other things, it was a political speech about multiculturalism and celebration of differences. I said I was gay. I just came out.

MR: You came out to the entire graduating class and assembled parents and dignitaries?

Lowenthal: Yes.

MR: My. That's a grand flourish. I like that. The first one of your young life, I might add, judging by the interview thus far.

Lowenthal: It was *wunderbar*. I thought I did it quite tastefully, and I did it kind of in two steps.

MR: What did you do after you graduated?

Lowenthal: When I graduated, I worked at a summer camp.

Then I moved to Northampton, Massachusetts, and worked as a dishwasher.

MR: Is that where you started to write erotic fiction?

Lowenthal: I think I need to talk about whether or not I do, and what that means. I actually did start to write when I moved to Northampton, and the first thing I wrote was a story called "Stallions," which is still one of my favorite things I've done to date. And I think it was a good example of the way I tend to write things that include a lot of sex, but are not necessarily erotic, or certainly not pornographic. The story centers on a woman whose occupation is jerking off stallions to capture the sperm by which mares will be impregnated. And so it is a lot of that kind of sexual imagery, and then the climax of the story, to coin a phrase, involves the woman's rape by a male attendant at the stable. So clearly, full of sex.

MR: Published?

Lowenthal: Not yet. Lots of nice rejection letters and lots of personal rejection letters.

MR: How did you meet John Preston? For what it's worth that seems to be launching point for your sexually explicit published fiction. Is that a correct assessment?

Lowenthal: If we're talking my published fiction, we're not talking a very wide range of fiction. I haven't really published any fiction. [Shortly after this interview, Lowenthal received word that a piece of his short fiction was to appear as part of *Men on Men 5*, edited by David Bergman.] I answered a call for submissions that John had placed in *Lambda Book Report* for the anthology *Sister and Brother*. And I sent him a letter proposing an essay that I would write, about a dyke who worked as a waitress at that music hall where I worked in Northampton, on whom I had an excessive crush. So I thought I would write about my experience as a gay man deeply attracted to this lesbian. And John wrote back and said, "Fine, give it a whirl, and by the way, I'm really glad you wrote because I've been meaning to get in touch with you. I heard about your graduation speech, and really wanted to get in touch with you, but had no idea how." So that was nice.

MR: And that relationship eventually blossomed into a mentorship and a close friendship. You have a story in *Flesh and the Word 2*, called "Better Safe," about a young man who is fetishized on latex condoms. This story is particularly poignant in the context of safe sex, and how safe sex can be very hot. Very erotic. How has the whole safe-sex movement impacted on the lives of your generation? Is "Better Safe" based on a personal fantasy?

Lowenthal: What I would say about that story is that it's not based so much on the personal fantasy, as it is on a personal cultural response. And a political response. And I sometimes call it—not to be ungracious—my "Fuck You, Fire Island" story, or my "Fuck You to the 1970s-Generation Gay Men" story. I couldn't be more appreciative of what my forebears have done for me, politically, sexually, and culturally, but I do feel that I am of a distinctly different generation, and things are different. And so if I hear one more forty-something gay man say to me, "Oh, you young guys have it so tough. If only you knew what was real, and what sex was like back then..."

MR: You mean, when sex was "Mansex"?

Lowenthal: You know, I'm going to strangle somebody.

MR: Well, your remarks at the 1993 OutWrite Conference indicated a certain hostility to that whole body of work. And that whole attitude.

Lowenthal: Yes. I've kind of got to deal with that.

MR: In what sense?

Lowenthal: Well, I feel so bad. I guess I appreciate their work for what it is, but I want to make some distinctions, or have the right to say it doesn't feel particularly relevant to me. And that is the way I feel.

MR: Run with this idea, would you? A lot of the pornography that was written in those days was very reflective of the attitude toward sex that you grab it when you can, before someone catches you, and with your generation it's a lot more taken for granted. I'm wondering whether you think that our literature, perhaps, reflects that?

Lowenthal: For example?

MR: I'm looking at something like Will Leber's story in *Flesh and the Word 2*, "Sucked In," about the ACT UP activist who seduces the Secret Service agent, ostensibly the enemy. It's an unbelievably erotic, and also beautifully crafted, piece of writing. I wondered whether you think your generation actually has perhaps more freedom to bring good writing to the pornographic experience. What do you think about that?

Lowenthal: I think that point has many possibilities. It might really hit on something. Before, I talked about really obvious observations that porn writers in that kind of classic school were so concerned with getting to the come shot that they did just that, hammered it to its physical details, and so on. It may be that it was all so fast, so new, and they just put it right out there. And now we have more time in life, more freedom, to get what we want; and so, in our writing, it's more a more thoughtful and leisurely path we can take to sexual arousal. And so, yes, I do see that, especially in the work of someone like Will Leber.

MR: It's intriguing to me that this should happen in the middle of an epidemic, where time is something that we definitely don't have.

Lowenthal: In one way, yes, time is something we don't have, and people's time is running out. At the same time, it has put sex in slow motion, and occasionally in freeze frame. People now stop before they have sex, and think about it, and take time to analyze the risks, and decide what they really want and how badly do they want it, and how much is it worth to them. And how they are going to contrive to get what they want, given the impediments we all have to deal with.

MR: Quality over quantity.

Lowenthal: Quality over quantity. You know, people have come up with some real creative solutions. I think, in that sense, it really has slowed things down, or opened them up.

MR: Where does the whole feminist ethic about pornography being degrading come from, and what do you feel your duty as a gay man toward it is?

Lowenthal: Yuk, yuk, yuk!

MR: You are a graduate of an Ivy League school, Michael, and well traveled, as we know from reading *Steam*. Articulate, please.

Lowenthal: I think the anti-porn feminists essentially get it all wrong, and attack people whom they perceive to be their enemies who [actually] are not. As for my duty as a gay male writer, a large part of me has given up on trying to have a dialogue with the hard-core antiporn feminists. Another part of me thinks if any men are going to be able to open up their minds, it is going to be gay men, and probably gay men who support erotic writing. And so maybe I should really make an effort to try to explain things, and to create work that speaks for itself in refuting their claims about pornography.

MR: Which brings us to the ultimate salient point about whether or not you view your work as pornographic.

Lowenthal: (*hums*)

MR: By your own admission, you are a highly sexualized individual. There is a large part of you that is, in fact, pornographic.

Lowenthal: I guess the simplest way of saying it is, I don't view what I write as pornographic, but I think I write pornography, and I am happy to be seen in the role of the pornographer and to claim the label "pornographer." Let me try to explain that! (*laughs*)

MR: How do you see erotic literature vis-à-vis literature? Porn has taken a terrible beating over the years in terms of reputation, and I wonder if you would like to comment on why you think that is.

Lowenthal: I don't know that I have anything particularly new or original to say on that subject. All writers have a goal in mind when they are writing. Usually I would say the goal is to move their readers. Porn writers have that same goal. As to the traditional problems with porn being taken seriously as writing, I think that sometimes the writers focus too much on the ends, rather than the means, and they forget all the things they need to do to be successful at achieving them. The subtlety and finesse is lost, and for me—and I suppose it's related to my abilities to just watch someone across a bar and become obsessed with him but not actually touch his flesh, although it would be nice at some point—that subtlety is much more erotic than hearing about how long his cock is, and what it could be doing in my "hungry chute."

MR: What kind of writing turns you on? Is there any specific writing—erotic writing—that does, or that you relate to?

Lowenthal: Umm, I don't know if I can describe it, but it's often the kind of writing that approximates the feelings I've tried to describe. For example, a book that I read recently is Paul Russell's *The Salt Point*, which is about someone who is obsessed with this teenage boy, and it deals with the tension about whether or not the boy is attracted to the character, and whether or not they will sleep together. And so, for me, I get off between the lines. And just the slightest hint of possibility sends my mind off into somersaults, you know, erotic titillation. So I'm a big fan of subtlety and not in the "dot-dot-dot" lesbian school of subtlety, as in "She reached over to kiss her partner, dot-dot-dot. 'Do you want some orange juice,' she said, when we woke up in the morning."

MR: That ties in with what you said about your adolescence. Because sex, for you, obviously happens very much in the mind, and it can take its full fruition and growth in there, without necessarily being acted upon.

Lowenthal: Without the disappointing logistics.

MR: Does the old pornography appeal to you on any level at all?

Lowenthal: Yes, it appeals to me, and I love reading it, but more in a sociological/historical/cultural way.

MR: Does it seem to be an anachronism?

Lowenthal: Yes. I just generally—you know, I don't beat off to it.

MR: To close it off, I wonder if you could be persuaded to do something quite presumptuous, and make an estimate of where you think pornographic erotic writing is going? What is your generation and the generation possibly crowding behind you going to do with this, in your estimation?

Lowenthal: Well, I'll start, and see if I believe what I am saying. I think as society opens up, continues to open up, and I mean that in terms of the freedom with which we declare our sexual-ity and have sex, with which books get published and which sexual images get projected on the screen and television, the sexual will finally begin to take the same place in our art that I believe it takes in our minds, which is namely front and center, constant, ubiquitous, and ever-present. Maybe I am just presenting my own twisted view on things. Then you could call this the mainstreaming of pornography, although I think something about that terminology misses the point, or makes it seem as though it's just a question of forcing the market. But I think that for me, life is sexual. Every waking moment. And you know that not every waking moment is geared to the goal of having orgasm, but everything is sexual or sexualized. That's the way I look at everything. So I feel that should be a part of all writing, and I think increasingly it will be. I think we are seeing that. A large number of novels, for example, that are out there, just address sex as a normal part of anything that happens.

MR: Is that good or bad?

Lowenthal: I think it's great. I still think there will be a place for—and a need for—writing that is more directly addressed to sex at the exclusion of nonsexual parts of life, if there are any.

MR: And you're not ready to concede that there are?

Lowenthal: Right. And more out there, challenging, fringe depictions of sex. And even if we do talk in terms of the market, the spectrum is shifting there, too. I mean you have someone like Dennis Cooper writing books about really dark sadomasochistic—you know, dirty sex—and they are being published between hard covers with marketing campaigns behind them.

MR: Maybe pornography is losing its ability to shock, except in heartland America.

Lowenthal: I think you probably underestimate people's ability to be shocked. Outside of the circle that deals regularly with this material, I think even huge segments of the gay community continue to be shocked and horrified by the prevalence of sex in our writing. I think the concept of pornography is still very useful because it remains such a loaded term. That's why I say I am happy to play the role of the pornographer. And in this I, as you know, am consciously following directly in the footsteps of John Preston, who adamantly claimed his label as a pornographer, and proudly owned that label, even when he wrote things that had no sexual content, and nonsexual fiction.

Now, my mother, bless her heart, is horrified by all of this. She says, "Honey, it's like a tattoo, it may be what you want now, and it may look great, but when you're fifty, would you really want that?" So she encourages me not to label myself a pornographer, but it's not going to be. But at the same time—and I think I am reminding myself now of what I wanted to say. I alternate between using pornography in the sense that society uses the word, in the sense in which I think of it, which I'm not sure I can explain, but I don't view what I write as pornographic. I don't think of what I write as pornographic because what I write is eminently natural to me. It's what I think about, and so I write it. And, in fact, stories I write that have no sexual content, if that's possible, feel to me exactly the same way as stories that have some erotic content without explicit reference to sexual organs. It feels roughly the same to me as stories I write in which sex acts are described. It's all an expression of the same mental view of my surroundings, and it's all of a piece.

MR: So what is pornography, then?

Lowenthal: I always think of pornography as something that exists only within one class, restricted to one end of a spectrum. And I think I have society's baggage here. But I think of pornography not only in terms of its position in the world, but within itself. Pornography limits its view to explicit sexual acts, toward the end goal of orgasm. And for me, all my work is much broader than that. And, in fact, in the stories in which I have described sexual acts, I don't see the end goal as really having much to do with turn on.

MR: That brings us full circle to what you were saying about yourself before. You yourself don't always have orgasm as a goal in terms of your sexual expression.

Lowenthal: Yes. I think it all feels kind of the same to me, and everything is kind of bittersweet. As I said, in terms of my life, I like nothing more than seeing the guy across the crowded bar and just watching him and thinking about him; but of course I find it completely frustrating, and I get off on the frustration, but I also get legitimately frustrated by the frustration. And that is the feeling from which I write most of the time. So it's all personal.

Scott
O'HARA

*I have said from the beginning, we talk about the most contro-
versial things, because they are the areas that no one else is
talking about, or defending, or dealing with.*

Looking back over a working lifetime in one aspect or other of
the sex industry, Scott O'Hara can offer a perspective on erotic
imagery unlike any other. After retiring from a video porn career
that flourished between 1983 and 1988, he repaired to Wisconsin
to focus on writing and living a country life. A few years ago, he
launched *Steam*, a quarterly review of sex clubs and bathhouses.
Not unacquainted with controversy, O'Hara has watched his
magazine evolve into, among other things, a forum for articulate
and insightful essays on censorship, book banning, and sexual-free-
dom issues. At the time of our interview, he was preparing to
launch a second magazine, more "lifestyle" oriented than *Steam*.
   As a writer, Scott O'Hara's work has appeared in magazines
and reviews. His essay "How I Got AIDS, or, Memoirs of a
Working Boy," which appeared in *Flesh and the Word 2*, details
his life as a porn star. With *Steam*, he has moved into the next
phase of his career, nurturing the voices of new writers, and
sparring with the hypocrisies and silences of a society that would
willingly keep sexual issues in dark places, away from the light.
   From his home in Cazenovia, Wisconsin, he explores his

evolution from porn star to writer to editor, and explores his feelings about the need to discuss and celebrate sexuality at a time in our history when gay sex and the ethic of sexual freedom are looked upon as anarchic and dangerous.

Michael Rowe: Most people know you as either Scott O'Hara, porn star, or Scott O'Hara, publisher of *Steam*. Guide me, if you would, along the peripatetic path which led you to go from porn star to writer, then magazine publisher.

Scott O'Hara: I suppose almost everyone has the feeling about his or her life that it was inevitable. That is exactly how I feel about porno and writing.

MR: You feel that *now*. Did you always feel that your life was inevitable? Are you fatalistic about the direction that your life has taken?

O'Hara: I certainly didn't expect, when I was twenty-one, that I would be in porno films, or that I would end up writing as a profession. Or, for that matter, editing a magazine. But as each of these things happened, I saw it as a perfectly natural next step. Now, in retrospect, I think that all the steps I took before were just a necessary preparation for this.

MR: What was your family like?

O'Hara: Very conservative, religious.

MR: Where did you grow up?

O'Hara: Oregon. On a farm. Not a working farm, but a large piece of land in the country.

MR: Were you close to your parents?

O'Hara: I think my parents did a good job of raising me. I just don't think much of most of their ideals.

MR: Do you say that out of duty, or is that the way you actually feel? I mean, do you feel you were actually well raised, and if so, how? In what way do you mean? Values?

O'Hara: Certainly I don't say it out of duty. I feel no duty toward them, and very little affection. But I do see the ways in which they did instill values into me that I respect. They also had many beliefs that I certainly do not respect, and in fact loathe. But they were able to teach me how to distinguish between things that I believed in and things that I didn't, and to believe in myself, which is important.

MR: Where does the lack of affection come from?

O'Hara: It wasn't a very affectionate family, I can say that. A very Puritan family. I don't believe I ever saw my parents kiss. But they just are not people I would normally choose to spend time with. They are conservative Christians, not my favorite group.

MR: What particular denomination?

O'Hara: Free Methodist. It's the John Birch church.

MR: Did you play any sports?

O'Hara: I was manager of the basketball team one year. I got to hand out towels. (*laughs*)

MR: Laying the groundwork for the future, I see. Who says you never get anything out of high school?

O'Hara: I got a lot out of high school. I enjoyed it a great deal. It was the part of my childhood that I really did like. I was a typical straight-A student who spent every spare moment in the library, and actually took—I don't know—two or three extra courses during most of my high-school years.

MR: Your parents must have been very proud.

O'Hara: No. That was just expected in the family. My older sister was valedictorian, and it sort of went on from there.

MR: Did you think about becoming a writer?

O'Hara: I wrote poetry in high school and actually won second prize in the South Oregon Eisteddfodd Competition.

MR: What is that?

O'Hara: The Eisteddfodd? It's the name of a Welsh poetry competition. No big contest, but it was the first money I ever earned outside the home. You might say a professional writer was the first thing I ever was.

MR: Did none of this give your parents any pleasure at all?

O'Hara: Well, it must have. But at home, I was always—from the time I was thirteen—quite rebellious. And sulky, so I think they were more worried than proud.

MR: Did you have an isolated childhood or did you have a lot of friends? By childhood, I guess I mean adolescence.

O'Hara: Not a lot. I had at least two or three, and I certainly didn't feel isolated. I thought I wasn't popular by any means, but I remember my school life as being very enjoyable.

MR: Well, it would be a world that would be free of the repressive doctrines you were getting at home. All about books and language and everything.

O'Hara: Yes.

MR: Were you a sissy?

O'Hara: Yes. Definitely.

MR: Bookworm?

O'Hara: I'll never forget the time when, for the first time in my life, I actually did not manage to come up with an appropriate excuse, and I was forced to play football. I don't remember what I did exactly, but I broke some very obvious rule that everybody else knew about, and they weren't pleased.

MR: Oh, God, I can relate to that so well. With me it was soccer. I scored on my own team.

O'Hara: It was something like that.

MR: Did you experiment sexually in high school?

O'Hara: Not until I was fifteen. I wanted to, long before that.

MR: A good time to start.

O'Hara: I was trying to when I was twelve.

MR: Were you sexually active in high school?

O'Hara: I never actually had sex with anyone in school. All my sexual partners were much older at that point.

MR: Where did you find them?

O'Hara: One was through a friend of one of my older sisters. My older sister was gay.

MR: You were identified as gay to her at that age?

O'Hara: Yes.

MR: So she was sympathetic?

O'Hara: She was a sort of counselor to me, and it was very good to have her.

MR: How did your parents feel about two gay kids? Or were you very closeted?

O'Hara: I was not completely out to them in high school. I was to everyone else.

MR: How did that go over in Oregon? It's not known as the most liberal climate at the moment. Was it different back then?

O'Hara: I had no problems. By the time I graduated, I'm sure almost everyone knew.

MR: Did you experience any hostility at all?

O'Hara: I would occasionally have people come up to me and say—or ask—questions, and they would ask them in fairly homophobic ways. But...I don't know, in a strange way, I think I was sort of respected. I'm sure they were all sort of intimidated by my reputation.

MR: Which reputation are we talking about?

O'Hara: As a brain. Which I was, then. And just by being out. It's hard for them to insult you by calling you a faggot if you say, "Yes, I am."

MR: That's a very highly developed concept for the late seventies, Scott. You and I are the same age, thirty-two. It's hard to imagine anyone our age taking such a proactive stance in high school. That's terrific. Did you go to college?

O'Hara: I went to college for one year, but ended up dropping out before the year was over.

MR: Where did you go?

O'Hara: The University of Dallas. It's a Catholic school. The only reason I went was that they were willing to give me a scholarship. And it got me away from Oregon and away from my family.

MR: Into a nest of Catholics?

O'Hara: I had no problem with that. They were entertaining people; and, of course, by the time the first term was over, I was informed that if I did not start being more discreet, they were going to ask me to leave.

MR: The school's governing body?

O'Hara: The dean.

MR: What sort of indiscretions?

O'Hara: I was in a dorm, and I don't remember if they...they must have heard about my having sex on campus, which I did, several times. No one ever caught me, but I was told that if they did, I would be out of there so fast, and so forth.

MR: What was your reply to that?

O'Hara: I smiled and said, "All right, thank you for telling me." That's all I remember of it; it didn't make a big impression.

MR: And you left because you were bored?

O'Hara: Bored? It's hard to quantify exactly why I left. I realized I wasn't learning things that were important to me.

MR: What were those things?

O'Hara: At that point, I wanted to get out and see the world, and I did. I took off on my motorcycle and started traveling around the country. Hit Provincetown, the bathhouses, and ended up in Chicago. I was in Chicago for eight months, and sort of worked the back rooms of the bars, the bathhouses.

MR: Work? Or *work?*

O'Hara: When I say "work," I didn't mean employment.

MR: I see.

O'Hara: I *worked* the back rooms.

MR: You were exploring your sexuality?

O'Hara: That's what I was spending all that time doing, yes. There was a period of about a year when most of what I was doing was fisting and SM. That was the most outrageous, radical thing I could think of and as a—let me see, how old was I?—nineteen-, twenty-year-old, I was highly valued in the back rooms of the Gold Coast.

MR: Top or bottom?

O'Hara: I have always been what I consider to be an absolute bottom, in that I can do absolutely anything as long as someone else tells me to do it. I can play a top if someone tells me what he wants, and I did. But I don't have a lot of interest in sex unless someone else expresses desire.

MR: So you are the ultimate submissive?

O'Hara: Yes.

MR: And you were young and beautiful, and this was the early 1980s we're talking about?

O'Hara: Yes. And there were lots of drugs offered to me, and lots of men took me home, and I had a number of great times.

MR: Did you keep a journal or anything at this time? Did you do any writing at this time?

O'Hara: I kept a sex journal of everyone I went home with. But it didn't include a lot of generalities.

MR: Tell me about the sex journal. Was it descriptive? Did you enjoy the writing of it?

O'Hara: It was intended strictly as an aide-mémoire, so that I would know what I did and with whom.

MR: For your own enjoyment, or just for a record?

O'Hara: Just for a record, really. Now I can go back to it, as I have a couple of times recently, just to look over it and smile fondly, but that wasn't its intent.

MR: How many volumes are we talking about?

O'Hara: (*laughs*) Three or four, probably.

MR: My goodness!

O'Hara: Notebooks, you know. Small notebooks.

MR: Right. Probably single spaced.

O'Hara: Yes.

MR: How did you get into the films?

O'Hara: I moved to San Francisco in May of 1983.

MR: Did you have a lover, or were you single?

O'Hara: I was single.

MR: Were you chronically single, or did you have a lover at any point?

O'Hara: I had at that point one lover and we had been together for all of, I think, five months. So I was pretty typically single, yes. I moved to San Francisco and immediately saw an ad in the *Bay Area Reporter* for jack-off shows at Savages. My eyes got all big, and I went *wow!* I saw the shows, and came back the next night and the next night and saw the shows. Then one of the performers said to me, "Hey, why don't you get up onstage and do a show?" And I did. They hired me. And I had a marvelous summer doing performances. Sometime during the course of the summer, the manager of the theater got the idea of doing a porn flick. Since he had the talent right there, he thought he might as well make use of it. He got a bunch of us to agree to it, and we all went down the coast to a nude beach near Santa Cruz and had ourselves a ball on the beach.

MR: You've actually described that quite graphically in your stories—what it's like to have sex on the beach. With all of the sand.

O'Hara: (*laughs*) That's right. Then I won the "Biggest Dick in San Francisco" contest on Labor Day, 1983.

MR: What a busy summer you had, Scott.

O'Hara: It was rather a marvelous summer.

MR: And a talent scout saw you?

O'Hara: And asked me if I would be interested in doing a Falcon video. I said sure, why not. That was the infamous scene where I gave Randy Page an enema with a garden hose, and for years I would shudder if anyone brought it up.

MR: You've already indicated that you were highly sexual and an adventurer. Did the work in porno films come naturally to you? Was it like having sex for pay, or sex in front of a camera, was it a thrill, or what did it feel like?

O'Hara: It was only just a lot of fun to me. It was not that different from having sex with someone I liked because, why not? We were both horny. I'm quite sure it's different for lots of people who are in front of the camera, who are working in the business, but for me it was always just fun.

MR: And it became a fairly comfortable source of income after a while?

O'Hara: I suppose one could live off of it, but I never really tried. I was fortunate in that I didn't have to. My trust fund brought in enough income so that I didn't need a job. As I say, I was doing it because it was fun.

MR: Were you writing any scenarios in your head at the time? Did you ever think about how it would look, or how it would read?

O'Hara: Scenarios? For videos?

MR: Or print stories. As you were doing it, did you think about words? Did you think about stories, or anything that could go along with the picture? Was the experience the sort of thing that would naturally make you think about words? Sometimes you walk down a street and you see a great-looking guy, or a dog, or a tree, or something, and you describe the thing in your mind.

O'Hara: I do that all the time now. I don't remember paying much attention to it then.

MR: Did you have a good memory? Did you lock these experiences in your mind?

O'Hara: I've never had a good memory. It's kind of one of my regrets about myself, that I don't remember all those wonderful experiences that I know I had. For instance, the year and a half I lived in Hawaii, much of it is just gone. It's one of the reasons I do write now. I know that going back and reading the writing that I do now will be even more vivid to me in ten years than it is today. Even if not necessarily entirely true.

MR: They say that memory improves with age, and that images become more vivid as years go along.

O'Hara: I hope so.

MR: Tell me about HIV diagnosis. At what time in your life did this happen?

O'Hara: Oh, it was such a long process. It wasn't one shocking diagnosis for me. For years, probably beginning in about 1985, I started telling people, and assuming to myself, that I was HIV positive.

MR: Where did that come from?

O'Hara: From pragmatism. Whether I was or wasn't, it was better to behave as if I were. I had been, well, engaging in a pretty indefensible rationalization for some time.

MR: Which was?

O'Hara: I phrased it to an interviewer in more than one case as *"Oh, sorry, sex is just an occupational hazard."*

MR: Okay...

O'Hara: And I was using condoms in my private life, but on-screen I had decided that it was just a risk that one had to take if one wanted to be in films, which was true.

MR: Was that a prevalent attitude at that time?

O'Hara: My attitude?

MR: Yes.

O'Hara: I don't know how many of the performers even thought about it. Obviously there was no one I knew, except Richard Locke, who was campaigning seriously for safe sex, and Richard Locke wasn't actively doing films at that time. He was retired. Where was I?

MR: We were talking about your gradual awareness of your HIV status.

O'Hara: Yes. It wasn't until 1988 that I actually had a pretty startling realization. I was modeling for the Gay Men's Sketch group in San Francisco in September...could it have been 1989? I don't know, I can never remember if it was 1988 or 1989.

MR: The bad memory again.

O'Hara: I was sitting around in a particular pose staring at my foot for twenty minutes, and sometime in the course of that twenty minutes I realized that spot on my foot was not just a scar, but a lesion. I went down to Southern California for the winter for six months, found myself a little shack on the beach, oceanside, and didn't see anyone for six months. Wrote and thought about it.

MR: What did you write about?

O'Hara: (*laughs*) I'd have to go back and read it to find out. I don't know at this point.

MR: Was it a lot of diary stuff? Was it fiction?

O'Hara: A journal, mostly. I did write several short stories during that period, I think.

MR: Had you published any by that time?

O'Hara: Oh, yes.

MR: When did you start publishing?

O'Hara: The first short story was in *Advocate Men* in 1984 or 1985, I can't remember which. It must have been 1985. It was published under the name "Spunk," the persona they had invented for me. And then there was something else, I think, in *Inches* a year or two later, and a poem in the *James White Review*, and a piece in *Drummer*.

MR: All as "Spunk"?

O'Hara: No.

MR: You had other pseudonyms as well? Or were you writing as yourself?

O'Hara: I think it was all Scott O'Hara.

MR: Did that carry any cachet?

O'Hara: I suppose it must have, but I don't know how much.

MR: Didn't anyone say anything to you about the advantages of being a famous porn star writing erotic fiction for a gay erotic magazine?

O'Hara: (*laughs*) Well, in *Advocate Men*, of course, the reason they wanted to name me "Spunk" was that they had run a photo spread of me, and I suppose that it added some novelty to actually have a model who could write. And probably the same with *Drummer*.

MR: I should think so. What kind of pictures were they in *Drummer*?

O'Hara: The photo spread they ran of me was me getting my head shaved by Patrick Toner.

MR: Did you find that writing cathartic? Did you do it as catharsis?

O'Hara: I did it just to figure out what I was doing next. Because porno was very important to me, and that was the point at which I knew I was going to have to get out of it, retire.

MR: Did you feel any initial sense of revolution against the HIV, or did you freeze up? John Preston was not able to write porn for the first couple of years after he got his diagnosis. Did you have any similar experience?

O'Hara: No, not at all. It really didn't affect how I felt about sex. I guess I had just been too used to the idea of AIDS.

MR: You expected it?

O'Hara: It was not entirely unexpected. Or a shock to me. It was just, okay, now it is time to make these changes. For years I had been thinking about what I would do after I got too old to do it in front of the camera anymore, and that was just the point at which I said, "It's time to make concrete plans." So I spent those six months trying to tie up loose ends in my former life and start a new one.

MR: In *Wisconsin?*

O'Hara: I actually had fallen in love with Wisconsin the previous summer. I had just been on a round-the-country motorcycle tour. On the road through Wisconsin, I just fell in love with it. It's as green as anyplace I had ever been, and this was in August, mind you, and there was water everywhere: creeks, streams, ponds, lakes, beautiful. And then I stopped and picked up a real-estate catalog and saw a house advertised for $10,000 and said, "Perhaps I should investigate living here."

MR: Was there something about living in the country that appealed to you?

O'Hara: I've always chased this particular version of paradise. I grew up in the country. I know what country living is like, and after a couple of years of living in big cities, I began to realize that, yes, I was a country boy, and I would end up eventually back in the country. There were too many things about nature and solitude that I loved. And there were too many things that I wanted to do that I would never do in the city.

MR: Such as?

O'Hara: Particularly writing.

MR: Had you thought of what kind of writing you wanted to do at that time? Was there any sense of the great American novel, or anything like that?

O'Hara: No, I've never wanted to write a novel. Poetry, short stories, essays, journals and letters. Letters are something that for years I wrote quite assiduously, and very well if I do say so myself. I have almost entirely stopped writing them since I've been working full time on the magazine.

MR: Since we're on the topic of letters and writing, have you ever had any flak at any time about people taking you seriously? Because you are very erudite and you choose your words very carefully and you're obviously well educated, but there is a stereotype...

O'Hara: Bimbo.

MR: Did you ever run up against that?

O'Hara: I may have, but I don't believe I ever saw it.

MR: You don't seem to acknowledge negativity.

O'Hara: I don't see it. And yet, the flip side of that is that my friends have been amazed for years that I don't see it when people are, for instance, cruising me, either. There's a lot that goes right over my head, and I suspect that if people are thinking of me as a bimbo, they probably are treating me well, and so I smile and say "thank you." (*laughs*) And never notice.

MR: You *are* a country boy.

O'Hara: Well, yes, I am.

MR: Did you think of yourself as a writer? Is that an identity that you've ever actually embraced physically? We're getting into the territory of labels here, but it seems to be important for some people.

O'Hara: There's a distinction there. Most writers will call themselves writers. Then there is the author, and to me the author is someone who gets published regularly. And a writer is someone who writes because he feels he must write. I've always been a writer and I've always written, but I've never written for publication.

MR: But you haven't exactly thrown it away when it's happened?

O'Hara: No, not at all, but I have never, until quite recently, written for a particular purpose, for a publication. Even knowing I could do it was a relatively new thought to me until, oh, a year and a half, basically, the beginning of *Steam*.

MR: Tell me how *Steam* came about.

O'Hara: When I retired here to the country, I intended to write. I intended to write a great deal about sex. And my travels. I had traveled a lot and was continuing to travel. A friend of mine jokingly said to me, "Gee, you should start a journal about Scott O'Hara's sex travels." And I thought, *That's a nice idea, I like it*. And then another friend, about a year later, actually made a concrete proposal for starting a magazine along those lines. That was Keith Griffith, and we did it.

MR: The format that you've chosen is intriguing. You've made it look very much like an academic journal, or a literary review.

O'Hara: I have to credit that brilliant idea to yet another friend, Richard Borrance.

MR: And now you're the Grace Mirabella of sex. Many people would perceive your creation of *Steam* as a very in-your-face indictment of a sex-phobic society.

O'Hara: That's exactly how I see it.

MR: That may seem commonplace to you, but a lot of people would find it interesting.

O'Hara: Well, that's exactly how I intended it. A declaration that sex is not bad, no matter what people may think of AIDS. Sex continues to be seen as violently negative. And yes, that is an indictment of society.

MR: Was it a *conscious* indictment of society? Was the indictment an unavoidable by-product of the magazine's theme?

O'Hara: It was *very* conscious.

MR: You haven't just started a porno magazine, you've staked out some very politically combustible territory, because the magazine is all about sex clubs and bathhouses.

O'Hara: I have said from the beginning, we talk about the most controversial things, because they are the areas that no one else is talking about, or defending, or dealing with.

MR: Do you get strength from that? Do you find that a galvanizing experience?

O'Hara: Well, yes. Anytime there is resistance, you push harder. And we have encountered the occasional bit of resistance, but not nearly as much as I would have expected. I really had expected that by this time we would have been denounced—and possibly prosecuted—all across the country.

MR: There might be some temptation to see you as a sort of gay *Marianne*, the symbol of the French Revolution, with your dress off one shoulder, sort of fighting the good battle against the forces of repression. But that would be a bit time-consuming.

O'Hara: It would. Frankly, I don't have the strength. I want to have a life. I've said this from the beginning—all during my porn career—that nothing could make me happier than to put myself out of business. I think the goal of making porn films for me was to free up people's sexuality to the point where they do not require porn. Because porn is an aid to sexuality that in an ideal world—I don't think—should be necessary.

MR: What makes you angriest?

O'Hara: Government. Government of all sorts: IRS, persecution of bookstores, anytime government intrudes in lives. Is that the answer you expected?

MR: Maybe. What about censorship? Let me play devil's advocate for a while here. There's a whole school of thought that would say that you're actually promoting the spread of AIDS by pushing bathhouses and public sex in the magazine. How you would address that?

O'Hara: I have difficulty even responding to it. I don't see the connection. I mean, obviously these people do not believe in safe sex. We've been hearing it for years, but I guess it hasn't penetrated to some people. It's not who you do or where you do it, it's what you do. Trying to repress sexuality, I think, is the worse course you can take. In the first place, it destroys a person's psyche; and in the second place, it probably will not work in keeping you safe.

MR: Do you have any plans at all for fiction? Even in the future? You said you weren't going to write novels, but what about your story collections?

O'Hara: I think I don't have the length of continuity to write in novel form. I write the occasional short story and continue to write poems now and then. And the short stories will, I am sure, eventually find publication somewhere.

MR: There is a flourishing of erotic publishing right now. And your appearance in *Flesh and the Word* hasn't exactly hurt your reputation as a writer.

O'Hara: (*laughs*) Well, I'm glad to hear it. I was quite surprised by John Preston's choices. He told me that he wanted to reprint both the *How I Got AIDS* series and the one in *Flesh and the Word 3*, which is something from *Steam*. I haven't seen either one as really appropriate for *Flesh and the Word*, but, hey!

MR: Do you like editing? Bringing other people's work to publication?

O'Hara: I'm finding it entirely too seductive, yes. I mean, you know how we as writers are supposed to feel about editors. And I find myself enjoying it far too much.

MR: You like working with writers?

O'Hara: Yes, I do. That really has been one of the unexpected but wonderful pleasures of *Steam* as we have found new writers. Three that I can think of offhand who declared quite genuinely to me, "Oh, I'm not a writer! I've never written anything!", and who have written some of the most exquisite stuff I've ever read in my life. And that's a pure joy to know that I am partially responsible for that.

MR: In terms of the sexuality, is the written word as important to you as the visual image? Are you pursuing the written word now with the same vehemence as you went after the visual?

O'Hara: Words have always meant a lot more to me personally than images. Words are sacred; words are my reason. Porn films were fun, but they are more meaningful to other people than they are to me, I think. I enjoy them. I've enjoyed them, and enjoy watching them now, but I don't think they were as significant to me, even then.

MR: Do you miss being in front of the camera?

O'Hara: Now and then I do. Yes, if I were offered a chance to make a comeback appearance in a film now, I would. Well, I'm not sure what I would do....

MR: Do you feel the inclination?

O'Hara: I certainly would. And I suppose I would, at this point in my life, at this point of my career, have to have preconditions on it. I am a more political person than I was ten years ago. Aside from it having to be safe sex, which of course every porn maker has to do, I think it would have to acknowledge that I am HIV positive. That's probably something that wouldn't happen these days.

MR: What do the good citizens of Cazenovia think of having a porn star and magazine publisher in their midst?

O'Hara: Well, I don't know. I do suspect I am a subject for discussion. I don't actually live in the town; I have forty-seven acres out here, eight miles south of town. The town itself has something like 250 people.

MR: Do you keep a distance from people? Are you a privacy-oriented person?

O'Hara: I'm very private and solitary. In four years, I have met oh, three or four people who live around here. Like, for instance, the three little old ladies who tend the voting booth. They are very nice, and they ask how I'm doing.

MR: Sounds very Golden Years.

O'Hara: Yes.

MR: Do you live alone?

O'Hara: Well, no, I live with someone. (*laughs*)

MR: Are you in a relationship?

O'Hara: I am now, yes. Whether I am by the time this book comes out will be another question.

MR: You do have kind of a short-term relationship history, have you not?

O'Hara: That is very much my history, yes. This one was supposed to not be, but…

MR: How long has it been?

O'Hara: I met him two years ago.

MR: Well, that's a very long relationship, Scott.

O'Hara: Yes.

MR: That's a relationship with a capital R.

O'Hara: It feels long.

MR: You know how it is with us early-thirties or mid-thirties people—we have to start getting serious about life and everything like that.

O'Hara: (*laughs*)

MR: But you've already got the farm. You've bought the farm, so to speak.

O'Hara: (*laughs*) I refer to it that way occasionally myself.

V. K.
McCARTY

I love the cane, and I love schoolroom training sessions, and military interrogation scenes. I want to see some ballet, debate aesthetic issues over supper and sip a little wine, and I like to be bathed properly. I like to be laced and dressed slowly, and I like a little massage and I like my hair brushed. I will gladly practice my aim in order to enjoy those things.

V. K. McCarty, aka Victor King, aka Mam'selle Victoire, has earned herself a unique place in the *demimonde* of classic erotic writers whose work spans the 1970s and the 1980s.

My own discovery of the legendary V. K. McCarty, editor of *Variations* magazine, was somewhat circuitous. In the early 1980s, I was flipping through a copy of *Drummer* magazine, and I happened upon a photograph of a strikingly beautiful woman, slender, with white skin and dark hair. She wore a revealing black dress and a top hat with a veil. She held a riding crop against the throat of a leather-jacketed man who looked up at her adoringly. The photograph was stunning, and not only because it seemed out of place in a magazine like *Drummer*, which was so devoted to extreme masculinity. Who, I wondered, was this woman? And how had she infiltrated *Drummer*'s shrine to macho? A couple of years later, I read John Preston's *Entertainment for a Master*. One of the characters was an elegant cane-wielding dominatrix referred to only as "Madame." Although I did not associate the character with the photograph in *Drummer*, I was once again struck by the image. Who was this woman, and how was she important enough to infiltrate the work of a man who has admitted that "when ladies appear in my fantasies, I have to walk them to the door and, with as much gentlemanly poise as I can muster, ask them politely to leave." By the time Preston revealed the identity of the woman he called "my dear friend Victoria," I had already read the work of Victor King, and I was under the spell.

Although V. K. was initially wary about talking with me, I felt that it wasn't the usual interviewer-interviewee power struggle. Rather, I had the oddest sensation of vertigo—for one crazy moment, I felt as though I were addressing my late grand-aunt, a Victorian matriarch of the old school who steadfastly maintained that a lady's name appeared in print only three times: at her birth, marriage, and death. I would later discover, from others, that this odd sense of chronological dissonance was not unusual in dealing with V. K. McCarty. So strong is the force of her persona, rooted in another, more formal era, that it is easy to forget she is the author of such stories as "Shackled Nap" and "Knife Litanies." The cane, so to speak, may be hidden at times, but it is always close at hand.

Talking with V. K. McCarty is very much like experiencing the sweetening power of cream and sugar in bitter coffee. Her intensely feminine persona and her exquisite speaking voice somehow bring out—with shockingly erotic results—the flavor of her dark, rough-textured, intensely masculine prose. This is not a question of typecasting "strong" prose as male and "soft" prose as female, but a case of V. K.'s almost literally *becoming* a ribald gay male raconteur when she writes as Victor King.

It's a little eerie, but it works. And that is, after all, the contradictory essence of Mrs. McCarty. Like the Edwardian era she embodies so effectively, the reserved facade only occasionally hints at what she herself has described as "the fire underneath."

Michael Rowe: Now, you had expressed some concerns about things you wanted to talk about, and things you didn't want to talk about. Your life has grown more complex...you're involved in many different things outside—and perhaps less compatible with—the sexual arena. Is there any particular direction in which you'd like to guide the conversation?

V. K. McCarty: No. I've found over the years that I do better letting the interviewer guide the conversation. We'll just see how it goes. It's easier to get rougher in either pseudonym [Mam'selle Victoire and Victor King] than it is as V. K. But I think we are talking about V. K. here. So let's just talk.

MR: Can you tell me a little bit about your background? I understand that you were born in Boston.

McCarty: I was born in Boston, but basically I was raised in Michigan in one of the university towns.

MR: Right. And then, years later, you forged a theatrical career for yourself in New York.

McCarty: I did. I was in theater for many years, and I really only stopped singing oratorios and doing acting in shows when Guccione wanted to develop a magazine about alternate sexual practices of American couples, and I started *Variations*. That's what I always say. However, I'd like to step back, and be a little more honest, and say that I didn't actually dream up the name *Variations*. It had begun as a special magazine, and in fact the erotic writer Marco Vassi, whom I dearly wish you could be interviewing for this book, did the first couple of issues when it was a still a special edition that came out of *Forum*. I developed it into its own magazine.

MR: You had been something of a sexual pioneer in your earlier years. You've written erotica both as a gay man and as a woman and I'm wondering—

McCarty: I started writing on the straight female side when I was in theater. I started with poetry, actually, as a lot of people do. Maybe I'm not quite compassionate enough with my writers about their poetry, but I came from that, too. I was in various literary journals, you know, got paid two copies and all that, and pursued it very seriously. But then I began to realize if I could make this erotic writing into short stories, I could sell it. And I did sell quite a few stories there before I started *Variations*. That was through the 1970s. I did most of my gay writing in the early 1980s.

MR: Do you identify yourself as a bisexual woman, or as a heterosexual woman? Or do you not identify yourself that way at all?

McCarty: Well, I might offend someone by saying this, but I identify primarily as a heterosexual woman, even though I am in a primary relationship with a woman. Then, next to that, very quickly after that, I identify as a male, as a gay man. And I am most comfortable with that identity. When it comes to wrestling about it, I kind of back off, but I consider myself not bisexual at all. Given the kind of unisex philosophy and physical behavior that I think is involved with bisexuality, I'm really quite heterosexual. I identify with top and bottom.

MR: Your interest in sadomasochism goes back how far?

McCarty: A man helped me come out in it in 1977; but now that I look back, I see that I was interested in an accumulation of erotic pressure, and of intense rituals and intense men who experienced manhood ordeals in their culture, from the time I was quite small.

MR: What is your religious orientation?

McCarty: I didn't get started on a spiritual path until just a few years ago. I don't come from a family that was very religious at all. Each of us girls has kind of found our own way. And in the last ten years, I've been quite swept up in the Episcopal church.

MR: I'm intrigued by your attraction to ritual. Quite often that is a by-product of a religious background, either Catholic or Anglican.

McCarty: Not in my case. I love rituals. I love monasticism. I love ballet. I love many ritualized forms of behavior.

MR: The subtext of all this, of course, is discipline?

McCarty: Yes, well, in my life now, probably the subtext would be more religious service. But at the time in which I was acting out more of my SM life, it would have been SM.

MR: Can you tell me a little bit about that?

McCarty: I was most active in SM in the late 1970s and early 1980s.

MR: In New York?

McCarty: In New York, yes.

MR: I saw a photograph of you in *Drummer* many years ago, wearing, I think, a top hat with a veil.

McCarty: Yes. That was in San Francisco, but most of what I did was in New York, in the time since I was divorced.

MR: Things were a lot freer back then, pre-AIDS.

McCarty: Yes, they certainly were. Some of what we did then, we don't talk about now, because it was not only unsafe, but there were sometimes elements of coercion and unkindness which don't really fit with the consciousness we have about these things today. I don't know that I would be very interested in playing now. After I had long since stopped going to clubs, I took some friends to one, and I was just amazed to see that people could be doing SM with no poppers, and no penetration, and no yelling, and no grass. It was very strange. It was hard to accept. It was quite different from the days when we used to sidle up to a sling, and push a fist into a stranger, and it worked or it didn't. Usually it did.

MR: Was there a more receptive culture in SM back then? And more interactive relationships between heterosexuals and homosexuals? And—

McCarty: No, there was no interaction at all. My heterosexual leather partying was more what I would call private. It was more a matter of very intense relationships.

MR: With young men?

McCarty: Some of it with older men, actually. Some of it was with older British men. Sometimes they fell into a pattern, with some wonderfully startling exceptions. Then I just wanted something else, and I wanted to be doing this in the gay world. I think people were very tolerant and gracious to allow me to sometimes be a part of the gay men's clubs, and to be a part of the parties, and to be a part of the midnight ceremonies at the piers, and so forth. I think it was just very tolerant. I wouldn't want to go anyplace where there were women. So I'm just grateful that people were as accepting as they were.

MR: Why no women?

McCarty: I don't know. Now we seem to have grown beyond so much of what I was most interested in. I think it was probably just a level of immaturity, or a prejudice, but I wouldn't want to be partying in a room where women were.

MR: You have a very highly developed persona: very old-fashioned, very Edwardian, very Henry James. It carries through in your speech patterns. I understand that this is also the way you comport yourself. I'm wondering what it is about that particular era that so appeals to you that you've assimilated it to the degree you have.

McCarty: I don't know where that started. Sometimes I can look back, and see some of it might have to do with wanting to sculpt myself into a woman that my father would be interested in seducing. He has expressed interest in the women in [Howard Chandler] Christy drawings. Christy was doing drawings at the same time as Charles Dana Gibson. So Christy drawings are like Gibson girls. But why did I land there, and not be a flapper, or an Elizabethan? Why Edwardian? I'm not quite sure.

MR: Perhaps it's the trappings of the era?

McCarty: I like taking my hair down for a man, and baring my shoulders for dinner, and imparting traditions to the next generation. I like having Edwardian housemaids about me, and butlers, and puppy dogs. I'm not quite sure why. Where did I get the role model for that?

MR: It's not entirely incongruous to imagine you in that particular time, given your attraction to the things you've described—the starched corsets, the propriety, the rigidness...

McCarty: The fire underneath.

MR: Yes, exactly.

McCarty: Earning the empathy.

MR: Can you remember your earliest erotic thoughts? What are the earliest erotic thoughts you can remember?

McCarty: I remember discovering in college that I must have been doing something that, for me, was masturbating, as early as five years old. As I remembered it, when I first went to bed and was finally alone, I would pile up things on top of me, and have fantasies about being imprisoned and then released. Then, somewhere along the way, it switched to me getting on top of something—a certain shape—but I never imagined at the time that there was anything sexual about this. But I did this many times when I went to bed, and I did it until there was a release, which I don't think was orgasm, necessarily. But something was happening. And I did it consistently through grade school, and all through high school. I actually remember the time I did it in a dorm, over which piece of furniture, and so forth, and suddenly the light bulb went on and I realized *this is masturbation!*—what the men do with their cocks. This was the thing you're not supposed to do. I was horrified to discover that when you piece it back together, back to my father being in medical school and so forth, that I had been masturbating in this infantile way, all the way back to five. I was very confused about what sex was, or what it would be, and I remember even lying in bed in high school trying to imagine how men and women would fit together, and just having a lot of fear about it. I may have actually eroticized a lot of that fear.

MR: Were you aroused by the usual erotic totems of adolescent girls? What sort of got you going in those early days?

McCarty: The notion of how a cock would ever fit inside me. How could that be possible?

MR: The question aroused you?

McCarty: Yes. The terror of that.

MR: It's almost clinical.

McCarty: Yes, it was. I was very confused, very frightened, and very inexperienced, until college. And after college, too, but certainly in college, I saw a lot of cock, but I didn't do much with it.

MR: And your interest in SM, specifically—came about how?

McCarty: It was after my divorce. I was making up for lost time, and I was seeing a man who took me to an off-Broadway show where we thought we would pick up one of the actresses. And she came out after the show and spoke to us, and I spoke to her and figured out that she was with her husband, and he was the producer of the show. So we made a date to go over and maybe do a three-way, or a four-way as two couples. By the time I got there, my lover was out of town, and his wife wasn't there. So I was having a date with this producer.

MR: How was it?

McCarty: It was mildly disappointing, and as I got up to leave, I hugged this guy good-bye. He kind of melted under me. As I went to catch him, he sighed and whimpered, and as I caught him more and got him against the wall, he got hard.

MR: What did you make of that?

McCarty: It was intriguing.

MR: Did you identify it as dominance? As topping?

McCarty: There are different ways of topping, but what he was showing me was a kind of topping where if I hipboned myself into his cock, to a painful extent, he was panting and begging and hard. What we were doing was a little cock-and-ball work, and that was his thing. That was interesting.

MR: Was there an answering response in you, in terms of the feeling of power?

McCarty: Yes, there was.

MR: The power appealed?

McCarty: Well, I think to begin with, I have been so societally trained to please men that initially, the kick of it wasn't that I "had power." The kick of it was that I had pleased the guy with something new. This was just one more thing, but I enjoyed it. And I liked him. I went back several more times. And then, astonishingly, I met Marco Vassi. He was quite a figure in the sexual world, and he had an amazing misunderstanding about me. I was basically just a little heterosexual geisha type. I mean, I was pretty intense but I was certainly no dominatrix. I'd had these experiences, but I hadn't even had a half-dozen of them. I had a little leather. I'd been to some clubs, but I was not in any way SM-identified. I did want to know more about men's SM, but I had absolutely no interest in being a woman in SM. And Marco Vassi got it into his head that I was some sort of well-known dom. I learned very quickly. I learned to fill his need and actualize this persona in the blink of an eye. We had many other techniques. It was quite astonishing. I love coming clean about that. It really amazes me, the phenomenon of erotic infatuation, and how we blossom in the light of it.

MR: He was a submissive?

McCarty: He was a submissive, and also was very interested in possession, and in being beaten with many kinds of things, and being marked, and being fisted. And with being tied up in different ways, and with different levels of intensity, and different techniques. On the heterosexual side, he was into topping in terms of possession, and certainly in terms of fucking... so he was pretty incredible.

MR: So this was your introduction to SM?

McCarty: I became networked in the SM world at that time, and I also began to enjoy the friendships of certain cultured sophisticated gentlemen, mostly from England, who had a specific kind of need.

MR. Canes?

McCarty: Yes, I love the cane, and I love schoolroom training sessions, and military interrogation scenes. I want to see some ballet, debate aesthetic issues over supper and sip a little wine, and I like to be bathed properly. I like to be laced and dressed slowly, and I like a little massage and I like my hair brushed. I will gladly practice my aim in order to enjoy those things.

MR: It sounds like what you're talking about is something very sensuous.

McCarty: Oh, it's very sensuous. I do it all for my own selfish pleasure, negotiating what it is I want for me, and expecting the bottom to negotiate what he wants by stretching himself to obey me. So, one of the things that is sometimes awkward to incorporate is that a lot of the men I see have known professional dominance, and that's a much different situation. The man can *expect* his whims to be fulfilled rather than pleasing me to satisfy himself. Often they are far more experienced than I am. But I am always going for my own pleasure.

MR: Do you feel your femininity when you dominate men?

McCarty: No. I feel more feminine in nonsexual situations. I think I feel the most feminine being escorted by a man whom I have allowed to touch my waist, and to lead me around corners, and in and out of chairs and cabs. I feel feminine offering my waist in public, or my throat between the sheets. And I feel more feminine, I suppose, in conversational communion. Of course, it isn't the way it *has* to be. But the way I am wired, I feel more like a preyed-upon mammal in sex, and I like that. I don't particularly feel feminine. I feel like I am about to be killed and fucked.

MR: We're essentially talking about the feelings of a dominant. I would have thought that you would have felt more like the aggressor, more like the killer and the fucker.

McCarty: Well, I think that when I top, very often, although I'm in long black petticoats and sometimes a naked back, I still imagine myself as a man. For anyone who has done scenes with me, I either have no sex when I do scenes, or if I do have a sexual identity and have sex, I fuck. Basically, when I top, I don't identify as feminine at all.

MR: Do you prefer to top men or women?

McCarty: Oh, I prefer either. I guess I envision three separate categories, actually. If I could choose, first of all I would like to top cute gay boys. I'm very comfortable with where the pleasure of that will lie, but I also love what I can get from topping a very accomplished, financially achieved heterosexual man. And then, bless their hearts, I certainly love to ravish little girls, but I kind of think of them as separate species.

MR: So you're sexually omnivorous, then?

McCarty: No, *sexually* I still persist in identifying as a heterosexual woman. Then, as a top, generally as a gay man.

MR: I'm really, really curious about why, aside from the obvious strength factor, it is that so many accomplished female writers are so successful writing as gay men?

McCarty: I don't really know.

MR: You've done it, Anne Rice has done it, Pat Califia has done it, Laura Antoniou has done it—

McCarty: Well, that's a sweet sentence, near Anne and Pat like that. I'll always remember you having said that, Michael. I don't know why it is. I think it's an incredible mystery.

MR: I was rereading your story in *Flesh and the Word 2*, and of course, when I talked to Anne Rice in 1992, she told me it was because she enjoyed taking on the aspects of freedom that men have to pursue their sexual ends in a society where women's sexual freedom has been somewhat curtailed.

McCarty: That's part of it, but one of the things I see in this consciousness-raised time, which all of us are supposed to be in, is that there would be a lot more freedom for me if I would allow it. And I don't want it. There is the top/bottom aspect, and the predatory aspect, those are all artificial things that I add on because I have eroticized them. In a freer way, we know that we are team members in intimacy—I'm just not there yet. In the Zen sense, I will be a less miserable person when I let go of some of that. But I'm not ready. And there is actually more freedom as a woman to be had, but you have to be willing to take responsibility for it. And I still want to be overwhelmed and ravished, and I want to overwhelm and to ravish, and I'm not ready to let go of either of those things. I've got to fuck, and if someone is willing to try it, I still love to be overwhelmed.

MR: When did you first start writing?

McCarty: The poetry is when V. K. started. I started writing poetry at fourteen. I was doing a lot of poetry by the time I was out of high school. I didn't start doing short stories until I was in New York, divorced. A lot of poetry came out during the divorce. But the short stories didn't start until I was here in New York. I was in theater, and I realized that if I were to describe some of the things that happened last night, nobody would probably believe me, anyway. But we had a short story there.

MR: And you kept your nights busy enough to be able to write these stories?

McCarty: Oh, not all of them. Solitude is probably the single most nourishing thing I feed myself with.

MR: Do you have a wide circle of friends outside the sexual field?

McCarty: Yes, I do.

MR: Do you find it a release?

McCarty: No. They don't understand a lot of things. That's how I ended up in my primary relationship. I get talking with somebody about something very dear to me, and I'm amazed that they wouldn't be able to translate it laterally, and talk about the same thing in another discipline. But very often they can't. So I don't find that my theater friends necessarily understand my ritual life, or that my liturgy friends understand my ballet enthusiasms, but many of them do.

MR: Do you have brothers and sisters?

McCarty: I do. I have three little sisters. Achieved young ladies.

MR: What was your family life like?

McCarty: A little rigid.

MR: Aha. One of the famous V. K. McCarty "periods." I've heard about these. They warned me that when you don't want to talk about something, *c'est fini*. You're not going to tell me anything else about this, are you?

McCarty: (*silence*)

MR: Okay, let's try another question. Tell me the story of how you wound up as a character in John Preston's *Entertainment for a Master*.

McCarty: In a flusher economy, Guccione sent me, each year, to either L.A. or San Francisco, and I received writers, interviewed writers, and either reported on one of the big sex-education conferences or participated in erotic-writing workshops. John used to enjoy the hotel that I was always put in in San Francisco, and we thought that Anne Rice would get a kick out of it, and we dreamed up the idea that we would have a large tea party—a high-tea party or cocktail party—and that we would invite some of our favorite people, certainly including but not exclusive of Anne Rice and Sam Steward. And that each of us would have various of our boys serve. The American Booksellers Association was coming up in San Francisco that year, so we put an ad in *Drummer*.
    We were quite serious to begin with—we were going to have

this party, and it was going to be to honor Sammy and Anne, and we wanted men to serve and be silent and wear harnesses, or maybe 1920s bathing suits. They would serve canapés, and they would wear gloves. So we put an ad in *Drummer* for boys to interview to serve at this party. That's about how far we got in actuality. Then John put the party in his book, and he also met several of those boys as they answered the ad and auditioned for him, in fact. I tell the story from time to time, and then I have to ask—are you one of them?—because there are a couple of wonderful people in our lives that he met because they answered that ad. It was sort of like *Looking for Mr. Benson 2*.

MR: And your character—your persona—was very much available to the world through that story, personified by Preston's character, Madame.

McCarty: Mam'selle Victoire. She was out and about a bit then.

MR: Did you write fiction in her voice?

McCarty: Oh, yes. My heterosexual fiction is as her. It's tame stuff, but I like it. She did a lot of poetry, too.

MR: Do you experience life as a different person when you are writing under the different personas?

McCarty: Yes. And I remember. In a lot of the writing I am trying to accurately remember, now that I'm on less drugs, and reconcile the intensity and ambiguity of my feelings at those times. One of the ways I integrate it is by imagining that I am a different person. But when I am trying to understand the incredible intensity and longing of those times, one way to reconcile it is to realize I was a man. Or that I was a school marm, and yes, when I am writing, I usually am very intensely into my Mam'selle or my Victor King persona.

MR: Tell me about the Mam'selle persona.

McCarty: She is—they are both—older people. Mam'selle is looking back over a life of having formed and brought out the best gifts in young men.

MR: Does she have a preference of acts for her men?

McCarty: All of that is extra stuff. The first thing she wants is to see, and smell, and bite, and control, a velvety, muscled boy's body, and to know that she can spank and fuck it. Then if such a person could be trained to be a devoted butler, or a German shepherd, that's really a sideline.

MR: And Victor King?

McCarty: Victor King I made up as an homage to Sammy when I saw his Phil Andros picture, the one with the petulant young fellow leaning on a lamppost, smoking, in the cutoff sweatshirt. I thought, who is this boy coming home to, while he's out doing whatever he's doing and being bad? Who does he come home to? To be forgiven and punished by? Who does he come home to? And I imagined that he comes home to a man who is retired from—I want to say "hustling," but that he sells boys—

MR: A procurer?

McCarty: A procurer of hustlers. And I picture him as blond with a bit of a stomach. Uncut. And then, add-ons that are unnecessary in the 1990s are that I imagine him drinking quite a bit, and certainly enjoying pissing and being mean, with moments of kind memory, but surly outbursts all the time. The Victor King stories are kind of about Sammy.

MR: Is the writing rougher?

McCarty: It is. Actually, this is something that John Preston uncovered, because he was sometimes rougher, and yet sometimes more urbane. Those are two sides, and John has tried to make me get honest with myself about when those two sides come out. Sometimes he likes the more urbane side. And then when I am on the surlier side, the writing is a little rougher. Now as for the sex, you can certainly have rough sex and speak about it in either a sophisticated or a rough way. But it is interesting that Victor King sometimes speaks in a rougher way and sometimes in a more urbane way, and I never realized that until John made me come clean about it.

MR: And what does Mam'selle Victoire sound like?

McCarty: Probably she sounds just like me. I don't think she is any different from me, talking.

MR: With all these personas, do you ever have a hard time remembering which persona you are writing in? Do they ever overlap?

McCarty: Not at all. Everything is very compartmentalized. I think the more that we integrate sides, probably the healthier we are, but in fact I am quite staunchly pigeonholed about it all.

MR: What do you think about the furor and controversy right now about women writing pornography? Your personal orientation, certainly through your Edwardian persona, is from a different era. And you've actually broken the rules of that era as well, so it shouldn't really be too much of a shock to you, breaking rules of this one.

McCarty: I worked on that front for a while.

MR: The anti-antiporn front?

McCarty: Yes, they used to send me out. I used to do more work against "women against pornography." That, again, was in a flusher economy. *Penthouse* used to send me out to do the morning talk shows.

MR: Do you still do them?

McCarty: I have come to realize that there are more professional, better informed, more intelligent women on our team,
who are better advocates about censorship debate. I have taken
a step back about it. I let the professionals do their work, and
we have a couple here who are very, very good. And I used to
talk just extemporaneously about it, but this is a critically important debate that is happening, and it is crucial for women that
we don't lose on points, and that we send out the right people
to do this precious work.

MR: What is different now than then? From when you were
doing the talk shows?

McCarty: The attacks upon freedom of speech are much greater
since the Meese Commission, in particular.

MR: Different people making the attacks?

McCarty: The government, the Justice Department, but certainly
the fundamentalist Christian Right. And in some cases, women's
criticism of the erotic is so extraordinary that it would make
you feel as though women had no right to even choose to
purchase—much less read—erotic material. If we expect to
maintain this right in our society, we must speak up and defend
it, or we will be deemed unequal to that right.

MR: Do you think that pornography today is different than it
was when you were more involved in your sexual nightlife, in the
late 1970s?

McCarty: No and yes. It's there, it's beautiful. There are beautiful examples. It's not better than it used to be, or worse, but
there are fibers of ethos running through it that I wasn't aware
of from previous decades.

MR: Have issues of safety become more prevalent?

McCarty: There certainly weren't as many condoms and safe

words in pornography, or in erotic practice in general, in the 1960s and 1970s as there are now.

MR: Have you ever encountered hostility from other porn writers, other male porn writers, toward you as a woman writing porn, and especially rough-sex porn?

McCarty: Actually, writers have been very gracious and kind. I've found the fraternity of writers to be very, very nourishing. Particularly the old school.

MR: What do you think of the work of the younger generation?

McCarty: I like some of it.

MR: Anyone in particular?

McCarty: I like all the Steven Saylor material.

MR: What about some of the new young writers, Will Leber, or Michael Lowenthal, or Owen Keehnen, or Patrick Carr?

McCarty: Let me see if I have a *Flesh and the Word 2* here. No, not over in this office. I think I'd rather study some of that a little bit more before stating an opinion.

MR: That sounds reasonable.

McCarty: But as to favorites, who I read with my own dick in my hand, I'd certainly go along as far as Steven Saylor.

MR: I've found this very intriguing, this generational slant. Certainly I've discussed it with both Will Leber and Laura Antoniou, who are my age...early thirties. And with Michael Lowenthal, who's a little younger.

McCarty: I see. And are you talking to anyone of my generation?

MR: You haven't actually told me your age, Mrs. McCarty, and something in your demeanor leads me to believe that you might interpret the question as less than gallant.

McCarty: I'm—I suppose I play it that I'm—I wouldn't necessarily want my age published, not because I mind being that old, but because I usually play older.

MR: Yes, ma'am. I would never be so ungentlemanly as to ask. One of the things I've talked about with the writers I've interviewed is the idea that pornography, some years ago, was the primary literature of gay culture. Now it is an adjunct, and perhaps freer to develop into really good writing. I wonder if this generation will succeed, in your opinion, in—

McCarty: Well yes, it was *fine* writing a generation ago!

MR: That's fabulous! Rage at me! Cut me to the quick! Let loose!

McCarty: No, no, look at Gertrude Stein! And Sammy Steward!

MR: Of course, you're right. But maybe it's the publishing itself that is better now. Is it better published now?

McCarty: Yes, better typesetting, and page layout and printing excellence available. But not always enough consideration given to proofreading and copy editing.

MR: Is there anything you feel that our literature, our erotic literature, has to look forward to, at this juncture in our history? Is there any mission that should be undertaken?

McCarty: I don't know. That's a perfectly wonderful question. But I don't know if I'd have an answer for it tonight. That's quite lovely. That's the kind of thing where I'd like to have a written answer under my belt and talk about it on television.

MR: You form beautifully crafted sentences, and you are about as evasive as I expected you to be.

McCarty: (*laughs*)

MR: But then, I was well warned.

McCarty: By whom?

MR: Well, you're a very famous person, V. K. It's not all that difficult to get a view on you. One doesn't have to scratch very deep to get an opinion.

McCarty: Well, we could have gone deeper if we were doing Victor King or Mam'selle.

MR: There you go. What a fascinating woman you must be.

McCarty: Oh, no, I'm really quite ordinary.

John
PRESTON

*Look, as a gay man, let alone as an SM man, I long ago learned
that I was never going to be loved by society, and I have nothing but pity for people who attempt to be loved by society. And
I think that for an artist who is a gay man right now, it is most
important that we are speaking to our own audience and not
to the society at large.*

I conducted this interview in the summer of 1992 at John
Preston's home in Portland, Maine. I was taking some courses
at Harvard Summer School, and before I left Toronto, I
convinced Dayne Ogilvie, the editor of Toronto's *Xtra!* magazine, that my summer studies would be a perfect opportunity to
interview Preston, who was enjoying the first flush of wide-
spread, mainstream fame. His anthologies, *Hometowns* and *Flesh
and the Word*, had introduced his work to a new audience, and
for his longtime readers, his new success merely validated something they had known since his first novel, *Mr. Benson*, appeared
in 1983. Preston was thrilled that his older work was about to
be rereleased by Badboy.

I traveled to Portland on the bus from Boston (gay journalism doesn't frequently pay transportation costs), and met Preston
on the steps of his apartment building. He was an effusive and
genial host, something I had not been prepared for by our brisk
telephone conversations in setting up the interview.

He took me out for lunch. Then we repaired to his apartment
and consumed several bottles of wine, getting quite drunk while

talking through three cassette tapes. My profile of John Preston, "Family Values" (the title referred to his book, *A Member of the Family*, which was released in the fall of 1992), appeared in *Xtra!* in December of that year.

When John Preston wrote *Mr. Benson*, he articulated the desires of his readers so perfectly that they followed him everywhere: to journalism, creative nonfiction, and finally, triumphantly, to Harvard University itself, where, on April 15, 1993, he delivered the Jon Pearson Perry Lecture. The title? "My Life as a Pornographer."

John Preston's erotic fiction—the *Master* series, *The Heir*, *The King*, *The Arena*, and his two short-story collections, *Tales From the Dark Lord* and *Tales From the Dark Lord 2*—as well as his nearly forty other books, stand testament to a gifted writer whose connection with his readership was unsurpassed. Over the course of the interview, he continually emphasized how important that connection was, and how he felt simultaneously exhilarated and humbled by his calling in life, which was to be "a scribe in the marketplace" and the voice of the gay everyman. "The only thing that makes sense of my life," Preston explained, "is to be a writer."

John Preston died of complications relating to AIDS on April 28, 1994.

Michael Rowe: Canadian Customs officials recently had something to say about your pornography, specifically *Flesh and the Word*, when Canadian author Robin Metcalfe, whose story "The Shirt" was included in the collection, tried to have a copy of the book mailed to him. Would you tell us about this?

John Preston: Robin Metcalfe, who contributed to several of my anthologies including *Hot Living*, *Personal Dispatches* and *Hometowns*, very straightforwardly ordered some copies of *Hometowns* and *Flesh and the Word* from the publisher, and this shipment was seized at the New Brunswick border and declared obscene. He questioned it and began the whole proceedings. As I understand Canadian law, he and Customs were on paths that should have been linear, although in opposite directions: Robin's to have the book declared legal in Canada, Customs' to have the book banned not only at this one crossing, but also at any border point in the country. As I understand it, the very fact that Robin questioned them threw everybody off, and they are now backtracking.

MR: There's another case in Canada that you're involved in, this time in Vancouver, B.C.

Preston: The case involves the Little Sister's bookstore, where one of my *Master* books was seized in a shipment to the store, and they are fighting it vehemently. The case is going to court, as I understand it. They've asked me to come and testify in Victoria, B.C.

MR: Is this something that you're accustomed to when dealing with Canadian customs officials?

Preston: It's been fairly common for my books to be seized at the Canadian border, and one of the ongoing issues that is very seldom looked at is that Canada Customs is a tail that wags the dog. I know that Canadians aren't going to like to hear that, but the Canadian market is approximately twenty percent the size of the U.S. market. And the profit margin of an American publication is often twenty percent of sales. I'm talking about magazines here, not books. And that means that if a magazine can cross the Canadian border, it makes money. If it doesn't, it doesn't make money. So what happens now is that sexually oriented periodicals that are published in the States have to be vetted by the Canadian federal government. And the most prestigious and widely circulated sexually oriented magazines do this.

MR: For example?

Preston: *Penthouse* and *Playboy*, for instance, send proofs of the magazine to Ottawa before they go to press. So there's this little man, sitting in an office, who decides what can or cannot get by Canadian Customs. Depending on what he says, the magazine then alters itself. It's an astonishing problem for American publishing which is never addressed.

MR: How does it differ from the American situation, specifically in the way publishers view how their work will be received by officialdom? Or is there a completely different situation in the United States?

Preston: The biggest thing in the States is against something we call "prior restraint." This means that you cannot say anything about a publication until it is actually physically produced. You cannot prior-restrain anybody's free speech. The Canadian system is diametrically opposed to that, and demands—or promotes—prior restraint. All of these U.S. publications that are attempting to get into the Canadian market are subverting United States values by presenting them to the Canadian government before they are printed.

MR: Cold, damp, white-bread Canada is a valuable enough market that publishers of erotic periodicals are willing to manipulate themselves this way?

Preston: Oh, yes. Especially for a magazine. It is the definition of profitability. So *Mandate*, *Playboy*, *Penthouse*—gay, straight, all of them—send these magazines to Canada. The gay magazines are quite simply not big enough business to redo themselves. It used to be you would suddenly find a big white spot in *Mandate*, in the middle of the text. And that is because it was determined that the Canadian Customs wouldn't accept it. So rather than redo it, they would just blank it out.

MR: Censorship is a white-hot topic of controversy in Canada right now, mostly due to the banning of books and the brutal harassment of gay and lesbian bookstore owners by officialdom here in Canada. John Scythes, the owner of Glad Day Books in Toronto, has said that he simply can't financially afford any more raids or court costs. To push one of the few gay-owned mainstream purveyors of gay literature in Canada to the wall this way is horrifying, and an argument could be made that this is not acceptable in a liberal society. Do you have anything comparable in the United States?

Preston: It's fascinating. If you take three of the most liberal societies in the world: the United States, Canada, and Sweden—and I think that one can make the argument that they are three of the most liberal societies—they have each evolved separately. And they have each evolved with different definitions of what is obscene. And the distinct difference with the United States is we are getting close to the point that the written word *cannot* be obscene. In the United States you can write about anything. And you "cross the border" and start getting into trouble only when you start doing photographic or other depictions of actions. What happens in that case, especially with videotapes, is that certain states of the union will determine that a certain kind of video material is obscene.

MR: Which states come to mind in particular?

Preston: Tennessee is infamous for having done this, as is Alabama. And then it becomes too complex and too expensive for a company to start marketing around them. In the United States, everything is aimed at a national market. It has now been determined that these individual states can prosecute people for production of certain materials and for sending them through the mail. So you get people backing off from video representations, especially of bondage or certain kinds of kink. But the written word, in the United States, is pretty vehemently protected now. That is not true in Sweden and Canada.

MR: How does the distinction manifest itself there?

Preston: In Canada, it's the depiction of certain physical acts which is the problem. Those include beatings. And the Canada Customs has a specific fetish against urine. Any water sports really drive the Canadians up the wall.

MR: And Sweden?

Preston: Sweden, on the other hand, has a prohibition of the written word depicting what it defines as violence. It's not so concerned about the physical act as it is about any depiction of the physical act as being nonconsensual. And those are three very different journeys from the same point.

MR: As the preeminent writer of gay male leather and sado-masochistic fiction today, how does that make you feel? For that matter, SM aside, how does that make you feel as a writer, as an artist?

Preston: I assume that the whole society is not intrigued with broadening its perspectives. And I assume that this is a kind of parameter that I am always, in one way or another, going to have to deal with. The issue for me, then, is to be able to create my voice and to deliver it to an audience. I have, at various times, written for the Swedish audience. I was very amused, because there was a certain point in history, probably about ten years ago, when I was better known in Sweden than I was in the United States. There are some limitations with which any writer can deal, without infringing on his voice or his integrity. And those are things that writers do all the time. It's not much different from acknowledging, for instance, space limitations.

MR: It sounds like you're trying to make several points at the same time here.

Preston: Actually, I'm going in a different direction from your question, because what I'm really talking about is the ease of doing safe sex.

MR: In life or in writing? Or do you mean in both? And do you feel that "safe sex" affects how erotic literature, or pornography if you will, is perceived by society? And if so...

Preston: Look, as a gay man, let alone as an SM man, I long ago learned that I was never going to be loved by society, and I have nothing but pity for people who attempt to be loved by society. And I think that for an artist who is a gay man right now, it is most important that we are speaking to our own audience and not to the society at large. So we're going to be hated, and we're going to be disdained to a certain extent. I think that all of the SM stuff, and all of the gay erotic stuff that I do is potentially censorable by somebody—Canada, Sweden, the United States.

MR: And recognizing that this potential censorability exists, how do you propose to react?

Preston: Except for relatively reasonable restraints, I am not going to consider it. I have long ago acknowledged that I am on the edge, that I am an outlaw, and I tend to embrace that. One also makes all kinds of decisions. I decide that I want to write certain things in a *form* that's not going to be acceptable to a commercial market. Or about a subject that's not going to be acceptable to a legal market, if you will. And I simply make those decisions. And I usually have a very good sense of when I'm writing something that only an avant-garde literary magazine is going to publish, or which is going to be censored at the Canadian or Swedish borders—censored in Canada and not translated into Swedish.

MR: How do these questions come into play when you are considering your audience and its access to your work?

Preston: The main thing is to get something into print. And if I were totally denied an access to my market, then I would feel horribly mistreated. To get only to my core audience, however, is sufficient for me.

MR: The whole issue of your work being published in the mainstream now, as it has been with your anthologies, brings me to a question that I have found intriguing for a long time. The simultaneous explosion of the whole right-wing Christian suppression of the erotic experience, particularly the whole gay erotic experience, appears to have coincided with a surge of mainstream enthusiasm for gay fiction. It seems to be quite unprecedented. The books are handsomely published, literate...you don't even need a "gay fiction" section in the bookstores. Can you give your take on this turn of culture? How can these two diametrically opposed forces erupt at the same time, and with equal vehemence?

Preston: There are two separate dynamics going. One is AIDS, which certainly made gay sexual experience a more viable stationary target. AIDS was supposed to have proved to the right wing that they were right, that God was striking these people down. There was this huge vulnerability that they were using to attack gay sexuality. At the same time, AIDS dragged many gay men in the United States out of the closet. And that feeds into the second thing, the intense commercialization of American society. If you can make money, it's worth doing. There are fifty gay bookstores in the United States, which meant that publishers could sell enough hardcover books to at least not lose money. And so, niche publishing began, all on this basis. There is also, one has to say, at least begrudgingly, a very powerful strain in American publishing in defense of expression.

MR: And how does this manifest itself?

Preston: One of the things that does happen with American publishing is, if you attack it, it responds. It doesn't fold. Mind you, this is the only segment of the media where this would happen. It would not happen, for instance, in television. But in publishing, if you start attacking publishers for doing gay books, their response is to publish more of them, not retreat. It is one of the few elements of dignity and nobility left in their industry.

MR: It's almost as if mainstream publishing has woken up and discovered that gay men do, in fact, read. And all along, we've thought of ourselves as a fairly literate subculture with an interest in buying books that deal with our experience.

Preston: I don't really know that stereotype of gay men at all. When I did *Hometowns* and I got these twenty-nine writers to contribute, people at Dutton got together to read the manuscript and all came back and said, "These men were all so bookish when they were young, and all so overweight, and all so withdrawn, and isn't this intriguing about gay men?"
And I looked at them, and my editor looked at them, and we said, "This has nothing to do with being gay. It has everything to do with being a *writer*."
   I think that there have been so few voices of gay men in our culture that we...well, the whole point of the gay existence was to be erased. We didn't have access to a lot of the other media. We weren't going to be on television. We didn't have daily newspapers. Mainstream magazines didn't want us. Our own magazines were pretty lousy and didn't nurture new voices. But we could write, and we could write books. So the major voice of gay men has, for some time, been the voice of writers. A lot of what have been in reality the stereotypes of writers have been assumed to be the stereotypes of gay men.

MR: Do you feel, then, that the two stereotypes are not natural allies?

Preston: I think that there's a built-in fallacy there. One of the great lessons I learned by moving to Maine, which is so far outside the literary mainstream, was to recognize how *not different* gay men were. And one of the great things about being here is to be so intimately attached to my audience, without the filter of a literary circle like Boston, or San Francisco, or New York.

MR: You're speaking, I assume, of a working-class, blue-collar audience here in Portland?

Preston: Oh, yes! Gay men in Portland have nothing to do with

the literary image we have of gay men. They work on the waterfront; they work for the Central Maine Power Company. They're
much more diverse. One of the fascinating things about gay
life in big cities is that as soon as you get a large population, gay
life begins to fragment. When I lived in New York, I easily went
for months without talking to anyone except white gay men
with college educations who were into leather. I could find that
group of people very easily, and they could find me because I was
one of them too. But you get into a small city like Portland, you
don't have that luxury of specialization. You have men and
women in the same bars, leather and fluff in the same bars.
They don't always love each other, but they have no choice.

MR: Okay. Fair enough. The one question attached to your
work that never seems to stop fascinating the literati or the
press, but which your readers, for the most part, don't give a
second thought to...

Preston: I think I see this one coming. Here we go.

MR: Bear with me, please. I have to ask. Would you define for
me the difference between erotica and pornography, *as you see it.*

Preston: I could probably find for you a difference, but the
difference I could find has nothing to do with any of the definitions I've ever heard in the debates. And, given the definitions
I've heard in the debates, I would want to just bluntly say that
there is no difference at all. I'm just now beginning to write two
books: one called *The Arena* [published by Badboy, 1993], and
another one which is as yet untitled. They very much have the
same theme. They're about secret societies of gay men who
commit themselves to SM sex. I understand that *The Arena* is
going to be published by a publisher like Badboy, and it's going
to be serialized by *Stallion*. It is pornography. I also know that
the pretensions of the other novel are such that it's at least
going to have a shot at being published by somebody like
Dutton. What's the difference between the two? Well, it's going
to take a hundred pages in the second novel for them to have a

hard cock that seeps come. And the first novel—*The Arena*—couldn't be published unless that sex was in the first ten pages.

MR: So the difference is commercial? Literary?

Preston: Commercially, there is a difference. There's going to be not necessarily more frequent sex in *The Arena*, but more measured sex. You won't go more than fifteen pages without a sex scene. So that becomes a certain kind of pornography. And I can understand how somebody is making that distinction. But those are literary distinctions. People want to make moral distinctions. I'm constantly being pressured to claim that my books are erotica, not porn. And I reject those. It's very similar to the pressure on gay men to separate ourselves from other gay men. As in, "You aren't one of *those*." When I was coming out years ago, that was an enormous, well-articulated pressure. *You're not the kind of terrible fag who goes to a bar looking for a one-night stand!* Even here in Portland, the city council just passed a gay civil-rights bill, and one of the most impassioned speeches in defense of the bill was by a gay man who, after an attack from the right-wing element, declared that he and the other supporters of the bill weren't the kinds of gay people who went to the park, and that they—the "good" supporters—didn't even know who those people in the park were. Well, I know every one of them. It's bullshit.

MR: And they know them, too, no doubt.

Preston: Probably. But they're not honest with one another. There's a willingness to sell out. "I'm not one of those pornographers, I'm a literateur." I find my need and desire to separate myself from that debate increases as I become more established and more "acceptable." The pressure to perceive myself as an "erotic artist" increases, and I don't want to buy into it.

MR: You could probably raise more than a few welts now, by digging your heels in and making waves in this debate now that you've acquired more mainstream clout. Does it become more important—or less—to make this point now that you have the power to do it?

Preston: It becomes less consequential. I'm not sure that my disinterest with making waves has anything to do with the publication of hardcover books at Dutton. I think it might have more to do with mortality, with having felt the kiss of AIDS, and having been very ill from that at one point.

MR: It doesn't sound like it's much of an issue for you anymore.

Preston: Anger is too much of an investment. What I'm much more aware of at this year in my life is that I have probably eleven books which are fully developed in my mind, which I want to write. And I now recognize that they'll all be published. That's what's important to me. So all of my stuff is to get those books written, and what anyone might think of that doesn't affect me.

MR: Are you saying that you're immune to criticism at this point in your career?

Preston: One still reacts to reviews, one still reacts to slights and pretentious academics. But I've won most of the rewards. I remember back fifteen years ago when I was living in New York, and the whole generation of gay writers who were my age were all starting out. It's very fascinating as I sit here and hold a copy of the reissue of *Mr. Benson* [Badboy, 1992] of all things, but I'm the one who got it. I'm the one whose books are in the Book-of-the-Month Club. I'm the one going off to book fairs, whose papers are being collected by Brown University. It's quite awesome. It's not what anyone expected.

MR: It sounds as though there is an element of détente—*You guys do what you do, and I'll do what I do*. I wonder if you're suggesting that staying true to your colors, in writing, yields rewards?

Preston: One thing that beginning writers never get, and I certainly didn't get in the beginning, is that publishing does reward perseverance. It really does. To stick with it, to write books, to get them published wherever you can. To do whatever you have to do to make a living is something that, after fifteen years, publishing respects. And I have done that. The only thing that makes sense of my life is to be a writer.

MR: Speaking of specific pieces of writing, specific characters you have created, would you care to hazard a guess at the appeal of someone like Mr. Benson, or the unnamed narrator of *Entertainment for a Master* and *The Love of a Master*? Both characters are electrifyingly masculine, older, affluent, slightly decadent and aristocratic, and completely dominant. What chord is struck in SM aficionados when these characters meet readers? The character of Aristotle Benson is an underground cult figure. Why? What is speaking to the readers?

Preston: I think there are many reasons. The appeal of the books, I'm afraid, is that what they're being compared to is so bad, especially in the beginning. There are some other gay pornographers who are just fabulous writers: Lars Eighner, Steven Saylor who writes as Aaron Travis, T. R. Witomski when he was alive. I consider those men my peers.

MR: What about women?

Preston: And certainly some women, like Pat Califia, and as a straight woman, Anne Rice. I think that we're doing things, and making dares, and taking risks that have in the long run paid off because we are good writers. And we cared very much about our material. But when I started, with *Mr. Benson*, which was the first fiction I ever wrote, everything around it was so rotten. So people responded to this halfway-decent material and somewhat provocative imagination, and by their response I had to take it more seriously. I remember so well giving a reading in Boston, and one man, one incredibly handsome young man in a black leather jacket, he looked so guilt-ridden that I adored him, raised his hand to ask me if Mr. Benson was a real person. And when I said no, he cried. The next book I wrote was *I Once Had a Master*. And I took that book very seriously. And I'm still intensely proud of it.

MR: Did you have a hard time getting it published?

Preston: I had a very hard time getting it published.

MR: Did you shop it around a lot?

Preston: No, there was no possibility of shopping it around. The only possibility of publishing it at that time, 1983 or 1984, was Alyson. So it became a question of convincing him to publish it. What I ended up doing was not writing a novel, but a collection of short stories with a common narrator. And the common narrator had a character progression, and an age progression, so many people read it as a truncated novel. It was very simple to do, and goes back to what I was saying about certain changes not affecting the integrity of the author. And I think it was only that common narrator and that progression which convinced him to publish it.

MR: And it sold well.

Preston: It sold very well. The *Master* books have generally done very well. For a gay book. A gay male book that does very well is 10,000 or 15,000 copies.

MR: And yet you and publisher Sasha Alyson came to a parting of the ways after *The Love of a Master*.

Preston: He eventually simply didn't want to do the series. Nor could we agree on a way to continue the Alex Kane series [currently published by Badboy]. And that all came at the same time as I was diagnosed and stopped writing, and in various different ways began to be picked up by mainstream presses. So we just parted.

MR: Did you attempt to publish any other porn after this parting with Alyson?

Preston: The problem was that then there was no place for me to publish my erotica. I tried with a couple of small presses, but they were truly incompetent. They were nightmarish. What I consider my best book, and what my mentor Samuel Steward considers my best book, *The Heir* [republished by Badboy in 1992], was totally bungled. It went out, and no one even knew it was there.

MR: What is your take on the appeal of SM?

Preston: Two things are in the forefront of my understanding of the appeal of SM. One is the drive by men to want to be part of a tribe. And to want to be part of a group. And SM—especially SM organizations—are the only places where that's really addressed in North American society. One gets to wear a uniform. One gets voted on by one's friends, or peers. And sexually one is told what to do, to a certain extent. It's very, very appealing. And the other thing is a reaction to the overly social-worked tradition of North American society, where everyone is supposed to be nice. Everything is supposed to be without conflict.

MR: Is the tribal element a male thing, or a societal thing?

Preston: I don't want to make any statements about genetics, but I think that men are really brought up needing a test of endurance. A need to prove something to one another. Needing a sense of combat. I think that all exists. And as a corollary to all that, I think that the role that men are put in by society, which is to be dominant and on top at all times, is simply not viable. A lot of men then retreat into a wide pendulum sweep, and walk into the waiting arms of a sadist like myself.

MR: Is sex more the currency of the gay psyche, or are gays already so far outside the mainstream that we simply follow through on basic human sexual instincts which others suppress? And have we been able to hold on to something sexual in our literature that has been bred out of straights?

Preston: Sex is so written out of North American society, a puritanical, repressive society that doesn't want this almost-anarchic force to be let loose. But the repression is simply too much for many of us to bear. So we broke out of the repression and became gay. Eric Rofes, who is now the head of the Ashanti project and used to be involved in *Gay Community News* and other political activities, has an intriguing statement. He says that those of us who came out at the very beginning of gay liberation did it because we had to. We were obsessed with sex; we were obsessed with revolution; we were obsessed by rebellion. We had no choice. So our coming out was part of the definition of what being gay meant. And once we were out, that was so contentious to society that we might just as well keep on going and being sexual.

MR: What about our literature? Do you think that sex is germane to gay literature?

Preston: I think that from a very specific point, sex is the definition of gay culture. It has to be germane to gay literature. It is the definition of society that gay existence is pornographic. It doesn't make any difference whether I'm writing *Mr. Benson* or whether I'm David Leavitt writing *The Lost Language of Cranes*. At a certain point, society is going to say, "This is pornographic!"

We recently had a situation where Texaco withdrew its sponsorship of an ongoing PBS dramatization of *The Lost Language of Cranes*. That is the definitive form of censorship in a capitalist society.

And a definitive statement on what is pornographic.

MR: You take a fairly bleak view of assimilation, then. The idea of fully integrated gay men and lesbians happily pushing lawn mowers in the suburbs doesn't strike you as being on the horizon any time soon?

Preston: There may come a point, after the revolution comes, and it certainly won't be in my lifetime, where you can say that all of the things that make up the fabric of "being gay" are just things that happen in the world, and therefore can become as neutral material as living in suburbia. But that's not going to happen in our lifetimes.

MR: Is it something to be looked forward to?

Preston: I don't know. I really do think that one of the most important things about being gay in our society is forming some sort of tribe. At some point we have to deal with living in a postindustrial society that has erased all forms of individuality, all forms of clanism. I think that looking forward to a time when there is no difference in people is looking forward to Huxley's *Brave New World*.

MR: How do you see our society responding to this eradication?

Preston: I think that there is a trend in the United States toward regionalism, and certainly in the two most powerfully defined regions, which are New England and the South. We're clearly all going back and embracing that regionalism terribly. And the regionalism is trying to override other differences.

MR: Where do you fit into this, both as an old-line Yankee and as a gay male writer?

Preston: I'm intrigued by the extent to which I am accepted as a Maine writer. And that it is becoming as important in the eyes of many critics and observers as the fact that I am a gay writer. And I think that has to do with how powerful a concept being a New England writer has become.

MR: Do you think that gay readers are more willing to give latitude to a gay writer who is both a mainstream writer and a writer of pornography? Certainly, do you think that heterosexual society would make allowances for a writer who did both?

Preston: I don't know that many people in heterosexual society would dare to take the risks that I have. Anne Rice did. But they are very few and far between. I don't think that the gay reader who is looking for affirmation makes the distinction between erotic and nonerotic material that the general society does. And I think that the man who is my reader, one of the 15,000 or 20,000 people who buy my books, is equally interested in what I'm going to do with *I Once Had a Master* as he is with the essays I'm going to collect for *Hometowns*.

MR: And yet there is this dichotomy to your life and work. Some of your most important books were resurrected when Richard Kasak, the publisher of Badboy books, approached you about reissuing some of your classics—most notably *Mr. Benson*—in new editions. And this happened just when *Flesh and the Word*, with stories from luminaries like Edmund White and Anne Rice, was being so elegantly produced by Dutton.

Preston: Well, the whole point of the dichotomy of my life really came back the last time I was in New York. I was going back and forth between mainstream publishers and Badboy. And I was euphoric! Absolutely euphoric! Because these were my two worlds. And they could never come together, but they were fabulous. I spent the afternoon with a friend of mine who is now the editor-in-chief of Avon. And we went to lunch at Rockefeller Center. We sat in this corner suite and drank cognac into the evening. From there, I went to Badboy to plan, with these quite disreputable leather types, the publication party for *Mr. Benson*. A part of me was separating and saying, how can I psychically deal with this. Going from Rockefeller Center to Paddles in Chelsea. And they were both figuring out my future. When you left the room just now, I looked at my mail. I have *QW*, the *Times Literary Supplement, Publishers Weekly, The New Yorker, Advocate Men,* and the *Tennessee Humanities Council.* This is somehow my life, and no part of it is separated.

MR: But doesn't that prove that it can be done? You flout a lot of rules by being successful in both worlds. I think you must make a lot of people nervous by not staying submissively in one niche.

Preston: It's not even that. A lot of writers are nervous because they're all trying to figure out what is the correct path. Everyone thinks there is a formula. And you're supposed to have a creative-writing degree from Iowa, or publish at Knopf. They want linear definitions of success. I think that people in publishing, much more than writers, are quite celebrative of how I do things.

I'll never forget, one of the great figures in gay publishing was a man named Bill Whitehead, who used to be the editor-in-chief of Dutton in a different manifestation of that company. Bill actually published most of the "literary" writers of my generation for the first time. Many of those folk, I remember, used to be desperately anxious and angry that I would spend so much time with him. But he would always have time for me, even though he would never publish me. Because I was doing things that he thought all gay writers should do. And that included giving readings in gay bars, especially in leather bars. He felt that his authors were trying to re-create Bloomsbury or something. Publishing not only rewards perseverance, but it also rewards an author with an audience.

I once went to L.A. and gave a reading to an SM group. It was held in a big auditorium, and there were hundreds of men there, in leather. It was from one of the *Master* books. At the end of the reading, they all applauded very respectfully. Gave me a standing ovation. Then took off their clothes and had an orgy.

MR: The word made flesh.

Preston: It was like magic. And I said to myself, this was what I wanted to do. I had a vision that I had driven these hundreds of men to orgasm. Even my good friends like Paul Monette and Andrew Holleran weren't ready to do that. And publishers love that.

MR: Do you still consider yourself an activist?

Preston: Very much an activist. I've just resigned as the president of the board of the AIDS project here in Maine. I was one of the founders of the Maine Health Foundation, and I've been involved off-and-on with various political and social groups in Maine since I moved here.

MR: What drives you?

Preston: Rage. Fury. The inhumanity of society.

MR: What about your writing? Do you feel that your erotic writing, and the distillation of gay experience that forms the premise of your anthologies, is activism too?

Preston: I'm only recently willing and able to hold up what I'm doing as something unique.

MR: Does that come with maturity and security?

Preston: I don't know. I suppose. Certainly it comes with a lot of support and having done a lot of reading. At a certain point it feels like you're the only one doing it and therefore it must not be of any value.

MR: Do you feel lonely doing what you do? Or did you in the past?
And by lonely, I suppose I mean isolated.

Preston: I've not felt lonely. I've always had such a strong sense of audience. I mean, no one who wrote *Mr. Benson* could feel lonely.

MR: Fair enough. I don't mean to harp on this "mainstream" thing, but is there not any difference at all in your outlook now that your books are on the shelf at Waldenbooks? Not that having your books in Waldenbooks is "better," just different?

Preston: What you're pressing me to recognize and admit,

which is intriguing, is a certain special victory that *Hometowns* and *A Member of the Family* represent.

MR: Which is not a very attractive thing to press you to recognize. Because morally I don't see a difference, and neither do your readers. But the question remains in the minds of many people as to whether or not the anthologies are more inherently valuable than the pornography.

Preston: It's a horrible cliché, I know, but the root of authority is "author." The biggest struggle I think any writer has is sitting down at the keyboard, or with pen in hand, and believing that he or she is going to write something that is worth reading and that people will read. And that the author's "take" is sufficient to assert that to the world. *Personal Dispatches* was a very painful book for me to put together. It was clearly a personal journey. And it really had to do with overcoming my fear of AIDS, and my fear of being diseased, and my fear of what the world was going to do with that.

MR: How did it lead you into anthology editing?

Preston: It really was subsidiary to that, that I discovered that I loved making anthologies. And that I so trusted my judgment that I could make an anthologies and present it to St. Martin's or Dutton. And that it would have a voice and a continuity. To be the editor of an anthology is to be a symphony-orchestra conductor. It's more than being one of the instruments. So I came out of that with *Personal Dispatches*. And I knew that something had happened. There were all these writers whom I adored, and there were these two pressing issues in my life: why am I living where I'm living, and what the fuck am I doing with my family?

MR: What were the circumstances with your family at that time?

Preston: I was reconciling with many people in my family at that time. I thought that these issues were so powerful that I wanted to know what these people whom I considered to be my peers thought about them. And I thought that they were books. Also, I felt that the power of what I wanted to do couldn't be communicated through a proposal. Most nonfiction books in the United States are sold on the basis of a proposal, not a manuscript. I decided not to do that. I went to the writers and said, "I want to know what you say about this." I got back some marvelous manuscripts, many of which needed a great deal of work. The average essay in *Hometowns* was rewritten three times. So I had this magical thing which was a book. And we had all taken this big risk with no money, no guarantee that it was going to happen. But no fear and trepidation. I knew it was going to be fine.

MR: Had any publishers expressed interest, or did you take it around after it was done?

Preston: I took it to publishers and talked to an agent, and the agent said, "This is too fabulous, and we're going to sell it." It was sent out to a half-dozen houses, and Dutton came in with a preemptory bid to stop the auction. And this book happened. You know, in the United States we have this thing about ego being a very negative thing, yet one needs the authority of an ego to be an author, and that includes the right to decide who the twenty-nine men were. I had the right to tell them what the parameters were, however minor they were. It's hard to explain to you, but I knew what this book was going to look like before it was done. I knew it. And that is an enormous risk to one's ego.

MR: What future do you see for gay writers?

Preston: One of the things that is so difficult, if not impossible, to explain to young people is that as much as we write about it— and please forgive the pretension—you have *no idea* what it was like twenty-five years ago.

MR: Perhaps, but—

Preston: One of the things that bothers me about young people is that you have no idea of the difference we've made. The first time I ever saw a gay publication, it was a Mattachine newsletter on a cigarette machine in Chicago, before Stonewall. It was four mimeographed pages. Two years ago, I compiled *The Big Gay Book*, and the manuscript was over 1,000 pages. It was nothing but names and addresses.

MR: From Mattachine to *The Big Gay Book*. Like the movement's historical bookends, really.

Preston: I loathe the word "spiritual," but I must use it to communicate this moment I had two years ago this October. I saw these two enormous typescripts sitting on this table, *The Big Gay Book* and *Hometowns*, and I said to myself, very unselfconsciously, very much aloud, I said, "This is enough. This is a career. This is nearly forty books, and these two books I am particularly proud of. And if this is the end, I have done enough." I continue to find the ways in which Samuel Steward is a profound mentor in my life.

MR: Samuel Steward, of course, is the author behind the pen name Phil Andros. You've mentioned his influence on your work many times in the past, and that you consider him your mentor.

Preston: As you know, I went to interview him in California years ago. And one of the central points in his life is that he wrote all of the literary entries to the original *World Book* encyclopedia. And when he had finished writing that, he decided that was enough. He quit being a college professor and became a tattoo artist. Then, from being a tattoo artist, became a pornographer. He did his own stuff, and that image and memory reverberates in my mind. But with those two large books, I had done enough. There's no more that you can do, as a writer, as an activist...

MR: Did that make you feel fulfilled?

Preston: Oh, yeah. Totally. And that is why I use the word "spiritual" so reluctantly.

MR: But the young kids who have done nothing?

Preston: Well, they're the ones who break my heart. The ones who aren't even old enough to ask the questions. I don't think I could define for you what "enough" was, but I had done it.

MR: And gay writers and gay publishing?

Preston: Gay writing. I think that a lot of things are going to happen. I think that increasingly a lot of books with gay characters are simply going to be published, books that have nothing to do with the gay experience. And that's just fine. It's like having black faces in American television commercials. It really doesn't make any difference, but it does. I think that a very few people—mostly men but a very small number of women—are going to start making major careers. Major careers, in terms of money and recognition and so forth. Very clearly, someone who is beautifully poised for a major career and deserves every minute of it is Dorothy Allison, whose *Bastard out of Carolina* is being accepted as one of the masterpieces of the decade. Just a brilliant book. Paul Monette has really broken some ground. Which, people forget, he did about fifteen years ago, retreated from it and came back and did it again. So there are many possibilities. One can have a career now.

MR: Is there any downside? Do you have any fears or concerns regarding the direction the field is taking?

Preston: My greatest fear is that there's a big thing that happens in gay writing and publishing in the United States. I feel like screaming, "The emperor has no clothes!" and I never get any validation from anyone else. The situation is this: when we refer to the "gay small presses," we project on them all of the romance of the fine small presses, when in fact they are quite viciously commercial. They often turn out good books, and they often turn out really wretched books. And they almost all produce really terrible books, physically. They're really not all that attractive. What's going on is that there is really no nonprofit space where gay and lesbian writers can be published without commercial pressure.

MR: Where does your writing stand within the spectrum of "commercial pressure"? Most of your work, especially the erotic writing, is highly commercial.

Preston: Commercial pressure is simply not relevant to a man like me. I am a definition of commercial. About two years ago, I realized that I was an ultimately middlebrow person, and I decided that was perfectly fine with me. But there is no nonprofit press out there to promote the new voices. And the new voices are often pretty lousy because of the kind of selection process we have.

MR: You've discussed your HIV diagnosis in several interviews already, and you've discussed how you were unable to write anything for about two years following it. You've also said that returning to your roots as a pornographer became something of a catharsis for you. Now, there are people who are going to say that you are speeding up your writing and trying to get as much written as possible before the virus takes a more destructive turn.

Preston: Well, first of all, that's absolutely true. However, most people don't realize that I've written twenty pseudonymous novels. So there were years that the public is unaware of where I wrote ten books a year. And I am very unsatisfied, on that level alone, that I hadn't written twelve books a year. But there is absolutely no question that I have a very astute awareness of my own mortality.

MR: Do you have any sense that you are in the winter of your life?

Preston: No. I went through the winter already, and I don't know where I am right now. I went through the winter, and I stopped writing.

MR: Can you tell me about that?

Preston: When I got my own diagnosis it was difficult, but I was very stiff-upper-lip New England about it. I was going to *go on*, and I marshaled my forces.

MR: But it affected your writing.

Preston: My diagnosis produced a paralysis, and I went into a deep, dark fall. I simply stopped writing. I went quite crazy. My whole persona as a professional fell apart. But I was like this rock-ribbed New Englander who didn't admit it till it became a total disaster. But it was about writing, it wasn't about erotica. And what I finally needed to do was use pornography to climb back out of it.

MR: What happened?

Preston: I had this absolutely fabulous doctor, a woman here in Portland who actually made my diagnosis. What actually happened was, six months into the diagnosis, I had a very damaging prostate infection. I was very sick from it. My doctor, this much younger woman, said to me, "When was the last time you jerked off?"

I said, "I don't know. Six months ago?"

And actually, prostate infections happen because your prostate gland is like this pool, and if you don't come, you don't flush the pool. In a totally physical sense, I was making myself sick because I wasn't jerking off. That's why monks get prostate cancer. So, I went to the dirty bookstore—

MR: *You* went to the dirty bookstore!

Preston: Yeah.

MR: You *are* the dirty bookstore!

Preston: I just went for the tapes. And I jerked off for medicinal purposes. And it dragged me back into my pornographic mind and made me well.

MR: Well, that's it, isn't it? Erotica is the safest fantasy arena for sexual expression and experimentation.

Preston: I'm concerned about your use of the word "safe"—

MR: I'm not talking about bland, Protestant, vanilla sex. I'm talking about the way truly hot erotic writing is sexually affirming and not life-threatening. And how it kick-starts fantasies.

Preston: Well, that's the big thing between Anne [Rice] and me. The thing we always agreed about was that sex should not be "life-negative." And that's why Dennis Cooper isn't in *Flesh and the Word*. That level of violence is obligatorily impossible to me.

MR: How do you see the connection between safe sex and erotica, specifically yours?

Preston: I produced two safe-sex books. I wrote one and edited another. When I wrote *Entertainment for a Master*, suddenly, without comment, everyone has a condom. Or all sex is safe. And that was simply "done." And all the way back to the beginning of this interview, that's what I was talking about, the *acceptable* limitations on an artist. If I am in fact the scribe to a community, I need to teach them, not as a rule, but as possibility, how to love a condom. Now that is a totally acceptable responsibility. I went back through the rough draft of *The Arena* and inserted safe sex into it. Big deal. It was just a couple of paragraphs, tops. And it worked for me. But I can also draw on certain experiences that people of your generation can't, perhaps.

MR: Such as?

Preston: When I was a teenage hustler on the streets of Boston, half the men who would hire me—and I've never gotten over this—would have me put on a condom just for the fetish.

When it wasn't really necessary, a rubber was a plaything. In the fifties, men hired me to wear one in front of them and to suck me while I wore it. If I'm half the writer I'm supposed to be, I can make safe sex that sexy again.

Leigh W.
RUTLEDGE

There has always been a sweetness to me about erotica. There has always been an incredible sweetness, a poignancy about sexuality. I have always been a bit obsessed, even in high school, by the hidden sexual nature of everyone. I was always pretty alert to it. I would be sitting there watching an English teacher who is sixty-eight years old; and without indulging in a ludicrous or purely prurient fantasy, I would be imagining what she would be like undressed and passionately involved with another person.

Although Leigh W. Rutledge, indisputably one of the most gifted writers to grace the field of short erotic fiction between 1977 and 1982, appeared at one time or other in nearly every one of the slick pornographic magazines on the market, he has remained better known for his numerous mainstream books. Both *The Gay Book of Lists* and *The Gay Fireside Companion* remain reference standards, and even readers who might not recognize Rutledge by name will recognize his titles. Given the fact that anthologies of gay male erotic fiction are a relatively new phenomenon, a reader could be forgiven for discovering Leigh W. Rutledge as late as 1992, when John Preston republished his stunning short story, "Brian's Bedroom," in *Flesh and the Word*, ten years after it first appeared in *Honcho*. The tale derives its erotic strength from what the narrator *doesn't* see.

Rutledge denies that voyeurism particularly appeals to him. The recurring theme in his writing is not necessarily catching sight of the forbidden, but rather the sexual power at the heart of what less imaginative people might dismiss as ordinary. From early youth, Rutledge has found himself attracted to erotic iconography that whispers rather than shouts. Over the course of this interview, Rutledge discusses his childhood as a shy observer of the lives of others, his debut as an erotic writer at twenty-one with the publication of his short story "Amaranthine" in *Blueboy*, life in Colorado in a decade of homophobia and intolerance, and his perpetual fascination with "the common erotic element all around us." The writing of Leigh W. Rutledge suggests that perhaps we often roam too far afield searching for our sexual icons. The private tokens that are so arousing in "Brian's Bedroom" are available to anyone with the imagination to look for them.

Michael Rowe: Can you recall your first identifiably pornographic thought? Was there any one moment where you thought of something specific that this was more than adolescent lust? The sight of a back, or the curve of a leg, something like that?

Leigh W. Rutledge: In the fourth or fifth grade, my teacher, Mr. Strode—whom I actually despised—was very good-looking. He had a crew cut and a very masculine manner about him. I remembered sometimes I would look at his haircut and his hands, and I would feel some arousal.

MR: Which came first, the desire to write, or the desire to be an erotic writer?

Rutledge: The desire to write. I was writing a lot of poetry in third and fourth grade, stuff like that. Actually though, the first erotic story I wrote was in sixth grade. And I'm almost embarrassed to even speak about this. It was a story about guys jacking off. It had some dreadful, *dreadful* childish title like "The Sperm Sheath," or something like that, and that was the first erotic story I wrote. I never showed it to anyone.

MR: Did you hold on to the manuscript for a long time?

Rutledge: I'm not sure what happened to that manuscript. I didn't get rid of it, or tear it up and throw it away out of embarrassment, or anything like that, for fear someone would find it. In fact, I think I tried to keep basically everything I've ever written even as a kid. But that one just got lost somewhere.

MR: What inspired that story?

Rutledge: I have an older brother about five years older than I am, so when I was in sixth grade, he was about seventeen. He and his buddies would come over to the house all the time, and they would be talking about "chicks" and "fucking." It used to turn me on a little bit. It made me really inquisitive. I used to sit and imagine a lot of his friends engaged in sexual activity.

MR: With each other, or with you?

Rutledge: Sometimes either way.

MR: But never with a "chick"?

Rutledge: No. It's funny, though. I wrote a lot of things that had erotic overtones through junior high school, and then in high school. In my sophomore year in English, we had to do a project. It was very open-ended. I decided to do a collection of short stories. I mimeographed them, bound them, and then sent them around to all sorts of people—teachers, students—along with the questionnaire asking what they thought of them.

MR: You're not going to tell me that you wrote a collection of erotic stories as a sophomore English project?

Rutledge: A large number of those stories were very erotic. In fact, one was quite explicit. They were all heterosexually oriented, but they were very, very explicit.

MR: What was the response to that?

Rutledge: The response, actually, was pretty good. One of the stories was about two teenagers—a boy and a girl—losing their virginity at an amusement park. It was very explicit. The other was about a man who had lost his wife in a car accident, and couldn't deal with the loss and the loneliness, so he would put on his wife's clothing and masturbate in front of a mirror, pretending he was making love to her. People thought the stories were very well written and enjoyed them.

MR: There was no fallout in terms of the adults around you disapproving or censuring?

Rutledge: Not particularly. I got censured for other things in high school. I was editor of the school newspaper for two years, and I instigated a column that reviewed teachers the same way you review movies. And that created an enormous amount of shit.

MR: Did it give you a charge to affect people that way?

Rutledge: You mean with the erotica?

MR: I was actually thinking in terms of the column. I was thinking of the first moments of power for a writer.

Rutledge: I liked provoking people, absolutely. When you are in high school you are still, despite all your illusions, fairly powerless, and it was a way to get back at some of those teachers. I was never unfair in those reviews. I always tried to be very objective, but that was enough. There were teachers who would physically abuse students, and I would point this out in the column. In fact, there were a group of teachers who were at one point considering suing me.

MR: Was this in a rural area?

Rutledge: Not exactly. I grew up in a town called Saratoga, which is about forty miles south of San Francisco. It's a suburb of San Jose. It was very upper-middle class. A small community, but it was not typically rural.

MR: This must have been mid- to late 1970s?

Rutledge: Right.

MR: It strikes me as odd that physical abuse would be tolerated in an upper-middle-class high-school classroom at that time.

Rutledge: There was one teacher who missed the process. He was a Czechoslovak, and he was an older man. He would go around with a large ruler, and he would hit people on the head, or on their hands, really hard. Or, in one case, there was a girl who hadn't done her homework, and she had her books stacked on the desk. He just shoved them all on the floor and made her get on her hands and knees and pick them up while he berated her. I couldn't stand that teacher.

MR: When did you start self-identifying as gay?

Rutledge: It's really hard to say. I always knew I was attracted to guys. There was never any illusion about that. I remember, when I was ten years old or so, jacking off to two pictures of Robert Conrad and Troy Donahue in my movie magazines. I never really tried to hide it, and I never really felt that uncomfortable with it. In high school, I was pretty open. I used to go review movies, controversial ones like *Myra Breckenridge*. Movies I wasn't supposed to be able to get into. At the same time, like a lot of guys, in spite of the fact that I had no sexual thoughts about women particularly, some part of me always kind of thought I might get married and have kids and all that.

MR: In some situations, it's a given.

Rutledge: I actually remember when all that came crashing down for me. I was nineteen years old, and read Mary Renault's *The Persian Boy*. I remember finishing that book and feeling an incredible revelation, realizing that I was gay in the sense that I not only wanted to have sex with men, but my whole romantic inclination was toward men. And that was a real revelation for me. I stopped thinking in terms of marrying and having kids.

MR: What kind of a kid were you?

Rutledge: I was painfully shy, incredibly awkward, super-brainy, and very much an outsider.

MR: Did you fall in love in high school? Did you fall in love with anybody where it was reciprocal?

Rutledge: No, not reciprocal. I fell so much in love with someone whom everyone in the high school knew. He was a wrestler, and his name was Clay. I was so enamored of Clay for two years, and everyone knew about it.

MR: Including Clay?

Rutledge: Yes. (*laughs*)

MR: How did Clay react?

Rutledge: Surprisingly, when I look back on it, with enormous moderation. I used to follow him on dates. I would follow behind in my car. I actually became very good friends with the girl he was dating steadily. The great irony of this was he was dating a girl named Jennifer—many years later, when *The Gay Book of Lists* came out, I got a fan letter from her. It turned out that she discovered she was a lesbian in college.

MR: Too bad you didn't know at the time. You could have divided up Clay between you.

Rutledge: It was terrible. I used to follow Clay around constantly, and all of my friends knew about it.

MR: Did other people know you were gay before you knew?

Rutledge: No. As I said, I knew pretty well as kid.

MR: How old were you when you decided to become a writer?

Rutledge: That's really tough to define. I actually think it was some time around the age of seven. Even in elementary school, I used to spend weekends, and afternoons after school, sitting home and writing.

MR: Did you find the writing of erotica to be an arena in which to release repressed sexual desires?

Rutledge: I'm sure in high school some aspects of the sexual stories I wrote, especially about the two teenagers losing their virginity, were definitely a blowing off of steam from a lot of sexual tension. Other than that, not particularly. It's going to sound very strange, but there hasn't been a period in my life, except childhood and early adolescence, where I would describe myself as having been sexually repressed.

MR: Maybe "repression" is the wrong word to use. What I'm actually talking about is the idea that as an artist—even a young, unformed artist—you might have needed a way of channeling your feelings, in this case, specifically, sexual ones.

Rutledge: There is no doubt that all the stuff I wrote from about elementary school up through college was my voice. It was my way of saying things that I could not say to people, because even through high school, even though I came out of my shell a bit in the last step of high school, I was still incredibly shy. If a teacher called on me, my heart would start pounding, and I would start shaking. So in a sense, yes, the writing was always my voice.

MR: What were the popular literary genres that attracted you?

Rutledge: I was really interested in science fiction. Which is really interesting to me, as I know a tremendous number of gay people who were into science fiction. I wondered about that for years, and it didn't really take long to figure out that it was because a lot of science-fiction writers write about a hopeful, optimistic future, in which a lot of the heaviness of modern society is no longer around. So I think that's one of the things that attract gay people to science fiction.

MR: What about horror fiction? Or romance?

Rutledge: Never horror. I was interested in a lot of sleazy bestsellers. I went through all of them: Harold Robbins, Jacqueline Susann—

MR: Rosemary Rogers?

Rutledge: Yes. And then I would sit and jack off over the little glimpse of male nudity that would occur in something like that. I had an unusual access to a lot of stuff because my parents had a bookstore when I was a kid. They had everything, from *Myra Breckenridge* to some of the Grove Press, more explicit erotic books. I had a lot of access to all of that stuff, and ate it up.

MR: Did your parents encourage you to be a writer? Did they encourage you in your ambitions?

Rutledge: Not at all. My dad couldn't have cared less what I did. He was very indifferent to me. My mom was very much against me being a writer.

MR: That's intriguing, considering that they owned a bookstore. Were they business people more than book lovers?

Rutledge: No, my mom loved books. But I think, for one of her own children to become a writer presented a problem to her. She felt that all writers were beatniks and odd people. She really wanted me to become an engineer, or go into the sciences or the military.

MR: What was your parents' political affiliation?

Rutledge: They were ultraconservative. My parents were devout Goldwater Republicans. I remember, when I was a kid, they were part of the neighborhood group to "lick the Communists" in the town. They were very conservative people.

MR: Good Lord.

Rutledge: I think some of the fantasies I had in high school of figuring I'd get married eventually, had to do with desires to please my mother and please my family. To do the right thing.

MR: Did this conservative upbringing affect the way you view men? Did you objectify the all-American crew-cut military sort? Or did you actually find yourself in rebellion against that rigidness, and find yourself attracted to sort of more ethereal types?

Rutledge: No. I was attracted to all-American crew-cut types for many years. It wasn't until my twentieth year that it all started to branch out. But definitely, for many years as an adolescent, I was attracted to football-player types, military types.

MR: As we discussed earlier, in your pseudonymous essay in the anthology *Friends and Lovers* ["My Entire Life, and My Father" by Albert Clarke], you talk about your relationship with your father and the horrific beatings and abuse that you endured at his hands. And yet, wasn't he also tied into what your first example of what "a man" was?

Rutledge: Yes, very much.

MR: I'm intrigued that you would use a pseudonym for your essay about your father, and yet not use a pseudonym for your erotic writing. I understand the lack of desire to cloak your erotic writing in a pseudonym, but one might think there would be more of a reason to tell your own stories—your life stories—under your own name. Then, if that is your choice, cloak your erotic writing in a pseudonym.

Rutledge: The reason for the pseudonym in the essay about my father has primarily to do with wanting to keep the focus on the story and none of the focus on me. By the time that essay had come out, I think that all four of my gay books were published, and I was pretty well known. I did not want to draw the focus to me. I just wanted to draw focus to this issue. That was the reason. It never occurred to me to use a pseudonym when I was doing my erotic writing. The erotica has always felt like a very natural part of me, and there isn't a piece of it that I am, in any way, ashamed of. So it just never occurred to me to put it under a pseudonym. The only time that I have used one—I think I used one twice—and the only reason that ever happened was because I had two stories in the same issue of a magazine, and the editor asked me if I would mind putting a pseudonym to one of them.

MR: You made the point in your essay that you found yourself, much to your chagrin and dismay, attracted to men who resembled your father in certain physical ways.

Rutledge: Absolutely.

MR: It's not difficult to imagine a father being a gay son's first sexual object, or his first identification of manhood. But I'm wondering how the life that you endured with this man affected your development and your perception of sexual violence?

Rutledge: I think it's pretty natural to have focused on men who looked like my father. The biggest pain inside of me that I can remember, when I was growing up, both in elementary school and later in high school, was the total lack of a father. It was so bad that when I was a little kid, seven or eight years old, I would sit in front of the television with my brother and sister watching everything from *77 Sunset Strip* to *The Man from U.N.C.L.E.*, and I would say to my brother and sister, "Gee, don't you wish Robert Vaughn were our father? Gee, don't you wish Efrem Zimbalist, Jr., were our father?" I was absolutely fixated on this issue. Even before I had real erotic feelings about men, really pointedly erotic feelings, I remembered having terrible longing for a father, and for a father figure in my life. So it seems natural that in looking at men, the men I would be attracted to would be men who looked like my father, to ease the pain of my real father being so difficult to deal with. It never troubled me particularly that I was drawn to men—and am still drawn to men—who remind me of my father in some way.

MR: Where did you meet your first lover?

Rutledge: I've had only one.

MR: How long have you been together?

Rutledge: Sixteen years.

MR: That would take you back very near to the end of your adolescence, wouldn't it?

Rutledge: Close, yes. In the beginning, even though I had resolved some issues about myself about being gay, I still had a lot of problems expressing myself as a gay man. A lot of that had more to do with shyness than with any issues surrounding my sexuality. I had a terrible time talking to people and meeting people.

MR: Had you actually had sex with men?

Rutledge: I actually had sex with a couple of guys before I was twenty-one. I really wouldn't say that I lost my virginity until I was about twenty-one. And I went through the baths for the first time. And even then, when I went to the baths, a friend had to practically push me through the front door. A straight friend.

MR: A *straight* friend?

Rutledge: A straight friend. A woman I knew. In fact, she took me to the baths one night when I was twenty-one, and I couldn't do it. I had to call her from a pay phone to come pick me up. A few nights later, I asked if she would take me again. And she took me, and I sat in the car, just shaking.

MR: This was exclusively a shyness issue?

Rutledge: Yes. I had the same reaction walking into classrooms in college, even sometimes talking to people. I was incredibly shy. It didn't have anything to do with being gay. She finally said, "Just go do it!" and I got up the nerve and went inside. And proceeded to shake while I was inside.

MR: And how did it feel to finally have sex? To finally make love to a man?

Rutledge: An incredible revelation. An incredible relief, I loved it. The first time I felt another guy's hard cock as an adult, it really was like a revelation. It was like magic. I knew that was where I belonged.

MR: Do you remember anything about him, specifically?

Rutledge: He was a fairly nondescript man in his late thirties. I was in one of the soaking pools, and he came up to me and started talking to me. I remember we were carrying on this long conversation. He was asking me about college, and my majors, while his hand was sneaking under the water, playing with my hard cock. And I thought that was kind of funny at the time. It was good sex.

MR: Your first published erotic fiction was a story called "Amaranthine," which appeared in the December 1977 issue of *Blueboy*. How old were you?

Rutledge: I was twenty-one.

MR: *Blueboy* seems to have been a launching pad for many erotic writers.

Rutledge: It was the first magazine of its kind, really. You had magazines like *Gay Sunshine*, which were extraordinarily literary. *Blueboy* was really the first class-act gay magazine, and it provided a market that really hadn't been there before. And it had a very receptive editor at the time, Bruce Fitzgerald.

MR: I was reading in your book, *The Gay Decades*, that the old *Blueboy* actually began to deteriorate, and got a bit crazy toward the end of its publication.

Rutledge: I never learned exactly what the problems were. By the time it shut down—and I forget what year that was—they owed me $800. They owed a lot of people money. They had started printing model photographs upside down, occasionally, with very bad, bleeding colors. It really deteriorated. But there was a period around 1976 or 1977 when it really was the only magazine of its kind, and it was a class act.

MR: They were also receptive to quality fiction. Writing which, except for its erotic theme, would stand on its own merits as good mainstream short fiction.

Rutledge: I think one of the reasons why I had editors really interested in my work was that the stories stood up on their own. Then also, the kinds of comments I would get from editors were that the stories were "refreshing." In the sense that they generally never relied on cliché settings. I'm not particularly interested in cliché encounters between men. I was always interested in much more realistic encounters, and I think that really did give me an edge.

MR: I'm thinking in particular of the two stories "Brian's Bedroom" and "Fatherless," both of which were anthologized in the *Flesh and the Word* series. There seems to be a strong voyeuristic tone to some of your writing.

Rutledge: That's strange to hear, in a sense, because I'm not really a voyeur at all.

MR: In these stories, you elicit an erotic response by describing things that actually don't happen.

Rutledge: I think that in fact what those reflect, more than anything, is the fascination I've always had with the common erotic element all around us. The erotic overtones in the commonplace that are everywhere. I've always been fascinated with that.

MR: What else?

Rutledge: I've been fascinated with how anything, from pieces of clothing, to books, to just a certain way a man inflects a certain word, can have an erotic overtone to it. I'm not sure why, but that's always fascinated me, and I think that comes out in both stories.

MR: Are there any items of clothing, or particular situations, that charge you?

Rutledge: Almost everything. I'm not saying I'm an erotic maniac, no; but I guess what I mean is that under any circumstances, absolutely anything can be erotic to me.

MR: Are you a fetishist?

Rutledge: Actually, in a sense, I am a fetishist, but I'm not a focused fetishist. In other words, I can't say that, for example, sneakers are a particular fetish for me, to the point where the actual object becomes more important than the person wearing it. I am a fetishist to the extent that if I am attracted to a man who's wearing something, everything he wears and everything he does can become sexually charged for me. So I think there is a big difference there.

MR: What about leather?

Rutledge: In a lot of ways, leather actually doesn't turn me on as much as ordinary clothing does. I've not been much into costume, even though I enjoy certain aspects of sexuality. And I like the look of leather. I think there is something much more powerful for me in a guy who's dressed in an ordinary way, who turns out to be into SM, than a guy who is dressed in full black leather and turns out to be into SM.

MR: That came out in another story, "Angel," about the "rowdy, randy, farm-town boy whose inexperienced dick leaps up reflex-ively—rockhard—at thoughts of sexual cruelty and humiliation."

Rutledge: Yes, that was the story of a kid I knew here, and he was an eighteen-year-old at the time I first met him, eighteen or nineteen. And you might, if you look carefully into his face, be able to read that he was into certain SM-type things. But there was no clue just looking at him in general, in the way he dressed. And he was totally unsophisticated in the sense that he knew nothing about gay leather magazines or gay leather bars. He knew nothing about any kind of SM subculture. But here was this kid who, when you would have sex with him, would imme-diately take on such a provocatively dominant and sadistic role that he was a character out of a porn story, even though he had never read any of those stories.

MR: Are you a natural submitter? Or did he bring some submis-siveness out of you?

Rutledge: That's a tough question to answer.

MR: I guess the further extension of that question is about the degree to which you have involved yourself in SM, or how much that has been a part of your sexual development. Are there parts of SM that attract you? Or is it the whole concept of domi-nance and submission?

Rutledge: I'm not sure I can define it by either one of those categories. I had SM-type fantasies when I was a teenager. They generally involved being dominated by a guy. It just seemed very natural.

MR: But those power politics don't permeate so much of your work that it becomes an identifiable part of it. Or does it?

Rutledge: Not really, no. Ritualized SM doesn't interest me that much, and there are encounters I've had with guys which had SM overtones which were so shockingly erotic to me, even though they involved no use of leather, toys, or even use of rope. It was just an attitude. A dominating attitude. Ritualized SM is not as much of an interest for me. I've written about it. I've written a lot of SM stories, but I've been strangely reticent to publish any of them. One other thing, and this is difficult to explain—

MR: Try.

Rutledge: There has always been a sweetness to me about erotica. There has always been an incredible sweetness, a poignancy about sexuality, and I think that was probably a more driving theme in a lot of the stuff I have written than SM issues. I have always been a bit obsessed, even in high school, by the hidden sexual nature of everyone. I always was pretty alert to it. I would be sitting there watching an English teacher who is sixty-eight years old; and without indulging in a ludicrous or purely prurient fantasy, I would be imagining what she would be like undressed and passionately involved with another person. That always fascinated me. I think if there is an overriding theme to my erotica, it's that. The erotic elements in people that are not expressed.

MR: Human nature—the human response—seems to interest you almost as much as the erotica does.

Rutledge: I don't think there is erotica without people, and I think that is one of the big problems with a lot of erotica. It takes stock characters and stock situations, and gives no indication that sex is a sexual interaction between two people's minds. I've never really been like that. I don't know why.

MR: Do you live inside your own head a lot?

Rutledge: No. I'm not what you would call a person who hasn't experienced a lot of life, in fact quite the opposite.

MR: That's not what I meant at all. What I meant is, do you keep quiet, do you just *observe* a great deal, and take it all in and filter it through?

Rutledge: Oh, I observe a great deal and filter it all through constantly. There are times when I almost feel like what goes on in my head is a constant profit of therapy. There is an enormous amount of observing, and an enormous amount of filtering, an enormous amount of trying to put together the meaning of what I see.

MR: And have you spent time in therapy yourself?

Rutledge: Yes.

MR: Has that been helpful, in terms of your writing, to sort things out, to figure out why you feel what you feel?

Rutledge: No, in fact at first, when I went into therapy—and the therapy had nothing to do with gay issues—it had to do primarily with issues surrounding my father. The abuse problem. I actually found that as things were improving inside my head through therapy, it was increasingly difficult to write. The impetus to write was evaporating. My therapist told me at the time that it was very common. It wasn't until I basically got out of therapy that the urge to write returned, and in its usual way. I wouldn't say that it helped me to sort things out at all in terms of my writing.

MR: I haven't detected any sense of sexualized father/son role-playing in your fiction. I wondered if you've veered away from it consciously?

Rutledge: No.

MR: Has having endured the type of childhood that you endured had any connection with the way you perceive SM, perhaps the aggression, the symbolic or ritualized violence that frequently accompanies SM, which, as you said, doesn't interest you very much?

Rutledge: For me—and I can't speak for other people, because there is some controversy around this issue to begin with, about why people are into SM—there has never been any doubt that a lot of my interest in SM has been a way of blowing off steam, psychologically, from all the issues surrounding the abuse I endured from my father. In that sense, I have come to grips with it. It doesn't trouble me, particularly. Because I can think of a lot less healthy ways of blowing off steam from that kind of childhood.

MR: Tell me about being a gay erotic writer living in Colorado. It's not a state that one naturally associates with tolerance or progressive politics these days.

Rutledge: It's been tough. It's been real tough, especially because when I moved to Colorado in 1978, this was a state that was really renowned for being very tolerant and very open about everything. This is where meditators, and very odd religious cults, came. Drugs were reasonably tolerated here. This state has changed enormously, and it was quite a rude awakening when amendments were passed. It was difficult to deal with. I felt that they were going to pass—people in the state seemed to be in a lean and hungry mood—but I was still flabbergasted. And I had some emotional repercussions from it, some pretty strong ones. I was very angry and very depressed afterward.

MR: Did you write letters and articles?

Rutledge: No, at that time I was pretty well focused on most of my nongay writing. I think there was a little bit of an avoidance mechanism going on, in the fact that I didn't write about it. I was actually encouraged by my publicist to do something for the *New York Times*, and she knew someone at the time who thought she could get it in. I sat down and tried to write it, and found that I just had this whole avoidance mechanism. I didn't even want to grapple with the issues, I was so angry. My lover has become very actively involved in the political situation. For a whole variety of reasons, I didn't jump into the fight. But it has been tough, and the ramifications are still going on, two years later. The papers still get letters to the editor decrying homosexuality. The whole state has become much more conservative, and that kind of shocked me. But I talk to people in other states. I have a very close friend in Oregon, and she tells me Oregon has always been a standard-bearer in terms of tolerance, and they are having terrible problems up there.

MR: It's ugly, what's happening.

Rutledge: It's very ugly and it's tough to take.

MR: Do you get a lot of response to your fiction? Do people write you?

Rutledge: They would write letters when the stories were published in magazines. I would get a fair amount of fan mail. What is amazing to me is that when *The Gay Book of Lists* and all the other gay books came out, I started to get a deluge of fan mail from those books. It would always astonish me that people would write in and say, "I love *The Gay Book of Lists*, I really enjoyed reading it. By the way, the story you had published in *Mandate* in 1982, titled such-and-such, is my all-time favorite porn story, and I've worn out three copies of the magazine jacking off to it." I always enjoyed hearing that.

MR: Which gives you more pleasure: being a gay historian or being a pornographer?

Rutledge: Probably being a pornographer. Being a historian is a lot of fun. I enjoy that kind of writing, and I love that kind of research. I am almost embarrassed to admit how much I am truly into writing books like *The Gay Book of Lists*. Pornography is a much more personal thing to write, and I love writing it. There is almost a part of me—without being a standard-bearer or an activist in this situation—that really somehow wanted to legitimize erotica, because I never understood, and still don't understand rationally, any of the objections to erotica. They are so foolish and so stupid. Comparing my feelings about sexuality and erotica, and all of those things, to other people's, is one of the primary things that sometimes makes me feel as if I am standing at a strange angle to the rest of humanity. I just don't understand it at all. But then, sex has always been incredibly wonderful to me, I love sex and I love good erotica.

MR: How do you respond to the notion, especially in this context, that pornography is degrading, or that it corrupts?

Rutledge: Bullshit, total bullshit. There is nothing corruptive about pornography at all. There are so many ways to start in on this issue, I don't know where to begin. I always think there is so much hypocrisy in the writing field. If someone sits down to write a story whose major purpose is to inspire hunger in you for a certain kind of food, to describe a wonderful meal, there is nothing about that which is a problem. But if a person writes a story that tries to inspire erotic feelings—arousal, lust—then immediately all rationality goes out the window. It's very strange to me.

MR: That particular negative response to erotica is the academic, or establishment-artist response. What about the antiporn feminist response? That pornography degrades women?

Rutledge: That's largely an example of a group of people who are trying to take a personal erotic issue and turn it into a political issue. I don't think it degrades people at all. I don't think it degrades women in the least. I think most of the feminists who say that have very little experience, or very little empathy, for what really goes on through someone's mind when he is reading pornography. Most of my friends in college were straight guys, and I can tell you what goes through a straight guy's mind when he is looking at a nude model in *Playboy* magazine. It's not that he wants her to "submit." Not that he wants to rape her, not that he wants to "defile" her. What most guys are doing is lying there, stroking their dicks, and thinking to themselves, "Wow, this beautiful woman is smiling at me, she really likes me, she really wants me." There is no corrupting of women for most guys through pornography. The people whom it *does* corrupt are people who would be corrupted anyway, and who have major problems to begin with. I feel pretty antagonistic toward the view of some feminists toward pornography. I think it is totally misguided and irrational.

MR: Are there any other writers in this field whom you particularly admire?

Rutledge: I really admire Pat Califia, even though she writes primarily lesbian erotica. I really enjoy her writing more than her writing style. I really have enormous regard for her whole sensibility. She is one of the smartest people, I think, writing in gay and lesbian literature at the moment. I've enjoyed the stories of Phil Andros, Aaron Travis. There are a couple of other writers—oh God, I can't think of the guy's name! He writes really raunchy SM which usually appears in the Larry Townsend anthologies, often with a Southern setting. I can't think of his name. His stories are incredibly hot, and very well written. But, I've got to tell you—it's very strange. I find very little written erotica arousing.

MR: Except yours?

Rutledge: I don't find mine particularly arousing, except while I am writing it.

Steven
SAYLOR,
writing as "Aaron Travis"

*I remember once, somebody commented on "Blue Light." He
said, "Well, you know, your reward for writing that story should
be to actually live it out." And I thought, "You're out of your
mind!" Not only would I not want to live it out, what would be
the point? I mean, if you have the fantasy, why do you need the
reality? The fantasy is just as valid.*

The name "Aaron Travis" needs no introduction for anyone
who has even a passing familiarity with gay pornography. As
Aaron Travis, Texas-born author Steven Saylor's position as
one of gay erotica's superstars is unchallenged. His erotic oeuvre
currently in print includes the novel *Slaves of the Empire*, and
three collections of erotic short fiction: *Big Shots*, *Exposed*, and
Beast of Burden.

"Blue Light" (first published in *Malebox* in July 1980 as
"The Blue Light," and anthologized in *Flesh and the Word* in
1992), perhaps Saylor's most famous short story, blends elements
of dark fantasy, horror, and pornography, with results that are
both terrifying and profoundly erotic. His SM novel *Slaves of the
Empire*, which was first published in 1982 and is currently in
rerelease from Badboy, became a standard by which all subsequent forays into historical erotic fiction would be judged.
Drawing on the spectacle of ancient Rome, Saylor's novel weaves
political intrigue and rebellion with the decadence and deprav-
ity of absolute ownership of slaves by their patrician Roman
masters. *Slaves of the Empire* is as noteworthy for its carefully

researched and knowledgeable attention to historical detail as it is for its razor-edged pornographic imagery. His mainstream novels of ancient Rome—*Roman Blood*, *Arms of Nemesis*, and *Catalina's Riddle*—written under his own name (as are his mystery stories in *Ellery Queen's Mystery Magazine*), have gained him a devoted following outside the sexual field.

Today, living in Berkeley, California, Saylor says that Aaron Travis is "retired," and Saylor is merely "his agent." During our interview in June 1994, we discussed his Texas roots, the origin of his pseudonym, and the disparity between "Aaron Travis" and Steven Saylor. Perhaps most revealingly, however, we explored the milestones in Saylor's life—his maturing and changing attitudes toward sexuality, and his life as seen from the vantage point of an acclaimed thirty-eight-year-old writer who lived through the heyday of gay sexuality in the late 1970s and early 1980s, and who now lives in a California college town where he is able to observe the emergence of a new generation of gay men.

Michael Rowe: When I read your story "Slave" in *Flesh and the Word 2*, I noticed that the scene on the ship, where Jonah is a galley slave, is almost exactly what the parallel scene in the film *Ben-Hur* would have been if it had been overtly sexual, and gay. I am wondering to what degree growing up with those Charlton Heston-type Bible films had an effect on your pornographic consciousness?

Steven Saylor: Oh, well, almost undoubtedly they did. I did grow up watching gladiator movies that were made in the early 1960s. Those definitely had an impression on me as far as my sensibilities go.

MR: What was it about them that appealed to you?

Saylor: First of all, the spectacle, the color, the beauty. There is a real Italian aesthetic at work in those films. But of course, on a sexual level, there are all those highly fetishistic elements. I don't know if you are familiar with them, but there is the costuming, the bondage...lots of chain, leather, things like that. I grew up in a very small town in Texas and there was a drive-in there. We would go to it fairly regularly, and I was really eager to see the film *Cleopatra*. Now it didn't play there until a year or two after it was released, so I think I was probably six or seven years old, something like that. The local projectionist, who owned the drive-in, would censor the films. This was when films were starting to get a little racy, in the 1960s. I guess he would watch them in advance, and either snip them, or cover the projector.

There's a scene in *Cleopatra* when she is being massaged. Mark Antony is talking to her, and she is on a table, obviously naked. She just has a little strip of cloth over her cleavage. I remember, that scene began...and it ended instantly! It was obviously censored. I must have made a noise like "Ohhhhh," and my older brother kidded me, "Oh, you really wanted to see that, didn't you?" and at the time, it was really more a completion thing. I hated the idea of anything being *cut*. I wanted the whole experience. But certainly it impressed itself on me very strongly. That whole thing about the way we think of sexuality and the Romans: pools, baths, casual nudity, opulence—all of those elements impressed themselves on me.

MR: Do you suppose that in those sexually repressed times, the 1950s and 1960s, those films came into being, partly at least, out of a need to blow off some erotic steam?

Saylor: I would think so. I'm constantly amazed by old song lyrics—Cole Porter and the like. I heard his songs as a child, and never thought about them. As an adult, I'll hear them and think, "My God! It's a really sexy song!" We've certainly lost touch with that whole idea...the double entendre being so sexual. I certainly came out of the fifties. I was born in 1956, but I really grew up in the sixties. I think there was a hangover of whatever repression existed in the fifties, which I did not experience firsthand. I always heard about it.

MR: How did you experience the messages of the 1960s in small-town Texas?

Saylor: In the sixties, let's face it, things were really starting to loosen up. The values I grew up with, in spite of family, church, and whatever, were always totally sex-positive. In fact it was almost like an obligation. I always felt that one had to experience sex.

MR: Was your family upbringing particularly religious?

Saylor: Well, not rabidly so. We were Methodists. It's not a highly ideological theological sect, but at the time I was growing up, it was a highly socially conscious sect. So even though I grew up in a town of 1,200 people, in the middle of Texas, where everybody was white, our lessons in Sunday school were all about other races and tolerating other races. You know, all these liberal urban messages which are not exactly in sync with rural Texas in the fifties and sixties. Thank God we weren't Baptists. I mean, we were always very conscious that at least we weren't *Baptists*.

MR: Was pornography a part of your sexual life right from the beginning?

Saylor: It was definitely a part of my sexual life because I experienced pornography before I experienced sex. There was a town thirty miles away from where I lived, where there was a liquor store which sold porno paperbacks. They came in in shipments, and they all just had monochromatic covers at the time. Out of a shipment of eight, there would always be two or three gay ones. I had friend who went there to buy liquor and stuff, even though we were underage, and we would always grab some. I always made a point of getting the gay ones.

MR: Did that raise any eyebrows at the liquor store?

Saylor: You could almost act as if you just didn't know what you were doing, because they all looked alike. I was an avid reader, anyway. I wanted to read everything, and I just thought of porn as being more reading material. It was just harder to get. Occasionally, when I would go to Dallas, I would make a point of visiting the big newsstand where you could buy porn. So I started with written porn and SM. Yes, it was always really appealing to me.

MR: Was there a lot of it available at that time?

Saylor: It was much less censored than it is nowadays, because nowadays there are these eternal restrictions on, for example, age. Nowadays you simply cannot publish things about, for instance, a guy about the age I was then—sixteen. Coming of age. You are not allowed to do that anymore. Back then, anything went. People had not been so thoroughly sensitized to age as a limiting factor.

MR: And now?

Saylor: We have been totally sensitized to it now, and if you are in the industry, it's the first thing you think of when you get a story. If it has an underage minor in it, sorry, no way. So it's the basic ground rule.

MR: What were the ground rules back then?

Saylor: I'm not sure. They probably had them, but they were pretty freewheeling, and I think, back then, there were fewer rules than we have now.

MR: Did you manage to incorporate the pornography in your head into your fantasy life on a day-to-day basis? Did you create scenarios in your head with people you knew? Or was it always nameless, faceless strangers?

Saylor: Oh, definitely with people I knew. You can't help noticing the hot football player across the way, you know. You see him every day.

MR: Did you find football fetishistic? Did the gladiatorial aspect appeal to you?

Saylor: No, I can't say that it did. I've never found anything gladiatorial about football. It just looks boring to me. Now, wrestling, yes. But we didn't really have that in my school. It was a very small school, so we had a limited sports program.

MR: Rural Texas enjoys a reputation as being a conservative Christian stronghold. Do you think that religious doctrine, particularly when it's intense and fundamental, brings a certain kind of sexual energy? I keep reading polls which indicate that conservatives have a richer fantasy life than liberals, as much as a by-product of their own repression as anything else.

Saylor: It is my belief that if perhaps there is a gay gene, I think there is also a fundamentalist gene. I really believe that people who are fundamentalists are a very particular personality type, and I don't believe they can be changed, just like gays. I think it's simply the way they are, and I suspect that they are pretty close to us in ways. I think they are people who have to control everything around them all the time. Obviously they want to control total strangers, the behavior of total strangers. They cannot tolerate the idea of people doing things they don't approve of. So they go through life with this mind-set, of having to control everything around them. So I can't begin to imagine what their sexual fantasies are like. I mean I don't really care, either, whereas they apparently care about *my* sexual fantasies. Because of their controlling nature, I have no real interest in them.

MR: Which came first, the desire to be a writer or the desire to express your sexual fantasies?

Saylor: To be a writer, because when I was a child, there was a rummy game called Authors. You would match three Dickenses, three whatever. I remember that when I was asked, in the second grade, what I wanted to be when I grew up, when other kids were saying "fireman" and "nurse," I remember I said "author." I didn't say "writer," I said "author," because I wanted to be like the people on those cards. So I don't know.

From a very early age, obviously, that's what I wanted to do.

MR: You published something in a Methodist journal, did you not, when you were a child?

Saylor: Well, there was a contest. I was probably eleven or twelve, and it was for a youth magazine called *Accent on Youth*, which was in all of the Sunday-school sessions. It was a weekly, or a monthly. And they had a writing contest. I entered it, and I won. It was a big encouragement. To be actually published, to see your stuff in print for the first time, is always an experience for anybody.

MR: *Accent on Youth* is a long way from *Slaves of the Empire*. How did you begin with erotic fiction?

Saylor: It happened when I was just out of college, and I was trying to be a writer. I was sending things to little magazines, and so forth, not getting anywhere. There's that old rule that if you are going to write for a magazine, you should write for the magazines you read, that you actually know. And I was thinking, I really don't read *Esquire* and I don't read these journals, I read every issue of *Drummer* magazine. The first thing I sent in to them was a pornographic novel I was working on, and I remember it was rejected specifically because, at that time, California was in the throes of whatever that proposition was to ban gay schoolteachers. They weren't going to *touch* this novel. It was about a high-school coach and a student and it was very SM because there again was the underage factor. They simply wouldn't touch it, but they encouraged me to please send them more. So that novel was buried away, and when I look at it now, I'm not very impressed. I was simply copying what I was reading in *Drummer*, and regurgitating it. Which I did up until "Blue Light." I think, really, that was the first story I really put everything I had into.

MR: Was "Blue Light" your first notable publication?

Saylor: Well, I had a few previous stories. From the beginning of my porn writing career, I never just tossed anything off. These stories always had a lot of blood, sweat, and tears. So, the first three pieces, you know, when I look at them now, it's a derivative style. They are going to be published by Badboy probably in the next year, under the title *Raw*. Which works for several reasons. These were raw tales, they were the raw work, but they are also raw-nasty. With "Blue Light," I don't know. With that story, I was really putting something more into it, and after that there was no turning back. I had to try to reach that standard.

MR: Can you tell me how you came about writing that piece?

Saylor: Probably not very satisfactorily. As I recall, I read a lot of fantasy when I was growing up. The whole range, whatever there was. Tolkien, Dunsany, James Cabell. I remember James Cabell had a big influence on me when I was young. His whole sensibility, his sense of humor, his fantasy sense. There is a part in one of his stories where the hero—I forget what he's done—but in order to pay a penance, or to get something from a witch or sorcerer, he has to be in their thrall. And what they do is remove his head from his body. This didn't originate with Cabell. It went back to Norse myth. You'd find headless beings, and people's heads which were taken for ransom. And it's funny, in all of the Roman research that I had been doing, this behead-ing had almost reached mania in the ancient world, partly because it was one of the ways that you could prove you could kill someone. If there is a leader, and you've killed him, you can take off his head and prove it to everybody that he's dead. So the beheading is a powerful psychological thing, and it obvi-ously goes very far back. So that somehow that was in my mind, that whole idea, the head being removed. I don't know if that was the original thing; but once I got that idea, the possibilities became quite obvious to me.

MR: And if you can see it happen, as it did to your unfortunate hero in "Blue Light," it becomes the ultimate objectification?

Saylor: If your own head is removed from your body, it allows you to experience your own body as an outsider. Plus a lot of other things. I think that was kind of the inspiration of the idea. It may have been that the removal of the cock was the original idea I'd had; but once I found a way to segment the body, the fantasy naturally grew. And, of course, it had to have a supernatural setting in order to make the story work.

MR: One of the things I find very intriguing about "Blue Light"—and this also relates to your novel *Slaves of the Empire*—is the idea of a dominant master becoming enslaved by someone stronger than him. And you use the actual word "slave" many times in that story. Does that have a particular sexual appeal for you—the idea of not actually starting out as a slave, starting out as a dominant figure, then being enslaved?

Saylor: I don't know. It's funny—in my own sex life, when I was much more active, when I had a regular SM partner, which I did through most of my twenties, I really didn't want any kind of role changing to take place. I really liked very strict roles, and anything that didn't interest me I found antierotic. I am old enough now that I actually rather like the idea of people going through phases. At that time, when I was younger, I didn't like it. I wanted everything to be totally stable. Why I would include the role reversal, I feel is almost a literary equation, rather than a sexual equation.

MR: And yet, some of the most erotic charges in your work are actually coming from that role reversal.

Saylor: Well, there's that. But the earlier stuff I did for *Drummer* —that's one school of writing. But there's a certain point when I was doing things for *Stroke* magazine, when the stories got much nastier, much meaner. At the same time, I was writing sweet romantic stories, I would sort of ying-yang back and forth. I would write something just absolutely horrific, and then I would write this sweet story about sexual feeling. So I was kind of doing both, and one thing I really noticed was that the top, or dominant, or menacing figure, was quite literally menacing. For example, in "The Hit," it's a hit man who is abusing this room-service waiter, and it becomes quite violent and scary. There were different ways I would deal with the top, and his relationship with the bottom. One was for the top to just totally triumph, and that made a downbeat, nasty story. But there would be an erotic charge to that. You know, total submission. But the other is to kill off the top, as in *Slaves of the Empire*. Magnus is capturing the youth, but we kill him off, and that's definitely a psychological act, freeing yourself from that whole equation. And it also happens in "The Hit." The antagonist is killed by the cops at the end, and a pretty amazing sex scene is happening even as the murder is taking place. It's very obvious, symbolically, what is happening. What the top symbolizes is a kind of ferocious, very dangerous sexual domination, which is both repellent and fascinating at the same time.

MR: Does that leave you open to any charge that you have a negative take on sex?

Saylor: I can almost see my stories being classified in some ways as sex-negative, because there are those scary things, and the sex isn't always pretty. And to the extent that readers get a hard-on reading them, that's something I want them to think about, you know? Why is that going on here?

MR: That sort of goes back to the earlier question about the feminist idea that sex is degrading. Is it too much of a blanket statement to say that SM is degrading?

Saylor: Well, I think the more interesting question is why would anyone want to be degraded, or to degrade another human being? The interesting question is why? I mean, the idea of simply never portraying such a thing strikes me as stupid. The interesting question is, why is that fascinating?

MR: Why *is* it fascinating?

Saylor: What can I say about that? To answer that question of *why*, in a literal way, doesn't interest me. If you want to know why, you just have to read my stories. It's an artistic question. I mean, one reads a short story in order to think about it. We can argue that this is because men are naturally aggressive. I've always found this to be very valuable just as a literary tool. I *do* believe that human beings have a natural drive to create, to foster, to nurture, to build things into larger and larger units— whether it's a family, or a civilization, or whatever. And to connect with other human beings in a fundamental way. And on the other hand, people have a natural urge to destroy things, to break them into smaller and smaller units. I think that's also a fundamental drive, and we have to live with both of those things. And because they are in opposition, it creates conflict. It creates SM. It creates literature.

But you know, once you start talking about those things and in those terms, that's all very interesting; but I think it is much more interesting to actually experience it by fiction. The people who want to talk about pornography only in terms of psychology and legislation are missing the point. They should read some pornography, and if they don't like the pornography they are reading, I think they should create some that they like. I think the only way to drive out bad porn is to create better porn—not to simply eradicate pornography.

MR: I'm very curious about your choice of a pseudonym. John Preston once told me that your pseudonym was far more to protect the identity of your family and your hometown, and that you didn't have any particularly strong feelings about masking your identity.

Saylor: Well, first of all, I chose to use a pseudonym because I felt that everybody did it. I think that's why John Preston used "Jack Prescott" when he started. I mean you just do it. It's a convention for one thing, like George Sand—she was not ashamed of being a woman, but she had to use a pseudonym. So I used one for that reason to start with. Also, growing up in Texas, and this was in the Anita Bryant years, you could be very paranoid. You could be actually frightened, and when you are starting up publishing things that have everything and the kitchen sink, as these stories did, I did want a layer of protection.

But what I found was that it had a very positive aspect to it. When you use a pseudonym, even if everybody comes to know who you really are, and the pseudonym is totally transparent, you play a psychological trick where you let yourself be totally uninhibited. It's sort of like wearing a costume. It's still you; but because you have a costume on, it liberates you. It's not a deception, really; it's the lie that tells the truth. It allows the truth.

MR: How did you pick "Aaron Travis" as a name?

Saylor: "Travis" from "Travis County" and the hero of the Alamo. So it's a Texas name. "Aaron" for two reasons. First, it's a Jewish name, and Rick [Saylor's lover of eighteen years] is Jewish. And that's kind of a homage—my Jewish half, in other words. Also, that's just a real old-time Texas name. The old people in my town would have been named Aaron. Just all of these old Texas names, a lot of them out of the Bible. So it just struck me as a very, very heartland-Texas name, Aaron Travis—you just couldn't get any more basic than that. It seemed to work pretty well. It seems to be a name that's easy to remember.

MR: Do you think of "Aaron" as being a separate entity?

Saylor: To some extent. I mean, that's one of the good things about having a pseudonym. You are able to compartmentalize certain things. I was thinking about this a while ago. I think everybody does this, whether they are right or not. I think everybody has ways of doing this. When you deal with your mother, you are a certain person, and we all had a different name for each of these relationships we have: our mother, our lover, our boss. If we had a name for the person we are in those relationships, it would be very clear to us what we are doing. But because we don't usually go to that extent—changing our identity for these things—

we don't see it so clearly. But yes, having a pseudonym does kind of allow you the sense of having an alter ego, so you are perhaps more adventurous than you would be otherwise.

MR: What is people's response when they meet you? Are they intrigued with Steven Saylor, or Aaron Travis? Or both?

Saylor: Well, of course, at this point, with the other writing I am doing, there are really probably more people who know me as Steven Saylor, the historical mystery novelist. A lot of those people don't know anything about Aaron Travis. People who know about Aaron Travis are sometimes appalled at how young I was because I wrote the Aaron Travis material starting in my early twenties. And people would meet me and not believe that this kid had done this. They probably thought I had to be old and grizzled, or something.

MR: Did you find that they felt afraid of you? Were they expecting to find some ferocious leather top?

Saylor: Because of the nature of the stories?

MR: Yes.

Saylor: Well, if anything, they were probably disappointed by the reality. Because I've been a writer for so long, I don't really have expectations of writers based on their writing. I realize that the writer—and the persona of the narrator—are two totally different things, so I just don't think that way. But I do believe there are probably people out there that confuse the two. And of course, there are writers who themselves work on that. Like John Preston, for instance. He *did* want to have those two things sometimes be the same: himself and the persona. With me, I've never really been interested in that. The writing is kind of my fantasy world that I share, but as far as living as Aaron Travis—that's not. It's never occurred to me.

MR: Has anyone ever remarked on the disparity between the

way you conduct your life and the way Aaron Travis might, if he were you?

Saylor: I remember once, somebody commented on "Blue Light." He said, "Well, you know, your reward for writing that story should be to actually live it out." And I thought, *"You're out of your mind!"* Not only would I not want to live it out, what would be the point? I mean, if you have the fantasy, why do you need the reality? The fantasy is just as valid.

MR: Do you feel a sense of regionalism flavoring your work? Is there a lot of Texas, the spirit of Texas, in your work?

Saylor: You see it in quite a few of the stories. There is one called "Eden," about a truck driver on a trip from Texas to California. Some of the stories are fairly regional, of course. "Blue Light" has a Texas setting. In fact, only a few weeks ago I went by the house which is the model for the house in "Blue Light." And there's this other story I wrote, called "The Frat Boy and the Faggot," which is about an Austin, Texas, UT frat boy and the faggot next door. I really got a lot of that out, a lot of that whole Texas thing out. I just have never experienced anything like it anywhere else.

MR: Were you a frat boy, or a faggot?

Saylor: A faggot, of course. And quite proud of it, you know. But of course, some people are both.

MR: And that wasn't you?

Saylor: No. When I was in college and in Texas, it was a political issue. It really was, and no, I would never have been a frat boy. I had long hair. At UT, it was very much a status and prestige thing, and a money thing, and frat boys were the most conservative. And they could get away with anything. There are constantly stories out of Austin about frat boys not only raping girls, but guys. You know, there's this whole homoerotic thing that's going on that they can never acknowledge. It comes out only in grabbing some poor student off the street and abusing him or something. And then, of course, who's the faggot?

MR: So your erotic sensibility is very much a product of your Texas upbringing?

Saylor: I don't see that kind of "frat cult," for example, here in Berkeley, or in most other places in the States. It's like football in Texas. It reaches manic proportions, so that, yes, that had a huge impact on my erotic sensibility, growing up.

MR: Do you think that the Texas-macho ethic is an environmental breeding ground for SM pornography?

Saylor: Oh, yes, and for SM behavior, I should think. Because, yes, it really has that machismo and repressed homoeroticism just everywhere. A place like California is more free of those particular neuroses, and therefore, in a way, less exciting. When I am back in Texas it's all heightened. And once again, I can't tell how much is my nostalgia, how much is real, but I think a substantial part of it is real. There is a heightened sensibility.

MR: Do you think the whole arena of erotic writing has become identifiably better or worse since AIDS? I am assuming that a good body of your erotic work must have been written pre-AIDS?

Saylor: Oh, yes.

MR: Do you yield to any sense of nostalgia or sentimentality about the years pre-AIDS?

Saylor: Oh, yes. If I could bring them back in an instant, of course I would.

MR: How much of that has to do with the idea of AIDS and its effect on the world? Is that whole intensely sexual 1970s era something you relate to as having been a man in his early twenties? Or was that a very specific and magical time in history? If AIDS hadn't happened, would you still be as sentimental about those years as you are now?

Saylor: I'm sentimental about that time, but it is impossible for me to separate the sentimentality of that, my own youth, and that historical epic. I do think it was an unparalleled experience in the history of the world. I moved here in 1980, and lived through the whole 1980s on Castro Street. My ultimate feeling is that I've seen history. I've truly seen this major transition in the whole world, and there is something tragic about it because we are losing the past.

What's good about it and what's bad. In a way, the fact that AIDS happened probably keeps me from being more envious of young people than I would be otherwise, because I do often wonder if guys who are in their early twenties now are having as good a time as I did. Part of me says they can't possibly be, because of AIDS. But another part of me says they are feeling things just as intensely, and they probably are kind of naturally working around this, hopefully, and being safe. They have their own institutions, their own grunge, all of that stuff. I see them. I live in a college town here in Berkeley, so I am very aware of the presence of youth. They are probably having the same misery, the same enjoyments; but on the other hand, I don't know. I think possibly it really has just permanently dampened having fun. I mean, we used to get VD all the time, and it was something you dealt with.

MR: How old are you now?

Saylor: I'm thirty-eight. And I felt myself sort of drifting away from SM starting in my late twenties. As I say, it's hard for me to know if that was because of AIDS. Also, my mother's death was about that time, so I became really acquainted with mortality. I think mortality gets in the way of eroticism; and when you are in your early twenties, you are immortal. I don't know if guys now have more of a sense of mortality or not. I think because it's their breeding years, it's perfectly natural that these guys think about nothing but sex. And as you get older, you really are past that, and I think that's a big problem for human beings. What to do after your breeding years. They provide such an enormous reason to live that once they are gone, we have all these cultural elaborations: making money, creating art, travel, but they all pale beside that sexual obsession of your peak sexual years.

MR: There are at least two schools of thought here. The first one is that in those days, anything went. And today there is a reaction against sex-negative material in favor of pornography. Have you noticed any difference between the two eras?

Saylor: Well, the differences I noted were very much on the inside of the industry. I was the fiction editor at *Drummer* from 1984 through 1986, and then I took a break, and then I started editing the fiction for John Rowberry's magazines, starting around 1987 on until last year. Magazines like *Inches* and *Stallion*. I saw that whole period both as a writer and an editor, so I did sort of have a panoramic view of what was going on.

And I have to say that I think a lot of people really choked up because of AIDS. I know, for example, Sam Steward—Phil Andros—more or less ran dry because he couldn't deal with the idea of writing safe-sex material, and I would say to him, "Well, set it in the fifties or whatever you want, and do what you want with it." But the intrusion of that extra step took a lot of the fun out, because if you are going to write porn, and you are going to do it well, you really have to have no holds barred. You have to get into the deepest recesses of your psyche and be uncensored, and get it all out. And that's hard enough just because of the psychological process. Plus the stylistic problems that you have to overcome, and the skills you have to learn as a writer. When you impose this extra step of thinking, *"Well if it's unsafe, I have to set it in a historical period; if it's really modern, I have to be very careful about it,"* it's rather like the whole job of putting on a condom for a lot of people. They simply stop sucking.

A lot of people I know, if they are HIV-negative and wanted to practice really safe sex, just gave that up because the extra step just took all the fun out of it. So, yes, I think it had a definite deleterious effect on pornography because it drove a lot of people away. They just stopped doing it, or they started doing it artificially. Safe sex would just seem very artificial, or they would just slot it into the story. Although as an editor I have to tell you, I did feel pangs of conscience about this, because when I was editing for *Inches*, for example, if I got a story in that was clearly fantasy material—typical fantasy stuff, like the college coach and the football player, firemen having sex with each other—the things none of us think are realistic, but just accept as typical fantasies, I wouldn't be that careful about wanting the author to introduce safe sex into the story.

MR: What about more realistic stories, stories that might actually be drawn from something we might recognize as real life? Did you react to them differently?

Saylor: If I got stories that were highly realistic, you know, about people you might really know, I would generally want the author to cooperate. For example, this would happen in the stories of William Cozad. I don't know if you know his work—he was a very good writer.

MR: I'm not familiar with his work, no.

Saylor: He's written tons of stuff, and is in all of the digests. He has a couple of pen names. I think he was in the last Preston anthology, or the next one, but his stories are superrealistic. They are all about living in the Tenderloin in San Francisco, and picking up migrant farm workers at the McDonald's. I really wanted him to start using condoms in those stories.

MR: Aside from the obvious, why?

Saylor: Because I wanted these people to start using condoms. The realism was a factor. But I am intrigued by your suggestion that now it's become ideological to be sex positive. It always was, for me. I am a gay man. I must have a lot of sex. I must have no shame.

MR: I see an industry response, too. For instance, the publication of John Preston's *Flesh and the Word* series, by Dutton. Or Anne Rice's Beauty series. And these books are being reviewed in forums where pornography would not normally be reviewed.

Saylor: Well, pornography has become more respectable. That is an interesting phenomenon, the relationship between pornography and AIDS. That's a big subject. Why it is that AIDS has sort of enhanced its value of pornography. I'll ponder that.

MR: Well, ponder that. Maybe we can talk about it later. Would you comment on the antiporn feminist idea that pornography is degrading to women, or that SM pornography is degrading to gay men?

Saylor: Arthur Bresson, the filmmaker, said that when making his sex films, if there was a degree of inequality between the partners, it generated heat. An older man, a younger man, a person with more money, a person with less money. Variations in status. That creates heat, and I think that that is very true. I certainly have always found, in my sex life, that even if the simplest things are different—hairy and smooth, for instance—it's exciting. I think that if you look at my fiction, my God! It's all about the exercise of power, and imposing humiliation on other people for pleasure. So, I just think it's better to face all that and get it out. Actually talk about it. I wrote so much on that subject, and I've had enough experience with it, sexually, personally, that I really feel as though I've come through the other side of the looking glass. It's not that those fantasies no longer have the power to move me, they do. But they don't possess me as they once did.

MR: Are you still involved in SM?

Saylor: For better or worse, not really. For me, SM was always a relationship. I had a very specific one for most of my twenties with a guy back in Texas. I moved out to San Francisco, and a couple of years later he moved out here, and we picked up on the same thing. It was never highly fetishistic or leather-oriented. It was very much one-on-one and that was the kind of sex I always really liked. It was just that: interpersonal, without all of the trappings. These people who get into very specific trips, with lots of props—I mean that's their trip, I suppose, but it was never mine. I think the imagination one invests in the roles—top and bottom—especially as a young man, say in your young twenties, is such a powerful engine. And it's just because of the hormonal factor. The obsession with certain specific fantasies and ideas was something unparalleled for me in later life. I just can't imagine being able to focus on it that way today.

MR: Does that have to do with growth? Experience? Aging? What?

Saylor: Whether that is a natural function of getting older, or my sex drive slowing down, or the imposition of AIDS into our consciousness and forcing us to rethink sex, I don't know. But I think a lot of it has to do with the fact that I really just got all that stuff out. And it no longer possesses me. Perhaps that's one reason why fundamentalists have really nasty fantasy lives. Perhaps it's because they will not allow themselves to investigate these things to their root. They always have to be in control. I mean, in a way, being freed from that—or not being possessed by it—is kind of disappointing. If we lose all of our neuroses, who are we? Who would we be?

MR: But issues of censorship, and the politics of suppression—whether for nominally good reasons, or bad ones—spring up exactly because of those things. Suppressors want to be protected from both their own neuroses, and the neuroses of others.

Saylor: When you start mixing politics and pornography, that whole subject just doesn't interest me. To the extent that they want to censor my writing, and other people's writing, I feel endangered by it, and I will fight it. To the extent that they feel that if they can eradicate pornography, they will change the world—that I do not believe.

MR: Pat Califia has written about the scathing ire she has drawn from feminists who view a woman writing pornography, writing SM pornography specifically, as being gender treachery. Dorothy Allison has encountered the same attention, and so has Anne Rice. The whole issue of degradation—is that power politics between men and women? Or does it apply to same-sex inter-action as well?

Saylor: Well, I have to say this: I am glad I am not heterosexual, especially right now. I think the confusion that heterosexuals are going through is nothing to be envied. I don't really have a solution for them. The imbalances between men and women and how that can be put out, or whether it should be put out—I do not have an answer for that. Also, I am not really interested in it. As a gay man, I am free of that kind of role-playing. I just don't like injustice when I see it. On the other hand, I am really thinking that probably the biological destiny of heterosexuals limits them to certain kinds of roles. If they are going to be heterosexuals, and propagate, there has to be male penetration, short of some technological interference which doesn't sound very erotic to me. As long as that penetration is at the root of their sex, and as long as penetration is seen by either party as a power play, then I am afraid they really need to deal with that. If they want to have nonpenetrated sex, then they are no longer breeders. They become queers, in a way. Deviants. So if they are going to solve the problem of that, how to be heterosexual and breed and not have anybody be on top, that's their problem. It's not something I have a suggestion for.

MR: Have you had any experience with censorship yourself?

Saylor: Only to the extent that under the Reagan administration, because of the activities of the Justice Department, everybody in the porn industry laid down guidelines about such things as no minors, because that became such a hot issue. There were stories that I could not accept for *Inches* magazine, which I would have wanted to publish, because of technicalities like that.

MR: What about your own work?

Saylor: I sent a novel to *Drummer*, and they wouldn't accept it because of politics, not because of any intrinsic merit. I think we should always be very specific when we talk about censorship. When we talk about censorship, it really does mean laws that do not allow the publication of certain things. When people say that some movie wasn't released because of studio censorship, that always rings a little funny to me. If the reasons for not releasing it are economic, it's not necessarily censorship. I understand that there are all sorts of other factors. I think censorship is often cried when it's not truly censorship.

MR: For example?

Saylor: For example, the Bret Easton Ellis novel that was so controversial—*American Psycho*—everybody said it was censorship on the part of the original publisher when they chose not to print it, but that's the prerogative of the publisher. They are under no obligation. They paid him an advance, and I believe he kept it, so there is nothing to say. He went to another publisher. I do not call that censorship. In fact, that is freedom of the press.

MR: Is there a hometown or family audience that is uncomfortable with your pornography in your own personal life?

Saylor: Well, I don't think my siblings really know much of my pornography.

MR: How is that possible?

Saylor: I think they know I've done it, but I don't think they've ever been interested in reading it. I don't think they ever have read it. It's not something I ever wanted to show them because, for one thing, they are not the audience.

MR: Do you feel a strong connection with your audience?

Saylor: A strong connection?

MR: John Preston always talked about getting to his audience.

Saylor: John was very different that way. John's whole idea of being a writer was not my idea. For me, it's very much getting into my own head. And if I could be left totally alone, that would be the ideal. If I didn't have to deal with editors, publishers, even readers (*laughs*), that would be fine with me.

MR: Do you feel that way about the readership of your mystery novels as well? Mystery readers can be as possessive of their authors as readers of erotic fiction are.

Saylor: In a way, I've connected more with the mystery audience because it's more organized. I've been sent on press tours and things, and have gotten feedback from writers, which has actually inspired me to write specific stories because of what they more or less requested. I've gotten more feedback from the mystery readership than I ever have from the porn readership.

MR: Where do your pornographic thoughts come from, and how do they find their way out?

Saylor: Well, that's hard to answer right now, because I am virtually retired as a pornographer. I like to tell people that Aaron Travis is retired; I'm just his agent. I am keeping his work in print. I haven't been writing erotic fiction, and part of it is because I really felt I came to almost a kind of closure with all of that.

MR: What is the main thrust of the work you're doing now?

Saylor: We can call it mystery and historical fiction, but it's really about politics, and about power. There is a lot of slavery in the books I write, because they are about ancient Rome, so it's still dealing with a lot of the same principles and dynamics, but it's just doing it in a different way, which actually interests me more now. As for the origins of my erotic fiction, when I was writing erotic stories there were various ways it would happen. "Getting Tchimchenko" [anthologized in *Flesh and the Word*] came to me in a dream and it took me a long time to elaborate it. Other stories, like "Slave," I wrote over a long period, because I had this original fantasy. "The Hit" started in my head, however, because I saw an old movie with Vince Edwards, in which he played a hit man. And there is a scene where he has been working out or something. We've seen some beefcake. And he's in his hotel room, just wearing a terry-cloth robe. The room-service waiter comes in. The room-service waiter is this guy in his fifties, and he's a real dweeb. Vince Edwards sort of verbally abuses him and humiliates him, and that's the end of the scene. Well, something went off in my head and I said, *"What if the room-service waiter were actually nineteen and a beautiful little blond, and it doesn't stop at the verbal humiliation?"* because obviously that scene had somewhere to go. So I just kept elaborating that in my head until I had a novelette, and took it as far as I could. And that story ends up having two sequels, and it's sort of a short novel. So really it's the elaboration of a fantasy.

MR: Do you have any current fantasies?

Saylor: I have some current fantasies. I don't know how other people's minds work, but I think a fantasy is comfort. I had some fantasies which I have not written down, and these will be the Aaron Travis stories that are never told, perhaps. Because I don't know if I'll ever work these into a story form. Don't most people have currently running fantasies which they resort to?

MR: I certainly do.

Saylor: I think the importance of these fantasies is often very underrated, and these days people are told that they shouldn't think in certain ways, and to some extent that is good. We should learn to overcome certain prejudices. But those basic fantasies—I don't know, I think people have to be free to have those.

Caro
SOLES,
writing as "Kyle Stone"

I'm not trying to pretend that I'm Mistress Whatever, and I don't want people to think that....I remember I was one of the judges at Mr. Leather—where the hell was it?—and what was it that somebody said? Oh, yes, I had my handcuff earrings on, one of which was open, and I hadn't noticed, and frankly hadn't given it much thought. Well, he came over very solicitously and said he thought I was sending the wrong message.... (laughs) It's the little things that you assume.

"Kyle *who?*"

A well-meaning friend in Boston had handed me a copy of a paperback novel with the rather unprepossessing title *The Initiation of PB 500* by Kyle Stone. I had never heard of Kyle Stone, and I didn't like the cover photograph featuring a man's tattooed back. I regarded the book dubiously, but I didn't want to hurt his feelings.

"It's SM sci-fi porn," my friend enthused. "It's incredibly hot! You have to read this guy." I smiled tightly and pocketed the book, thanking him. I loathe science fiction with a passion bordering on the pathological.

The novel caught and held me from the first. The skillfully written story of Micah Stariron, a galactic warrior caught and enslaved by a barbarian warlord named Attlad, merged all the best elements of a romantic epic with some of the hottest porn I had ever read. Some months later, I read an item in Toronto's gay magazine *Xtra!*, identifying Kyle Stone as "local writer Caro Soles."

Interviewing Caro Soles was fascinating, and I have interviewed enough people in the last decade to be rarely, if ever, still fascinated. Here was a woman, a suburban wife and mother with an impeccable patrician WASP background, a product of Branksome Hall (one of Canada's oldest and chilliest girls' schools) and Trinity College, writing lustily (and with disconcerting authority) about—among other things—sadomasochism, dildos, and sex in outer space. During our conversation, she led me on a deft and merry chase while I tried to get her to reveal the source of her fantasies. Ever the lady, she wheeled and dodged. The subtext was quite plain: everything Mrs. Soles wanted to reveal was in her books, thank you very much.

Suddenly Kyle Stone/Caro Soles is everywhere. She has since released the sequel to *PB 500*, called *The Citadel*, as well as two other pornographic novels, *Rituals* and *Fantasy Board*, and at the time of this writing, she is set to make her debut in *Flesh and the Word 3*. As an editor, she recently released *Meltdown!*, an anthology of erotic science fiction and dark fantasy. In Canada, she is best known as the editor who engaged Timothy Findley, an award-winning Canadian author and a pillar of the Canadian literary establishment, to contribute to her anthology *Bizarre Dreams*, which attracted a great deal of media attention in Canada when it was detained at the border.

If interviewing Caro Soles can be a little like taking high tea with Katharine Hepburn in a leather bar while on very clean acid, reading her writing is a sexual act. It is enthralling and powerful. In a relatively short time, this prolific woman has made her presence very much felt in the field of gay male erotica. What interesting times we live in.

Michael Rowe: Let's begin by discussing the pseudonymous aspect of your work. It's intriguing to me that you have written these erotic and powerful gay male SM novels as a man. Did you feel the books would not be as well received by a gay male readership if you had been billed as a woman?

Caro Soles: I thought that they would be viewed differently, received differently, and that's what I did not want. I did not want anybody to say it was "a good book, even though it was written by a woman." I've seen these discussions, and I've heard them, and I've been involved in them. I just didn't want it to come up until I was sure that what I was doing was being accepted.

MR: Do you have any aversions to the word "pornography"? Do you use "erotica"?

Soles: I use that term when I don't know people because the "P" word puts people off. I've also discovered, to my horror, that if you do say it's "erotica," people have no idea of the kind of strength it has, and how powerful and disturbing it is for some people.

MR: You are a married woman, and you don't define yourself sexually as heterosexual, or bisexual, or gay. Furthermore, you are, by your own admission, not part of an SM community. Do you think of yourself as somehow transcending all of this?

Soles: I like to think that, yes. The fact that I'm not really part of the SM community bothered me at first, because I thought, once again, that people might question it. I think most people who write it are a part of the community.

MR: Tell me how you actually came to write this specific kind of pornography—hard-core, SM-leather, science-fiction-influenced novels and stories.

Soles: It all came about when I was trying to write a romance novel, which may seem very strange, but that's the way it happened. I simply wanted to get something in print that gave me some money; because the stuff I was doing, though all very interesting, was not getting me anywhere as far as money was concerned. So I wrote this romance—this Harlequin thing—which didn't work at all. I kept trying, because they kept encouraging me—they liked the writing. I wrote a second one. Well, that didn't work, so I wrote a third one, which was almost there. At this point I could not stand it anymore, and I thought, "I'm going to write what I want to write."

MR: What was wrong with the Harlequin romance?

Soles: I did not understand their idea of sexual tension! (*laughs*) I had no idea what they were talking about.

MR: Were your...tastes...intruding into the Harlequin?

Soles: Well I *tried hard* not to have them intrude. I mean, there was nothing SM in it, but I saw a lot of SM things in ordinary Harlequins, which they didn't seem to see. And I honestly could not figure out what they wanted. To me, it was all a lot of game-playing stuff which didn't seem real at all. And although my own writing of the Harlequin was very smooth, it obviously was very clear to them that there was no heart and soul in this thing because I was just trying to do what they wanted, and it wasn't working.

MR: And that's when you wrote *The Initiation of PB 500*?

Soles: Yes. If you analyze it, if you've done any reading of Harlequins—which is highly unlikely—you will see that *PB 500* is structured exactly like a Harlequin romance: the length of the chapters, the length of the book, the sparring between the characters.

MR: There is absolutely no way that I'm going to let you just leap from writing a Harlequin romance to writing hard-core gay male SM pornography without explaining yourself.

Soles: Well, obviously not. But that's the actual physical way that it worked. I neglected to say that I had already written a gay novel which was not at all sordid. It's a love story about a young man in a small town coping with this much older man.

MR: Who published this?

Soles: Nobody has, yet. This novel is called *A Mutual Understanding*, and it's the one that was accepted by Knight's Press.

Eventually they went under before it came out. Then it was accepted by Los Hombres Press. Then they went under. It's now been accepted by Spectrum Press—now just watch them go under. (*laughs*)

MR: The cursed manuscript of Caro Soles.

Soles: But about *PB 500*, when I was looking around for something I thought I could do that would actually make money, I saw that what I was writing at that point were love stories, basically. So that's why I thought I could try to write a novel like *PB 500*.

MR: That's a fairly rebel notion, isn't it? The idea of pornography being about love? It's supposed to be about violence and degradation.

Soles: Well, of course that's bull as far as I'm concerned.

MR: Did you reach instinctively toward the gay theme?

Soles: It came in stages, now that I think back. I can see the same things in my work all the way back. I originally started writing science fiction because it was easier to get outside and look at things that way. I did three science-fiction novels, one of which was also accepted by Knight's Press. In my mind, they were basically gay novels.

MR: Did you find that writing in a gay male voice was particularly empowering? Anne Rice has said that she enjoys writing as a male character because it gives her a certain freedom to do things and say things that she would not normally get a chance to say.

Soles: Writing from a gay male point of view makes me feel more free to pursue things in a different way than I could otherwise. I think that's the main idea.

MR: Had you known many gay men?

Soles: I thought that was assumed. I was actually getting more and more into the community because it was at that point that I went with the AIDS Committee of Toronto, and I started doing a lot of work for them. I was on the board of directors for a couple of years, and then I was doing fund-raisers like Dancers for Life. So I knew an awful lot of gay men. And in my—I was going to say flaming—youth, I used to do theater.

MR: You were raised to be a proper Rosedale matron, Caro. Theater and pornography are not the sort of anarchic pathways that well-bred Canadian maidens are encouraged to follow.

Soles: Well, that never really worked. (*laughs*) The seeds of all these things really go all the way back, and began to develop sort of subconsciously. I'm not, as you've probably realized, one of these people who sits down and plans things out consciously. I'm not a wildly concrete thinker. I'm not a structuralist. As for the writing, it just got deeper and deeper into the psychology of relationships.

MR: And you went from the psychology of relationships to SM?

Soles: Yes, because *A Mutual Understanding* is also about power—a younger person with an older, very authoritative person. How does the younger person manage to keep his independence while still submitting to et cetera. Even in the science fiction, there's a lot of SM.

MR: How did you develop your understanding of the whole SM dynamic? How do you relate to all that, being a wife and a mother living in a suburb? Do you find yourself in conflict with the messages you are sent by the society in which you live? Given your background, and the reality of your world versus the reality of the world which lives inside your head, I would think the two would be at odds.

Soles: Except I think this comes down to how one sees oneself, and I have never seen myself as somebody who lives in the suburbs. I see myself as somebody whose house and garden happen to be someplace that takes a while to get to. But it is not "my" neighborhood, not "my" people, not "my" friends. It never has been.

MR: Do you have any involvement at all with the community in your suburb?

Soles: In a way. I have tried to find out about these things. We are part of the community—the Homeowners' Association, and all that kind of thing. It's not as though one lives in a total vacuum. But it means, I guess, that I have not been able to relate too well to neighbors. Most of the time I actually fall asleep at neighborhood meetings. (*laughs*) That's how bad it is.

MR: So much for the neighbors.

Soles: Well, actually they have kind of adopted me as the neighborhood eccentric, so it sort of backfired. They call to make sure I don't forget about things. I'm always forgetting to come to the jolly neighborhood meetings. And there are some nice people there. There are some people who regard it the way I do, you know. Quite enjoyable, occasionally. I've now totally forgotten the question—oh, yes!

MR: The conflict between your suburban life—which you've explained is not actually your life—being a woman, a mother, and a wife, a homeowner, and your life as a hard-core gay SM pornography writer.

Soles: Yes. You see, one's life is divided into periods. The period where I was sort of the homeowner and suburban mother is, as far as I am concerned, over. There was a time when I was all of those things. And I wasn't really writing then, you see.

MR: What does your husband think of living with a madwoman?

Soles: He's used to it. We've been married for twenty-five years.

(*laughs*) He doesn't read the stuff. Periodically he'll look at something, shake his head and walk off. He's mathematical and totally different. Doesn't read fiction, reads only manuals.

MR: And your children?

Soles: Well, it's just another crazy thing that Mother does.

MR: Do you prefer the company of women or men?

Soles: I'm very at home with women, probably because I was brought up in an all-female school. But, on the other hand, I enjoy men as well.

MR: Have you had any sort of flak at all, or any negative criticism of you as a woman writing gay male porn? Have you ever experienced any hostility about that? Have people ever said, "What do you know about us?"

Soles: That was one of the things I was expecting. So far, it hasn't happened. I think part of the reason is that a lot of people, when they read my work, don't realize that I'm a woman. Frankly, most people don't. For instance, at the launch, various people came up and said, "Lord, it was good!" and they hadn't realized that I was a woman. They were floored.

MR: Were they floored in a negative way or a positive way?

Soles: They seemed to think it was absolutely amazing.

MR: What did you wear?

Soles: For the launch? I wore a sort of black A-line dress thing, and I wore—let's see. I had my collar on, I had my handcuff earrings. I had my pearls. (*laughs*)

MR: All the conflicting messages in place. Were the pearls real?

Soles: No, these weren't. I have just a short strand, but there was no point in wearing the real ones. But I like that idea.

MR: So, there you are in your A-line dress, and you're sending these conflicting messages...

Soles: Yes, because I think that's a good idea. I'm not trying to pretend that I'm Mistress Whatever, and I don't want people to think that. I think some people automatically assume there is something. I remember I was one of the judges at Mr. Leather— where the *hell* was it?—and what was it that somebody said? Oh, yes, I had my handcuff earrings on, one of which was open, and I hadn't noticed, and frankly hadn't given it much thought. Well, he came over very solicitously and said he thought I was sending the wrong message. Because if it were open, I would be the bottom, not the top. He obviously assumed I wasn't. So I thought, isn't that cute? (*laughs*) It's the little things that you assume.

MR: Is there a Mistress Whatever inside you?

Soles: I don't know. I'm not sure. I never really wanted to try it. I'm more of a voyeur, if anything. A lot of my writing is about that, too. Maybe not so much in this lot, but in the short stories. I'm really not sure. Perhaps in another stage? (*laughs*) We'll see.

MR: Okay. Let's just take a wild swing in the opposite direction and talk about being a Canadian author and talk about our feelings about the whole censorship issue here in Canada. And how we feel when books are seized. Canada has the reputation of being censorious.

Soles: Well, I think as far as I am concerned, Canada has the reputation of being censorious on a lot more than just the seizing of porn. I think it's a given. I don't even bother sending anything to any Canadian publisher anywhere, and I never will again unless actually invited to.

MR: You had a bad experience?

Soles: I wouldn't exactly say *bad*. More like there was no sort of response from people. And I don't know—in some ways, I suppose I shouldn't really be so ferocious about the whole thing. It's just that the difference between Canada and the States is so marked. Even though the United States weren't exactly showering me with contracts, the actual response to what I was sending was so much more supportive. It was quite amazing.

MR: In what sense was it supportive?

Soles: In the sense of getting excited about what I was doing, even if it wasn't necessarily what they were quite looking for. They were encouraging.

MR: Was the Canadian response actively chilly, or was it form-letterish?

Soles: The assumption was that if you had been good, they would have accepted your manuscript. Or if you were a literary sort, which was quite ridiculous as far as I was concerned. And the major houses were totally nonforthcoming. There was nothing, no sort of personal anything. I also found other Canadian writers, like the writers-in-residence people, to be totally disconnected with marketing and the way things really are in publishing. The reality of things. Or just not wanting to give out information, I suspect, because they didn't want any rivals.

MR: What was their response to your subject matter?

Soles: It varied a lot. Mostly they simply talked about the writing itself; because, of course, that's safer and it was something they could extol. As for the subject matter, some of them had trouble with it. They didn't understand why I was doing this.

MR: Do you understand the impulse behind censorship and the book seizures? Because if you do, I'd love to be able to understand it. It's embarrassing to be a Canadian in the writing community right now.

Soles: I don't understand it. I've never understood censorship, anyway. I think that there is a natural kind of censorship—basically, you read things that you want to read, and if you don't want—or are not interested enough—to read them, then what is the problem? You know? Don't read it.

MR: I see a very interesting paradox in the fact that erotic writing should be so much better-received at a time when the Religious Right, and conservative pressure groups all over North America, are working so hard to sublimate sexuality.

Soles: I think one of the reasons why porn is getting published so widely is because it's useful for safe-sex reasons. And usually, in a time of Religious Right aggression, there is a great interest in this sort of thing.

MR: What about the notion that pornography degrades and uses women?

Soles: Well, I don't understand this at all. I must admit that I usually haven't said much because I don't understand what to say. It doesn't make sense to me. On the other hand, I also think they are going to look at me and say, "You don't write about women, anyway, so what's the problem? You don't know what you are talking about." (*laughs*)

MR: What do you suppose it is that makes male/male pornography more acceptable than male/female pornography?

Soles: Do you think it is?

MR: Good question. I think that gay men perhaps, if they don't care for it, view it as being something rather less than literature, whereas many heterosexuals see pornography not only as being less than literature, but also as being something particularly dangerous and seditious. I don't think as many gay men see pornography as being dangerous.

Soles: That's true. I don't see it that way either. But I don't understand why people view this sort of thing as dangerous, anyway.

MR: What about the idea that it's eroding traditional family systems?

Soles: What, pornography?

MR: Yes. The idea that sexual fiction is some terrifying force being unleashed into the midst of good, God-fearing, right-minded men and women of society, and is destroying things. Those are a lot of the criticisms leveled at pornography in general. And if pornography is satanic, then your brand of SM pornography is the seventh circle of hell.

Soles: Well, that's true enough. I can see that. (*laughs*) But to say that, you have to accept that it's that in the first place. I think this comes from a long tradition of repression of that which people do not understand, do not want to understand, or are not allowed to think about, and therefore are afraid of. I think that's probably at least where it originated. Because it *is* a strong force, a very strong force.

MR: Sex?

Soles: Yes. And also it is a very destructive force, if you are not going to acknowledge it, or if you are going to repress it. So it is dangerous in that way. But to my way of looking at it, pornography is a healthy thing because you get the whole thing out here. You can see it, analyze it, and play with it. And enjoy it. And then it's not dangerous anymore. That's the way I look on that.

MR: Do you consider yourself to be a highly sexual individual? Either physically or mentally?

Soles: I guess so. I've never really thought of it, but yes, I guess so.

MR: Readers are always curious about the root of a writer's work. What is your religious background?

Soles: High Anglican, wouldn't you know? (*laughs*)

MR: That doesn't really surprise me. Given what and how you've written, you seem to be in full rebellion against your entire upbringing. The way you've turned out is completely contrary to your background—patrician WASP, girls' schools, Trinity College, and an academic career. You should be a genteel "lady of letters." How rich was your fantasy life as a child? When you were supposed to be doing proper-little-girl things, what were you thinking about? Were you thinking about science fiction? Were you thinking about sex? Fantasy? How rich were your fantasies?

Soles: Very rich. One of the things was—and I think this will probably help you understand this—that I was alone a great deal. I was kept alone for various reasons. One of which was that they thought I was very ill with the illness of that decade, rheumatic fever. Where they got that idea, I'll never know, because I didn't have it. The next thing was, I was about to go blind any second. That was closer to the truth. So I had a very *Secret Garden*-y upbringing. They were keeping people away from me so I wouldn't get "too excited," and all this nonsense. I think that anyone who is alone when he or she is young—especially someone who reads a lot—is going to have a very active fantasy life. When I did get together with my friend—who is mentioned in *Rituals*—we played games based on stories. We did a lot of role-playing games. You'll laugh at this—because both of us had a similar education—the games were pretty classical. Fighting the battle of Troy, stuff like that. (*laughs*) I hate to tell you this.

MR: Did you switch gender in your games and fantasies?

Soles: Yes, actually I did, now you mention it. And I also danced the boys' parts at school. (*laughs*) And played the boys' parts in the plays.

MR: Did you find that—

Soles: I hadn't thought of that. It was just accepted. I don't know why, I just always did. Isn't that funny? I never thought of that before.

MR: I wonder, were you particularly attracted by certain images?

Soles: I think so, yes. But kids that age don't analyze. It all just sort of flew over, and don't forget, a lot of my reading, as I say, was classical. I mean, there are a hell of a lot of battle scenes and floggings. The images are there, now that I think of it. Not to mention all the Spartans. Yes! (*laughs*) Forgot about that! Hilarious!

MR: Were you attracted to any of the biblical films? You look back on some of those old movies—I think one of the greatest SM movies ever made was *The Ten Commandments*.

Soles: I remember *The Robe*, myself. That was nifty.

MR: Did your parents think you were an odd little girl?

Soles: Oh, God, my whole family is strange.

MR: So you come from a long line of eccentric people?

Soles: Oh, yes! No, I mean, they were eccentric in different ways.

MR: British, I am assuming?

Soles: Mmm-hmm.

MR: Very British?

Soles: Oh, yes.

MR: British eccentrics?

Soles: God, oh, absolutely. They are all very interesting, because, of course, they are all characters! My brother was quite a character himself in his own right. He doesn't know me most of the time, but anyway... (*laughs*)

MR: Is he still a character?

Soles: Oh, yes, absolutely. I've forgotten what I was saying.

MR: I was wondering if they thought *you* were strange?

Soles: I don't think that they particularly thought I was *strange*, they just looked at it as talent. (*laughs*) Which is what they looked for—people with talent. They saw different types of talent, and that was fine. So you know, we used to paint, play, sing—all that stuff. We had music, all that sort of thing. God, I used to sing solo in the choir, and so on. It was all very jolly.

MR: Speaking specifically of your sexual experiences before you were married to Mr. Soles, did role-playing play a part in your interpretation of your own sexuality?

Soles: Yes, but we're talking a long time ago here. I think there was a lot of role-playing with everybody, then. There wasn't the sort of "I am going to be this, you are going to be that" kind of role-playing. It was far more subtle. Very much more subtle. But there was a lot of it. Oh, yes.

MR: Did that intimidate the men?

Soles: Well, actually, I think that men were intimidated by me quite a bit, and I didn't realize it because I didn't connect with that sort of thing. But various people told me that they had been quite intimidated. I don't know why exactly.

MR: Maybe because women of that era were expected to be passive and virginal?

Soles: Maybe. I don't know. There was a lot more "going by the rules" in those days, and they didn't quite know whether I was, or wasn't, going by the rules. One appeared a lot more blasé than one was, I suppose, when one was twenty.

MR: You haven't manifested an overly high regard for traditional societal norms in your work. I mean, that's a given.

Soles: Well, probably not. On the other hand, I think structure is very important. And, strangely enough, I think tradition is important.

MR: Structure in what sense?

Soles: Well, I guess I was thinking of some kind of familial structure. That kind of thing is important.

MR: But you are also not a "lady who lunches." Something you could have been.

Soles: I lunch frequently.

MR: I was speaking less of the ingestion of food, and more the wearing of white gloves whilst readying oneself to ingest it.

Soles: I did that.

MR: It's hard to picture, at least at this moment.

Soles: Sure I did. I've done it all.

MR: Then maybe that's what enables you to send your mind off to explore more...exotic venues than would normally be available to you, had you followed a more traditional path.

Soles: I think so, and I feel one can say that one is not afraid of that kind of thing because one understands it very well. I think that's part of where the authority comes from, too. Structure and society and all that sort of thing. But, as I say, it also means I can't write about some of the things that other people do so well. You know, I can't write about working-class life. There's a story I have draft-written. It's a novel, and it's about a kid who is from a very lower-class background. It was somebody I knew, so I wanted to write about him and his family. But I remember one time, I was sitting there trying to describe the living room, and I couldn't think of a room without books in it.

MR: Both of your SM novels, *Rituals* and *PB 500*, are written from the slave's perspective. Is there a reason for that? Is that a comfortable voice for you?

Soles: I'm not quite sure how I would do it from the top's point of view. I've been thinking about that and wondering—I felt perhaps I'd try a short story first, to see how it worked. I think from a writer's point of view, it is perhaps more interesting to do it from the perspective of the bottom. For one thing, I have always liked to have a certain amount of mystery about what's going to happen and all the rest of it, and I'm not sure how that would work if one were doing it the other way around. I don't think it would work as well. Because, how would your main character keep control if there were too many twists and turns, and he wasn't expecting them? How would he come across?

MR: So you are saying there is no personal identification between you and the subjects you are writing about?

Soles: No, I wouldn't say that I think there is.

MR: Can you elaborate on that?

Soles: Well, I think that there is identification with every character that you are writing about.

MR: In a kind of very specific writing, there is. Let's stick to you and *your* writing.

Soles:

MR: You write about exotic sexuality with a degree of authority, and I am wondering where that comes from?

Soles: Experience! (*laughs*)

MR: Now if that's not a tease, I don't know what is.

Soles: Experience of *writing*. I think that's really—I think that's where one gets one's voice of authority. If you write with authority—now, mind you, it doesn't work if it's not genuine. It didn't work with my Harlequin, so that really falls apart, doesn't it?

MR: I think that you can see where my questions are coming from. You see what I am trying to get you to talk about, and you are not coming through with the kinds of answers that I would like to have. Granted, I came with preconceived notions, and I freely admit that it is insulting to assume that fiction writing is autobiographical. You don't have to answer the question, but you have to tell me what you are thinking about my question.

Soles: Maybe I haven't quite been seeing what it is that you are getting at. I mean, obviously that's what I thought you were getting at, and I don't think it holds water. But I think the authority of a voice comes from the psychological truth of what it is you are writing about. Which means, of course, presumably that one has to understand it. And perhaps for me it is easier to understand the bottom role than the top, in the context of a story.

MR: So your understanding of SM, then, is mostly psychological?

Soles: Yes, I think so. Doesn't it come through that way?

MR: It comes through with an authenticity that's a little discon-certing.

Soles: Yes, well, I think that's why. That's what it is.

MR: And that's where these questions really come from, because if your novels had been a sort of hack-SM job—where it was obvious that you as a writer didn't know what you were talking about, or didn't even find the subject matter erotic—and where the reader didn't really believe they were doing anything more than being conned out of $4.95, I don't think I would have the same aggressive curiosity about where you get your enthu-siasm for the subject matter.

Soles: I think it's part of a whole lot of stuff that I probably haven't even thought about, which comes from fantasy, which comes from a lot of reading, and lots of just wandering around in one's mind.

MR: Do you find it perplexes people more to discover that you are not a lesbian, or that you are not a gay man?

Soles: Oh, I think they are more surprised that I am not a gay man. I think that's right. I don't think they think about the rest of it until much later on.

MR: Are people intrigued about your sex life? Are they intrigued about the motivation behind the stories?

Soles: I think so, but most of them don't actually come out and ask—which is just as well, I'm sure.

MR: Said she, briskly!

Soles: Yes, absolutely. I'm sure it's just the sort of thing people think about, of course. I'm sure I'm not coming up totally with things you want me to say.

MR: Do you find power dynamics between people fascinating?

Soles: Oh, yes, absolutely.

MR: How far back does that go?

Soles: Oh, way back, I think, to the power dynamics of the family. For instance, I was always the one who was sitting on the sidelines watching what happened. You know families—there was nothing more fascinating than watching a family, you know? Ho, it's great! Talk about SM! So I was the one who was sitting in the corner and probably being forgotten, because at that point I tended to be quiet. I am an observer, believe it or not. And you begin to subconsciously try out some of these things in a sexual context, you know? Or watch to see how other people are doing it, and why it's working. It's all part of that.

MR: There is a section of *PB 500* which is set to appear in *Looking for Mr. Preston*, and you have another story set to appear in *Flesh and the Word 3*. Had you written other pornography, before you first read John Preston?

Soles: No, I hadn't. It was some years earlier that I found John Preston, and I was busy doing other things, and writing other things. I think that he was the only gay male porn I read before I wrote *PB 500*. I can't think of anything else. Then, shortly after I wrote *PB 500*, I discovered Aaron Travis.

MR: Tell me about that.

Soles: Well, the first thing I found of his was "Blue Light." I thought that was wonderful. *This is more like it*, I said to myself. (*laughs*)

MR: It sounds almost as though you were on some sort of a quest to find a pornographic voice that clicked with your perceptions.

Soles: Once again, it wasn't a conscious thing. It was just the way I do everything. You just sort of wander along, and things kind of fall into a pattern, and that pattern began to take shape. It seemed to make sense, and it was coming along at the same time as I was doing this other stuff, this other writing, which wasn't pornographic, but was sexual. It was about power, and relationships, and all the rest of it. So it kind of does make sense in an odd sort of way.

MR: Did you write *PB 500* all in one sitting? Did it come fully formed?

Soles: It came about three-quarters formed, yes.

MR: Did you find it exciting writing it?

Soles: It was very exciting, oh, yes. That's happened before with me, but not quite the same kind of story. But, yes, it was really exciting. I really enjoyed it.

MR: As you've already firmly explained, you didn't do any hands-on research. The Toronto branch of the National Leather Association was involved with the book launch for *PB 500*. How did you get connected with the Toronto leather community?

Soles: Sean Martin, a writer and the head of NLA Toronto, is a friend of mine. He helped organize the launch for *PB 500*. Once again, that sort of came about in a funny way.

MR: Oh, boy.

Soles: I began to investigate electronically, and a lot of the leather guys are on-line on various computer boards. All of the research on BBS, and on-line sex, went into my book, *Fantasy Board*.

MR: Had you gone to leather bars, or had you had any connection with any kind of SM community which would have acted as a sounding board for some of these ideas of yours?

Soles: I think one of the things I found interesting about leather fetish was the archetype. I don't know whether one really has to have been connected with this stuff in order to plug into it. I think that maybe not everybody could have plugged into it without being connected to it, but it seemed to work that way for me. I hadn't gone to any heady parties or anything like that. By the time I wrote *Rituals*, I knew a lot more about it.

MR: Ah...?

Soles: Yes. Because by that time I had gotten to know much more of the community and talked to people. I would not have tried to write *Rituals* at the time I wrote *PB 500*.

MR: *Rituals* seems to be the work of a much more mature writer. It has a much tighter theme and scope.

Soles: I am a better writer now than when I wrote *PB 500*. Basically, *PB 500* is an adventure story, which is the kind of thing I was working on. But it was a simplified structure, one point of view, and it was very interesting to write.

MR: Tell me about *The Citadel*, the sequel to *PB 500*. Is it along the same lines as *PB 500* or is it more like *Rituals*? Or is it something completely different?

Soles: It's not completely different. It's obviously a sequel—it starts right after the other one stops. There's a lot of really dark stuff in *The Citadel*. It's more claustrophobic because Micah gets into a situation, and he doesn't understand why he's there. He thinks he's been betrayed. He is given to a woman. I finally got some women in this deal! I wasn't too happy with the way it turned out, but never mind. (*laughs*)

MR: So you get some dominant women into the book?

Soles: Well, yes, but they are just basically nasty women, I don't know where they came from. I don't know quite how to describe them. I guess they are dominant, but in this society, you see, they own the land. So Attlad actually has to get married, or he's not going to have any status.

MR: That's a very interesting feminist twist, isn't it?

Soles: But that was not what I really wanted to do. I mean, I didn't really want to concentrate on that aspect. I wanted to take more time—if I'd taken a year to write the damn book, it would have been different. But everyone is really quite nasty, and this is where Attlad's evil twin brother arrives on the scene. There're a lot of archetypical things, too. It's dark and evil and all sorts of horrible things. Oh, it's just dreadful!

MR: What would they say back at old Branksome Hall?

Soles: They knew I was weird all along.

Larry
TOWNSEND

*I've been involved in this sexual behavior for as long as I've
been sexually active. I mean, a lot of the things of course I
couldn't do. I've written about cowboys, and about futuristic sex
in spaceships, and a lot of other things. But the basic SM sex, yes.
I've either done it or, in the case of the* Handbook, *I've sought
out people who are doing things I don't do.*

It seems fitting to close this collection with an interview with
Larry Townsend, one of the acknowledged éminences grises of
the field of gay male erotica, and certainly the writer most
frequently associated with SM porn. ("Porn" is a term Townsend
loathes; he prefers "erotica.") If the field of erotica had a patri-
arch, Townsend would be the one best suited to assume that
mantle.

It would be difficult, and indeed quite unnecessary, to list
Larry Townsend's many groundbreaking books, published as far
back as the Greenleaf Classics of the 1960s, and extending into
the 1970s, 1980s, and 1990s. A random sampling might include
Kiss of Leather, his first leather title, *The Scorpius Equation*, and
the suspense novel, *Master's Counterpoint*. His novel *Run, Little
Leather Boy* (first published in 1971) and its sequel, *Run No
More*, have withstood the test of time admirably. Both novels
showcase the work of a mature and self-conscious writer who
treated his erotic writing seriously at a time in our history when
the name of the game was often speed and poor quality. There

is clearly a reason why classic erotic writing is classic. *The Leatherman's Handbook*, first published in 1972, remains a standard of the genre.

I interviewed Larry Townsend two days after he had returned home to Los Angeles (where he lives, and where he operates his publishing company) from San Francisco. I found him gruff and bearish at the start of our conversations, but as he moved into his stories, he warmed up and showed flashes of a genuinely ribald humor of the sort one often doesn't see in these politically correct times. From his tales of prep-school SM sex and clandestine Hollywood biker-leather bars to his political involvements in the early days of gay liberation, the interview shed considerable light on the persona of this man whose name has, for years, been immediately recognizable to cognoscenti of the best gay SM erotica.

For a gay male writer of my generation to be escorted across the pre-Stonewall, pre-AIDS, landscape of gay erotic publishing (in an era where "gay literature" was an oxymoron), and to hear the stories of his early days as a gay activist and writer, was almost as rich a sensory experience as reading the author's incendiary writing. Townsend, who doesn't consider himself "elder," is currently finishing a novel about the life of Ivan the Terrible.

Michael Rowe: You grew up, almost literally, from the East Coast to the West Coast. Tell me how that came about.

Larry Townsend: I was born in New York City. That was by accident, because my family never lived there; they were just there for a short time on business. I grew up halfway in Newton, Massachusetts, and in junior high, we moved to California, where my mother is from. I've been here ever since. Except for the time I spent in Europe.

MR: Was the family particularly religious?

Townsend: My mother was Roman Catholic, my father was Methodist, and because we were associating with upper-middle-class people in New England, I was brought up Episcopalian, until I reached the age of confirmation. Even at thirteen I balked at that.

MR: What was it about the idea of confirmation that bothered you?

Townsend: Because I had to repeat the creed, and I didn't believe a word of it, even at thirteen.

MR: How did your family respond to that?

Townsend: Well, my father said I was incorrigible, and I should be put in a reform school, but my mother was understanding, and it eventually blew over. It was a great family.

MR: Was your family politically conservative?

Townsend: Yes. My father was raised to be very conservative. He came from Virginia. I think my mother tended to be fairly liberal in her beliefs, but she went along with my father for the sake of peace in the family.

MR: Around what age did you first become aware of your homosexuality?

Townsend: It's really hard to pinpoint a time. I've always been homosexual. I can remember, as a small child, being excited by bondage that I saw in the Sunday funnies.

MR: You found bondage in the Sunday funnies?

Townsend: The old Tim Tyler strip.

MR: Before my time, I'm afraid.

Townsend: You see? I'm old. Tim Tyler was a white adventurer who was running around Africa, and they were always tying up the natives. The Tarzan strip also had bondage in it. Then I was given a wonderful little book, which is long gone. Something about Indians tying each other to stakes, something I found fascinating.

MR: What was it about the bondage that excited you?

Townsend: Who knows? It was just a very exciting thing, to see someone tied up in a picture.

MR: You must have loved those Romans-and-Christians movies?

Townsend: Yes, although they came along later. I never found them as sexual, actually, as the drawings. Largely because a lot of times the actors in the great Roman movies were not the ones who turned me on. I didn't turn on to any of the ones who were getting tied up, and I never liked Charlton Heston.

MR: What about Victor Mature?

Townsend: No, not Victor Mature either. And Richard Burton was much too dramatic. They didn't turn me on.

MR: Can you remember what would have been your first pornographic thoughts?

Townsend: Well, you know, I really don't like the term "pornographic." Erotic thoughts are, I think, very normal things for everyone. Certainly they were for me. Pornography is a loaded term and implies that something is "dirty." I mean, the root word means "whore," and I don't think this has anything to do with anything bad or negative. I just don't believe this, and I'm probably one of the major exponents of what they call "SM porn." I still don't like the term, and I really don't think it's appropriate.

MR: Those are strong sentiments.

Townsend: I suppose it's because I'm one who has never really had the guilt over who I am or what I am; although I've had jobs where I've had top-secret security clearance, so I've had to be very careful about what I did, so I didn't lose my job. It was always, to me, a contest of maintaining myself as I had to maintain myself, but I didn't feel guilty about it. I never have. I just don't think there is any reason why I should feel guilty for being created the way I was. I use the term "created" in a very biased way. I don't mean created by a Supreme Being, I mean created by whatever forces of nature brought me into this.

MR: Can you tell me about some of your earlier SM experiences?

Townsend: I would say, actually, I was playing around when I was in prep school. It was very Baptist in orientation, and it's quite fully described in my story, "Schoolmaster," which is in the *Dream Master* book collection. Several of us would play around after lights-out, and we would play little games of strip poker. And when you didn't have any more clothes to lose, you bet yourself. And we did a little nonsense there, did a little bit of macramé around cock and balls. The guy had to keep it on for a whole day. He had to go to gym, or whatever, and try to keep it hidden. Not real SM, but it sort of was on the fringe.

MR: What about after you got out of prep school?

Townsend: I didn't do much of anything for a long time after I came out of school because my family moved to California, and I went to public high school out here. I didn't really have much contact with any SM. I didn't know how to get into it. I was too young to go to bars.

MR: What about after high school, when you were old enough to pursue it? What then?

Townsend: Well then, I made the foolish mistake of deciding I didn't want to go to college right away after high school. I was going to work, and then go back to school. I didn't have a student permit, and I got caught when the Korean War came along. I would either be drafted, or I'd have to enlist. I went into the air force, which was a very fortunate happening, because I ended up in Germany instead of Korea. I was in the intelligence service, so I spent three years over there in civilian clothes, doing pretty covert work. But it was still away from any base. It was a wonderful experience.

MR: Did you enjoy the air force?

Townsend: Well, I enjoyed being in Europe, and the freedom that I had there, because most of the time I was in the British Zone of Germany. To a large degree, it was sexually a desert, because again, being an American in that area, I had to be very careful what I did. If they had caught me, I would have lost all my benefits. Anyway, I got through that and then went back to school, and at that time I really began to get into bondage SM because I was able to find people who were interested.

MR: Where did you find them?

Townsend: You went to bars where the motorcycle guys were.

MR: Are we talking gay bars, or straight bars?

Townsend: No, gay bars. I was never able to cruise the straight bars. I was quite successful in the old cinema with the bar in Hollywood at the time, and that was a very raunchy bar with a john outside. You had to go up the car lot to get to it, and people used to sit out on the curb and shine their headlights on us. They were afraid to come into the bar. They didn't realize we were all pussycats. They thought these were Hell's Angels, and they would be attacked with a beer bottle.

MR: And after the air force?

Townsend: I graduated from UCLA with a degree in psychology, and went on to do graduate work. I was working as a probation officer at the time, counseling kids. And then I was going full time to graduate school at the same time. So I was sort of both working and going to school in the same general area of study. But the more I got into it, the more I realized that these weren't the people that I wanted to be. As the various people began to drop out of the graduate school program, what was left was more and more of the people that I couldn't identify with.

MR: In what sense?

Townsend: I think a lot of them were professional students who were not very realistic in their perception of humanity.

MR: Their perspective was too academic?

Townsend: Yes. Academic snobbery has always bothered me. I really felt like an outsider. I just wasn't part of the "in-group." And I was uncomfortable with a lot of these people. A lot of them were women who just were in school because they could afford the time and the money, and they were very pseudo intellectual, which bothered me. I didn't like it.

MR: Were you an "out" gay man at this time?

Townsend: Oh yes, sure. When I say "out," remember I was working as a probation officer, so I wasn't out where everybody knew I was gay. But I certainly was leading a very active gay life. I'd had a lover, and we had split up.

MR: What time frame are we talking about now? Late 1960s? Early 1970s?

Townsend: Early 1960s.

MR: *Early '60s?* How old are you?

Townsend: Well, we don't have to go into that. I'm old—let's put it that way.

MR: What did you do when you were finished with the graduate studies?

Townsend: I got a job in industrial psychology with the Systems Development Corporation, involved with training the air force how to do things. How to counter Russian threats that we never had. And that's when I started writing on the side.

MR: Did you immediately turn to erotic writing? Or did you dabble in other things as well?

Townsend: I tried some other things, but the real passion was for the erotic. When I saw that they were being published, I started writing them. The first one was *Gay Adventures of Captain Goose*, which has just been rereleased by Badboy. Greenleaf published it as *The Gooser*, which I was infuriated about.

MR: What a perfectly awful title!

Townsend: I couldn't do anything about it. And then I did a string of thirteen novels for them.

MR: Under your own name?

Townsend: Yes. That little group who were publishing then are mostly gone.

MR: Did you all know each other?

Townsend: No, not really. I corresponded with a couple of them, like Peter Hughes. I liked his writing, and I corresponded with him. Never actually met him, even though he didn't live very far away from me.

MR: Your novel, *Run, Little Leather Boy*, has since gone on to become a precedent-setting SM classic. What was the response when it first appeared?

Townsend: It's hard for me to evaluate. I got some fan mail on it, which is always encouraging, because not very many people bother to write fan mail on books. I know that Greenleaf wanted me to do a sequel quickly, so they were happy with it. I didn't realize the impact that it had until several years later, maybe ten years later, when I suddenly found that a lot of people were saying, "Oh, yes, that was one of the first gay SM books I ever read," and so on. So apparently it had more of an impact than I was aware of at the time.

MR: Tell me about the emerging gay culture, and the climate of the times, into which these early books were released.

Townsend: I called an automobile agency that was advertising in *The Advocate*, because I needed auto insurance. I forget why I had to change companies, but anyway, the woman who sold me the insurance was a lesbian. Very nice. She said, "Oh, you should be involved with HELP Inc.," so I went to one of their board meetings.

MR: The acronym stood for what?

Townsend: It stood for Homophile Efforts and Legal Protection. I went to the meeting, and there were about six or seven people there and they were basically trying to put together a legal-aid group. They were lawyers committed to taking care of the people referred to them, without gouging them. They had a bail-bond program, where any member could be bailed out. For instance, drunk driving, which was really a gay offense in those days. But they had only about fifty members, and they were struggling for money. They didn't have anything going as far as publications, so I came in and started the newsletter for them, and we began mailing that out. Immediately, the membership started going up.

Then John Embry, who was the man who founded *Drummer*,

came back to California. He'd been in Hawaii, where he was publishing some kind of TV guide. He saw what we were doing, and he came in and really showed me how to do a newsletter. I was just doing it on a typewriter, and then it was offset printed. He showed us how to typeset, which wasn't expensive. He said, "You do this, and do that." He showed me how to do it, and did a lot himself. That newsletter really put HELP on the map. Then I became president of the group, and I was president for a couple of years. By then, the group was quite large.

MR: How many members did you have by then?

Townsend: We had 150 members, which was pretty good for those days, considering they were paying dues and actually supporting us. Because I'm politically a little bit more conservative.

MR: That's interesting.

Townsend: I was attracting money for contributions from areas where the Gay Liberation Front type of people weren't able to do it at that time, and I can remember how strange this was compared to today. Jim Foster was one of my best friends at that point, and was up until the time he died. Do you know who he is?

MR: No, I don't.

Townsend: Jim was the political director of SMR, in San Francisco. The Society for Mutual Rights. And it was a very large, very active group in San Francisco. Jim and I became very good friends, and we had a lot of things that we were trying to do together. This was probably 1972 or 1973. Jim said, "You know, the only Republican in the whole state who has a modicum of humanity is Milton March, he's the state senator. I'd love to get him down to Los Angeles and have a dinner in a nice hotel, like the Ambassador, to speak." We thought, maybe we can generate some interest in the more conservative, mainstream gay person, who wouldn't get out on the street and carry a sign. Anyway, I left the sale of these tickets to my vice-president, and HELP. I kept checking with him, saying, "How are you doing with the ticket sales?"

He'd say, "Oh, fine, going along fine."

Well, it came down to within a week of the dinner, and I went in and checked, and he'd sold about twenty tickets. So I called Foster, and he came right down. The two of us got on the phone, and we called *everybody*. We had made a deal with the hotel—it was only $15 for the dinner, and they got the bar. We weren't trying to make any money on it. We were just trying to put something together. I remember talking to Maurice Kite. I said, "Maurice, we desperately need some people to come in, why don't you get some people together and take a table?" He said, "Fifteen dollars is a lot more than most of our poor brothers and sisters can afford. I don't know that I would want, or could support, an elitist dinner like this." Today they send stuff to you in the mail at least three or four times a week, where they think nothing of asking you for $200 or $300 to come to something. And this is the way the movement has progressed, at least in the fund-raising area.

MR: Were you a Republican yourself?

Townsend: I was brought up a Republican, but I very soon realized that that was not my best interest. And again, when I say "conservative," I'm not talking Republican-conservative. I'm talking about mainstream gay attitudes in contrast to the people who are actually on the street doing battle.

MR: Is it different today than it was back then? The segregation?

Townsend: No. That's what I found when I came into the movement. Of course, so many people have come into the movement now. There is a good cross section of the whole community. But in those days, you really didn't have a cross section. I finally resigned from HELP and John Embry took it over as president.

MR: Did you remain an organizer?

Townsend: Later I established the Hollywood Hills Democratic Club, which was the first California Democratic Council gay club in Los Angeles. It didn't last very long, but it lasted long enough that people could see that it was viable. We did get quite a bit of money donated to us, because we had some important political campaigns that coincided with the founding of the group. We got enough money to take the centerfold in *The Advocate* to tout our candidates. Then the Stonewall Club and several others formed, so I just kind of let the Hollywood Hills club drift away. I really wasn't interested in doing this other than to stimulate other people to get into it.

MR: You were balancing this with your writing in the meantime?

Townsend: Yes. That's when I went through this long period where I really didn't write very much that anyone knows about, because what I was writing went into my self-published books, which were going out by mail order. And I was publishing other people a lot of times, so I didn't have time to write it myself.

MR: Did you ever find yourself politically out of sync with the movement? Did you find that people generally had the same political views as you?

Townsend: I don't really think I was out of sync with the mainstream. I always had the feeling that even though I might be in a minority in a particular meeting, where I was meeting people from various groups, my feeling was that I may be in the minority here but I'm in the majority as far as the community as a whole is concerned.

MR: That's a very intriguing perspective from a leatherman, because I think that much of the leather community feels very much on the outside. It's interesting to me that you would feel that you identified.

Townsend: If you're talking as a leatherman, then you're talking about something different. I really wasn't functioning as a leatherman, per se, in what I was doing, although everybody knew I was involved in SM. But I wasn't riding a motorcycle down the street in a parade. The only time I was in a parade, I was sitting in the backseat of a Cadillac convertible, which was much more peaceful than a street demonstration. But on the other hand I can appreciate what the more radical elements are doing. Today, I only donate for—what's their name? The nuts who are out there killing themselves for things today?

MR: ACT UP?

Townsend: ACT UP. I donate to them because I think that even though I don't agree with everything they are doing, I think it's a good thing to have them there because they certainly make people think, and be aware that there is a gay community that needs to be attended to.

MR: Did you read *A Place at the Table?* Bruce Bawer's book?

Townsend: No.

MR: It's been roundly vilified for espousing a fairly conservative viewpoint. There are sections which are similar in tone to the gay neoconservative view that suggests keeping leathermen out of sight on Pride Day, so as not to offend heterosexuals, or run the risk of them seeing fringe members of the community as its primary face.

Townsend: That's foolish, given that so much of the funding for a lot of the things going on is coming from the leather community. When I was in New York for Gay Pride, that was one of the big complaints the leather community had: they are shoved back to a more insignificant part of the parade, hidden as best they can be, whereas they have actually been the ones who really were responsible for funding a lot of it.

MR: How did *The Leatherman's Handbook* come to be written?

Townsend: Frances Green—she was the woman who now runs Renaissance House—called me up and asked me to do an exposé of gay SM. I said, "There's no way I'm going to write an exposé, because I'm part of it. That would be betraying my own community. But I'll certainly be happy to write a book telling about it." So I sat down and did an outline of all the subjects I wanted to cover, and I just wrote it. Actually it came together very quickly.

MR: Did you write about a lot of your own experiences, or did you let your imagination run free and untrammeled?

Townsend: I've been involved in this sexual behavior for as long as I've been sexually active. I mean, a lot of the things of course I couldn't do. I've written about cowboys, and about futuristic sex in spaceships, and a lot of other things, but the basic SM sex, yes, I've either done it, or, in the case of the *Handbook*, I've sought out people who are doing things that I don't do.

MR: Hands-on research, as it were?

Townsend: I got them to let me sit there and watch them do it. Things like fist-fucking, which of course, in those days, was very easy to get to watch. I never was much into electricity, but I found people who were, and who showed me what they were doing.

MR: Here's the old question about separating the dancer from the dance. How much of you is in the character of Wayne in *Run, Little Leather Boy*? Is that in any way autobiographical? Obviously, not the story so much, but the discovery of your sexuality?

Townsend: No, not really. By the time I wrote *Run, Little Leather Boy*, I had fourteen novels under my belt. I'd spread myself around, through these other stories. Wayne was strictly a character I created to be what I wanted for this particular story. Wayne was much more naïve than I ever was.

MR: Do you think that erotic writing has gone through any kind of significant change, post-AIDS? Was the fiction that was being published in the early issues of *Drummer* and *Mach* stronger, or more textured, than the stuff that's coming out now?

Townsend: I think it's changed. I don't read a lot of it, because a lot of the stuff they are publishing is really not very good. It's boring.

MR: Boring in what sense?

Townsend: Well, a lot of these guys are not writing with their balls. They are writing with their brains, and that doesn't work. Both brain and balls have to be engaged to write a really good erotic story.

MR: How do you feel about the prevalence of safe-sex in the erotic fiction coming out now?

Townsend: I do think that writing stories based on safe-sex can be kind of dull. I mean, there are two schools of thought. I prefer to write a story that just does everything that a guy would want to do because it's a fantasy; and if you can't really do it, at least you should be able to read about it. I just go ahead and write as good a story as I can write. I might have the guy slip on a rubber when he gets ready to fuck, but other than that, I really don't pay much attention to the AIDS epidemic when I am doing my fiction.

MR: Are there any writers writing today that particularly catch your interest in a positive way?

Townsend: Well, it depends. Lars Eighner is pretty good. I like his stuff. I've discovered some of the lesbian writers are really very good. Laura Antoniou is an excellent writer. I really enjoy her stuff. Her writing is wonderful, despite the fact that she is writing about a form of sexuality that is totally repulsive.

MR: When you say repulsive, what are you referring to?

Townsend: Well, she's writing about pussy!

MR: Any other lesbian writers come to mind? What about Pat Califia?

Townsend: She doesn't write the things that would turn me on, but she's a very good writer. She's a very male-oriented woman. Anyone who can write an "advice to the lovelorn" column for men certainly has to not be a mainstream lesbian with a hate-anything-with-a-dick attitude.

MR: That's interesting.

Townsend: My favorite, though, is my old buddy Preston. Of course, he's gone now. Preston and I sort of lost contact for a while, because he moved back east.

MR: He hated California with a passion.

Townsend: He was very poor. He couldn't afford phone calls. Then he started coming out here to promote his books, and that's when we saw each other. He stayed with us a few times.

MR: You liked his stuff?

Townsend: Yes. I wasn't crazy about *Franny*, and then when he got away from the leather stuff, he wrote a lot of things that didn't interest me. In a way, it's kind of like Hemingway. I can't say I dislike Hemingway, because I like the way he wrote, but he wrote about a lot of stuff that didn't interest me at all, so I didn't read all of it.

MR: Have you wished you'd written more about other things besides leather sexuality?

Townsend: Oh, I have.

MR: But you're not really well known for it.

Townsend: Yes, I know. That's why I would say, look what I've written! Science fiction, other things that are away from it. In fact, right now, I've gone back to a big novel that I've done on the life of Ivan the Terrible. I'm going through and I'm describing more of the sex and mayhem than I originally did. I did a lot of work on this, and I did a lot of research.

MR: You've got a pretty unique vantage point, because you've really seen pretty much the evolution, from Greenleaf Classics to Masquerade Books, in terms of erotic writing. I'm wondering what you think about the climate that is coming out into—the political climate, Jesse Helms et al., and the Religious Right. You started writing in the early 1960s, which was maybe not the most liberal of all times. And now, although a lot of new erotic writing is coming out, these are once again more conservative times.

Townsend: Except you're talking about the written word. Jesse Helms has never been successful in suppressing this. They can mount a picket line around a 7-Eleven store that carries *Playboy*, and they can take things off the market because of the pictorial content, but so far they haven't been able to do in any of us for the written word.

MR: But they would if they could?

Townsend: They would if they could, but I don't think that even at its worst moment anybody was going to do anything to me, no matter what I wrote. If I write something very controversial, and then put pictures with it, I'm asking for trouble. You have to give Greenleaf Classics credit for what they started, because they did publish *Song of the Loon*, which was the first very explicit gay novel to come out in a contemporary time. And they broke the ice with that. And so they just went on from there. And that's when a lot of us started writing. We suddenly saw we could actually get it into print.

And I don't think that's changed. I think the attitude of the overall community toward erotic writing has changed. A lot of the things Preston was doing just before he died sort of showed us that there is a degree of respectability to this now where there wasn't before. I mean, he was asked to give a lecture at Harvard. *The Leatherman's Handbook* was assigned as outside reading back in the mid-1970s by the University of Colorado, and the University of Chicago, and Long Beach State College. Evelyn Hooker used it at UCLA. It hadn't been a total turn-around, it's just that in the 1980s and early 1990s, it's gradually been building. The *Handbook*, at least, was not totally fiction. It's got a lot of pseudo-research. Armchair philosophies, observations, what you would call a scientific medley. I don't think it's any worse than Berger observing his grandchildren in the backyard of his upper-middle-class home and drawing all kinds of wonderful conclusions from that.

MR: Is this good or bad, this mainstreaming of erotic writing, in your opinion?

Townsend: I don't know. I guess the audience is there. The only reason anything ever becomes mainstream is because there are enough people interested in it, whether it's writing or political philosophy or whatever. So yes, I'm glad to see it coming because it means more people are accepting it.

MR: Some writers miss the days when the field was more clubby. The days of the old *Drummer*, when SM erotica was still considered something radical.

Townsend: It was more clubby, but they certainly weren't making any money out of it. You couldn't make a living out of it.

MR: People want their writers to be sages sitting on clouds, not worried about things like money, or food, or lodging, or anything like that.

Townsend: Well, that's foolish. If you want somebody to be

free to produce the artistic material that you are seeking—drawing pictures, or writing stories—the guy has to have enough to sustain himself in some degree of comfort. He's not going to be happy doing this forever.

MR: How did your own publishing company come about? How did you start that?

Townsend: Well, Olympia Press went belly-up in 1973, I think. I'd really burned my bridges with Greenleaf Classics at that point, because I really got into it with some of the editors there.

MR: Over what?

Townsend: They were doing things to my stories that I didn't want them to do. They were changing titles. I made them stop doing that. They were getting very picky with things in the text, and they were criticizing me for things that were not valid.

MR: Can you give us an example of the criticism?

Townsend: I remember the most outstanding example was when I had a circumcised Arab, and they just gave me all kinds of trouble. So I copied the piece out of the *Encyclopedia Britannica* on circumcision, explaining that all the Semitic nations practice circumcision. Of course, that didn't sit well with the editorial staff. Anyway, when Olympia went belly-up, I didn't have a publisher. That's when I was doing the newsletter for HELP with Embry, who told me to publish my own books. So I said, what do I do for a mailing list? At that point, the old Anvil list was available.

MR: I don't know Anvil.

Townsend: Anvil was publishing illustrated bondage stuff. I think actually it was Larry the Mad Welder.

MR: Larry the Mad *what*?

Townsend: Larry Young! Larry the Mad Welder, they called him. He made these metal restraints, and he made some deal with some Mafia publisher, whereby he put the thing together, and they published it. They gave him so many copies to pay him for his efforts.

MR: All right, I'm still with you here.

Townsend: Anyway, he had a mailing list—one of the first gay-SM lists, but he was going out of business at that point, so the list was available. John and I went together and bought it. I already had a little bit of a list, because I had been touting my books. When *The Advocate* first came out, I had about three hundred names. I had enough names so that I published the first of my own books, and went down the mailing list, and I actually made money from the beginning. Not a great deal, but it was enough to encourage me to keep going.

MR: Do you enjoy working without restraints of an editor, or do you have someone editing your work?

LR: Well, I don't really feel an editor is a restraint. Partly because at this point I have reached a status where they don't edit me, particularly. They'll edit me for content, they edit me for bad spelling, or something like that. I seek out an editor now because I do need somebody to go over it and say, "Oh, you didn't explain this!" An editor is a very valuable asset, if he's any good, and any writer is a fool if he doesn't accept editorial guidance. All of us need it because there is absolutely no way you can turn out your work without having somebody look at it before it's published, and tell you what's wrong with it.

MR: You're a conglomerate, aren't you? The activism, your own body of writing, your publishing company...

Townsend: Well, they've all sort of tied in together. I'm not involved in much of anything right now as far as the activism is concerned, because I never really enjoyed it. I did it because I felt I had to do it, but now there are a lot of other people with my political philosophy who are involved in this. And they are doing just fine. I'd rather just let them do it, and I'll contribute when I can to it, and hopefully that will be it.

MR: Do you see yourself as an elder statesman at all?

Townsend: I don't consider myself *elder*.

MR: Do you see yourself as a statesman, then?

Townsend: No.

MR: *No?*

Townsend: (*laughs*)

MR: Do you have any particular vision of yourself that you would like to be remembered by? Any contribution that you've made, any lofty visions you've had?

Townsend: Well, I'd like to get a few more things published in hardcover before I go. My Movement stuff...no one even remembers a lot of the things I did. I see all these books that have been written now, about the movement in the 1960s and 1970s. I never get mentioned, and partially that's because I really never had the attitude of trying to make a name for myself in the movement. I wanted the job to get done. I really didn't care to get credit for it. I'm really very honest about that: I really didn't care.

MR: I wonder if there's a perception that you don't really need other people.

Townsend: Well, possibly. Also of course I tend to be too vulgar.

MR: I can't imagine.

Townsend: Preston and I used to joke—before he got a Lambda Literary Award—that the only way either one of us was going to get a Lammy was to form our own group, and we would have to design a wonderful trophy, naturally for the male writers. It would be a large upright penis.